Sarah Jane Foster
Teacher of the Freedmen
A Diary and Letters

D0862146

Sarah Jane Foster

Teacher of the Freedmen

The Diary and Letters of a Maine Woman in the South After the Civil War

Edited by
Wayne E. Reilly

Foreword by
Jacqueline Jones

PICTON PRESS
ROCKPORT, MAINE

Cover Photo: This photograph is probably of Sarah Jane Foster's school in Martinsburg, W. Va. Taken by R. J. Rankin of Martinsburg and stamped with a revenue stamp from the 1860s, it is most likely the photo referred to in SJF's diary on March 23, 1866. It was found in a stack of postcards started by Foster's sister, Emma Ann Foster, and passed down in her family to Carolyn Crooker Reilly, her granddaughter. It was not discovered until after the original publication of the book by the University Press of Virginia in 1990.

All rights reserved
Copyright © 2001 Picton Press
Library of Congress Catalog Card Number 2001096943
International Standard Book Number 0-89725-445-7

This book was originally published in 1990 by the University Press of Virginia under the title of: "Sarah Jane Foster Teacher of the Freedmen: A Diary and Letters".

No part of this publication may be reproduced, stored in a retrieval system, or transmitted in any form or by any means whatsoever, whether electronic, mechanical, magnetic recording, the Internet, or photocopying, without the prior written approval of the Copyright holder, excepting brief quotations for inclusion in book reviews.

First Printing December 2001

This book is available from:
Picton Press
PO Box 250
Rockport, ME 04856-0250

Visa/MasterCard orders: 1-207-236-6565
FAX: 1-207-236-6713
www.pictonpress.com

Manufactured in the United States of America
Printed on 60# acid-free paper

∞

To my parents

CONTENTS

FOREWORD

"I am in love with my work." With these words Sarah Jane Foster expressed her passionate devotion to the cause of black education in the Civil War–torn South, a cause that eventually claimed her young life. Foster demonstrated her commitment to the former slaves through her work as a schoolteacher, a "womanly" occupation of great political significance during the Reconstruction era. A variety of her writings, including diaries, private correspondence and published letters, short stories, and poetry, reveal that the Maine native was dedicated in a very practical way to the principles of altruism and self-sacrifice glorified by proponents of the early Victorian "women's sphere." Yet as a teacher of the freedpeople, Foster emerged as a radical political activist, challenging the tenet of black subordination that had served as the cornerstone of southern society for so many years. In the process she also cast off the role as obedient teacher-missionary to defy the conservative policies of the northern society officials who sponsored her work. For her efforts she was rewarded with a peculiar combination of triumph and tribulation, thereby confronting the dilemmas of middle-class white women who sought to "do good" outside the sanctity of their own homes in these turbulent times.

Sarah Jane Foster conformed to the social and demographic profile of the "typical" northern teacher who volunteered for educational duty in rebel territory. In her late twenties and unmarried, a teacher by training and (apparently) temperament, she embraced the neo-abolitionism characteristic of one strain of Protestant evangelicalism during the mid-nineteenth century. The way south opened up for her by Union soldiers like her brother, Foster hoped to fight on the front lines of a new war, this one to redeem the minds and souls of black people from the degradation of slavery. Painfully aware of her own family's modest circumstances, she wrote "begging" letters to a religious newspaper, subsisted on a monthly pittance, and eschewed new clothes and small luxuries for herself in an effort to provide her pupils with books, other school supplies, and end-of-year picnics. In all these respects she resembled thousands of other young women from the northeastern, midwestern, and mid-Atlantic states, idealistic teachers who sought commissions from freedmen's aid societies to labor in the South for a year or two. Most then returned home to marry, resume teaching, or pursue missionary work elsewhere. Nevertheless, as Wayne Reilly points out in his Introduction, the bare outlines of this group profile hardly do justice to the complexity of individual teachers' motivations or to the high drama that often characterized their work among the freedpeople.

An avid reader with a romantic imagination, Foster delighted in Shakespeare and studied Macaulay, among many other authors; "I must read all that I can of useful matter," she wrote at one point. She was determined to make up in self-education what she lacked the money to buy at a female seminary or normal school. She enjoyed "rambling" about the countryside alone or in the company of friends, reveling in the beatific solitude of a cemetery (a favorite pastime of antebellum New Englanders), and collecting bunches of wild flowers. Although at times Foster's own words seem to paint an autobiographical portrait of a prim spinster, resentful domestic servant, and careworn teacher, she was in fact alive to the possibilities for social and political transformation in her day. Perhaps even more significantly, she possessed a vision (imperfectly articulated) of a new society in which black people would have a "white man's chance" to prosper and to preserve the integrity of their own families. In keeping with this vision, she incurred the wrath of southern whites who came to fear and ridicule all that she represented, and she endured a stinging rebuke from northern officials who considered her brand of racial egalitarianism imprudent, to say the least. Finally, Foster's commitment to black education literally killed her; in June 1868 she succumbed to yellow fever contracted in South Carolina.

Foster's multifaceted work in the South and the relationships she formed with blacks and whites there are the focus of the materials that Reilly has assembled and skillfully edited here. Elementary schoolteaching remained the core of her efforts. Through one of her letters we observe the sparse Martinsburg classroom one brisk winter morning; after a long walk from home, the smaller children arrived, chilled to the bone, and their teacher warms their hands in hers. Foster spent long hours in the classroom, day and night, instructing children and adults, pausing only occasionally to reflect, "It seems strange to serve God on the Sabbath by teaching grown men to read about cats, bats, and rats." Like most good teachers, she pondered, but never really resolved, knotty issues related to her own emotional involvement with her students, as reluctant disciplinarian and as a special friend to her favorites. The fact that her pupils of all ages progressed so rapidly is a testament both to her own skills as an instructor and to their great hunger for knowledge.

Foster remained sensitive to her pupils' physical and emotional needs and appreciated their capacity to learn quickly. She took an interest in their lives outside of school, as workers, churchgoers, and family members. A busy daily routine after school hours—visiting the homes of her pupils, attending prayer meetings, conducting Sunday School classes, socializing with members of the local freedmen's aid community, and corresponding with friends and supporters in the North—left her tired but exhilarated. Still, she suffered pangs of loneliness, "in want of a confidante," a friend who would understand her delicate responsibilities as a white teacher in a black school. At times she felt keenly her rather marginal position, in Martinsburg particularly—respected by the freedpeople, though not part of their culture or community; ostracized by southern whites; and never fully supported by the sponsors and Freedmen's Bureau agents who oversaw her work. Indeed, she was always hungry for approval from her superiors, and her longings gradually festered into resentment; "I know that I have labored and sacrificed as no other teacher has, and I tremble lest I not be appreciated by Mr. Brackett," who was the superintendent of Freewill Baptist teachers in the area. She admitted that she desired more than "colored appreciation." Ultimately, Foster discovered that she could not be true to her own principles and also win the wider public recognition that she felt she had earned. Recently, social historians have stressed the role of nineteenth-century schoolteacher as mother-away-from-home; but Foster's experiences emphasize another side of the teacher's duties—that of dutiful daughter within an educational bureaucracy manned by image-conscious administrators and clergymen.

Among whites who ventured south after the Civil War, no matter what their mission, Sarah Jane Foster was exceptional in her personal relations with individual blacks. She never condescended toward them, and unlike many Union soldiers and some Freedmen's Bureau agents and teachers, she came to understand the former slaves' commitment to kin ties and to recognize that they were "in all possible ways striving to care for themselves." She was respectful of their worship services, so different from the ones she knew in Maine, and she felt a special bond with fellow congregants regardless of race who, like herself, sought peace and renewal from a common faith.

Foster acknowledged that she walked a fine line between, on the one hand, embracing blacks as equals and, on the other, offending their sense of decorum by acting in ways they considered too familiar. She did try to conform to certain societal expectations that grated against her sense of justice and fair play—claiming as her "servants" the black children with whom she was traveling north one summer so that they would not be ejected from a "white" railroad car, politely welcoming white women visitors to her school "so that none can find fault with me about setting up the colored people above their place." Nevertheless, her efforts in the interests of equanimity eventually foundered, as they must have in any case in due time. The crisis of her professional career, indeed of her entire life, resulted from her habit of allowing black men, friends and older pupils, to accompany her on her way home during the day and in the evening after night school. Though not intentionally provocative, Foster's public behavior deeply offended the sensibilities of Martinsburg's white residents.

At times Foster seemed genuinely bewildered by all the fuss created by her strolls through the town. She felt the need of a nighttime escort and feared that avoiding all public contact with male fellow seekers after Christ would pander to the spirit of caste prejudice that lay at the heart of the rebel cause. Confederate sympathizers gossiped that she must be either black herself or carrying on an illicit sexual relationship with any one or all of the freemen who accompanied her. She could make light of the rumormongers but felt devastated when her supervisor, northern sponsors, and the local Freedmen's Bureau agent condemned her for, in the words of one man, creating "the *very appearance of evil*" by her indiscretions. When she was reassigned to Harpers Ferry, West Virginia, and her commission was terminated at the end of the school year, Foster struggled to come to terms with her "dismission." In 1866 she went public with her grievances, and to her dying day she considered herself wronged and betrayed by her superiors. The "disturbance at Martinsburg" brought into focus the cruel choices faced by this pious, hardworking teacher, so eager to please; she took seriously the cause of black advancement, too seriously for her own good.

Of course, we must also consider the perspective of the northern officials involved in the controversy. No doubt they wanted to avoid further inflaming the passions of poor whites and former slave-holders in the area, especially the men and youth who no doubt itched for a reason to torch the Martinsburg school and to subject its pupils to other forms of violent intimidation. Moreover, black parents might face retaliation as employees, all because a headstrong, naive country girl from Maine insisted on indulging her selfish whims without regard for the larger goals at stake in the enterprise of black education. Schooling for the freedpeople would suffer to the degree that public attention was drawn to it. It is also possible that society and the bureau agents were personally offended by Foster's actions; freedmen's aid workers varied widely in their acceptance of "social equality" between members of the two races.

Ultimately, Foster's critics knew only half the story about her strong "attachments" to the black folk of Martinsburg. The other half is not revealed fully in her diary, but we learn enough about her relationship to a young black man, the enigmatic John Brown, to know that her feelings ran far deeper than a simple evening stroll might indicate. A former Union soldier, Brown was part of a large family to which Foster grew exceptionally close (his younger brother Elisha was her school "pet"). Foster greatly admired John Brown, a self-taught, intelligent man, and she relied on his assistance in night school classes, describing him as her "faithful ally" and "firmest support." She followed his progress in "seeking the Savior"; after recording in her diary a discussion she had with him "about his soul," she concluded the entry by noting, "I am *so* happy tonight." And surely that happiness stemmed at least in part from her deep per-

sonal affection for Brown. Again, in the privacy of her diary she
commented on his "noble" bearing, "his fine, intelligent face" (another white woman was also "struck with his appearance upon first
seeing him"). One terrifying evening in January 1866 when a group
of rowdy white youths disrupted her school, Foster heard gunshots
and instinctively reached for Brown. She "caught his hand to hold
him back lest he should be shot" and later noted, "I could not
help it."

It is tempting to interpret the cryptic remarks sprinkled throughout Foster's diary in light of her relationship with John Brown—her
"wayward purpose" and "the secret" that she dared not commit to
paper: "Oh Lord thou knowest my heart." We discover that she continued to write to Brown (along with other friends, male and female,
black and white, young and old) after leaving Martinsburg and trea-
sured his photograph. She took pains to conceal her correspondence
with Brown from Superintendent N. C. Brackett. Considering the
nature of this unusual friendship, we might suggest that, in the end,
Foster was, ironically, much more discreet than her northern critics
ever imagined and that the threat she posed to the racial caste system in fact surpassed the unrepentant rebels' wildest nightmares.
Had her diary been made public at the time, the repercussions
would have been far more devastating than either official censure or
idle gossip.

During the 1867–68 school year the American Missionary Association assigned Foster to an isolated plantation school in South
Carolina, where she presumably could cause embarrassment to neither her sponsors nor herself. Foster enjoyed this school, after a dis-
appointing experience in Harpers Ferry. Sporadic accounts of her
year back in Maine between assignments (beginning in the summer
of 1867) suggest that her exciting months in Martinsburg would
serve as the standard by which she measured the rest of her life. She
became bored and frustrated by domestic duties, including rounds
of visiting ("six duller calls it was never my lot to make"), and seemed
torn between her desire for a home of her own and her disgust with
the drudgery required of a married woman to maintain one.

After Martinsburg, Foster took a keen interest in the great politi-

cal debates of the day and freely expressed her disapproval of the
conservative tendencies of President Andrew Johnson as well as the
pro-planter policies carried out by the Freedmen's Bureau. Yet she
apparently believed that women could most effectively exert political power not through the suffrage but through their "potent home
influence [which followed] men into the political arena and into the
halls of legislation." Foster thus seems to have resembled other active, reform-minded women like Catharine Beecher, women who
never married, lived socially productive lives, and believed in the
moral superiority of women over men, but shunned political activity
in the traditional sense.

Foster's short stories and poetry, published during the war years,
leave unresolved questions concerning the ways in which her so-
journ in the South might have altered or confirmed her classic
"women's sphere" ideology. Equal in quality and similar in themes
to the fiction found in recent anthologies of nineteenth-century sentimental women's literature, Foster's stories divide much of human
experience into opposing categories of male-female, public-private,
political-domestic values and actions. She populated her pinched,
predictable literary world with the stock characters of the period:
The virtuous heroine who was—choose one or some combination of
the following—crippled, orphaned, overworked, misunderstood,
unappreciated, poverty-stricken; the kindly, wise mother; and the
insensitive, brutish father. (We might wonder how and why the
compliant, wide-eyed boys featured in some of her stories would
eventually grow up to be such wretches.) In these pieces, a good
heart was rarely its own reward; romantic love, a favorable marriage, and a tidy inheritance were necessary for a happy ending.

We can only speculate whether, after Martinsburg, Foster came
to hail her own work as the melding of two "spheres" of endeavor,
the political and the nurturing, or whether she lamented her own
place in limbo, fully belonging to, or accepted by, neither one world
or the other. Certainly the circumstances of her death, a martyrdom
of sorts, would have appealed to her melodramatic instincts, and
they made a fitting end to her own life of lonely struggle. In this case
the heroine died vindicated not in her own time but by history. Stu-

dents and scholars in the fields of women's studies, Afro-American
studies, and social history owe a debt of gratitude to Wayne Reilly
for rescuing Sarah Jane Foster from the obscurity which she so
mightily feared; at long last she will receive the attention—and,
yes, appreciation—that she deserves.

Jacqueline Jones
Wellesley College

PREFACE

When I began to edit my great-great-aunt's diary and letters, my major goal was to reveal the human drama in the experiences of a single person whose life, at a time of personal crisis, became intertwined in the national crisis of Reconstruction. Later the project revealed itself as an opportunity to cast light on the aims and frustrations of a whole class of women, whose struggle for self-identity intimated the birth of the modern women's movement and the civil rights movement of the 1950s and 1960s. The significance of Foster's life lies not in great deeds or literature but in her own candid and accurate recording of what it was like to be a female at a crucial juncture in history, struggling to act on ambitions not yet shared by much of society, either in its conception of a proper woman's role or the proper relationship between the black and white races.

Most of the story is told in the scattered remains of Foster's writings, foremost of which are two diaries written in 1864 and 1866 that survived for many years in an old trunk in a Maine barn in the possession most recently of my cousin Minna Thompson. References in the diaries led to other sources including small but important collections of letters at the Amistad Research Center in New Orleans and at Harpers Ferry National Historic Park. The discovery of Foster material sometimes occurred quite by chance. My wife was told during casual conversation of the location of what may be the last set of *Zion's Advocate* in existence. Foster's published travel letters were located in that decaying pile of the obscure newspaper lying uncataloged and unprotected in the open stacks of the Colby College library in Waterville, Maine. They are now on microfilm at the University of Maine, thanks to the efforts of Eric Flower, former special collections librarian. What I have been able to find of Aunt Jane's (as she was called many years later by nieces and grandnieces who knew her only by reputation) published short stories and poems were located in a more orderly fashion in tattered collections of the *Home Monthly* at Colby and at the American Antiquarian Society in Worcester, Massachusetts.

The decision to include in this book only that portion of her 1866 diary from January 1 until August 4, when she wrote her last letter to *Zion's Advocate* about her experiences in West Virginia, was purely arbitrary, based on a desire to focus on her southern experience. The part omitted is a continuation of her time back in Maine after her return from West Virginia, followed, beginning on October 1, with an account of her experience caring for an invalid in Boston. I have been unable to locate any other diaries except for the 1864 account of her life in Maine. References to that diary are included in this volume when they shed light on her background and character.

I have made no intentional changes in Foster's diary other than to add some punctuation for clarity. Occasionally, her writing is so illegible or faded that it is impossible to see the punctuation that may be there. Illegible words are indicated by [   ]. The only changes made in the letters from *Zion's Advocate*, other than the correction of a few obvious typographical errors, were to correct the spelling of the Reverend Francis L. Cardozo's last name in one letter. The dates when her letters appeared in the newspaper are in brackets next to the dates on which she wrote them.

This project would not have been completed without the generous cooperation of numerous people including some descendants of Sarah Jane Foster's sister, Emma Ann Foster Thompson. Foremost of these was Minna Thompson. Her long-term loan of the Foster diaries and family photographs, coupled with her encouragement and advice, made everything else possible. Other family members who loaned materials were Lillian Jasper and my mother, Carolyn Reilly.

The search for other materials was greatly facilitated by many librarians and archivists, including Eric Flower, Libby Soifer, and Muriel Sanford of the University of Maine; Mary Riley of Bates College; Keith E. Hammersla of the Martinsburg–Berkeley County Public Library; Clifton H. Johnson and the staff of the Amistad Research Center; Hilda E. Staub of the Harpers Ferry National Historical Park; Beverly Carlson of the American Baptist Historical Society; Clifton Davis of Bangor Theological Seminary; Harold M. Forbes of West Virginia University; Harlan Greene of the South Carolina Historical Society; and Michael P. Musick of the National

Archives. Other librarians and archivists at the University of Maine (especially the Interlibrary Loan Department), the American Antiquarian Society, the Bangor Public Library, Colby College, and the Maine State Archives were particularly helpful.

Providing valuable comments on portions of the manuscript were Professor Edmund L. Drago of the College of Charleston, Professor John E. Stealey III of Shepherd College, the Reverend Robert Howard of Hampden, Maine, and Nancy Remsen, senior writer at the *Bangor Daily News*.

Other people providing various sorts of assistance included Ardeana Hamlin, Marion Roseen, Herbert Adams, Roberta Todd, John Day, Jack Loftus, Eric Zelz, and Robert DeLong. The latter's generous contribution of his skill brought faded family photographs back to life for this volume. Others providing valuable advice and information were Professor Jane H. Pease of the University of Maine; Margaret C. Sawyer and Charlotte B. Wallace of the Gray Historical Society, Gray, Maine; Martha Zierden of the Charleston Museum; Helga Vogel of the Preservation Society of Charleston; Tessa Perry of the College of Charleston; Leslie S. Rowland of the University of Maryland; and staff members at the Admiral Boarman House in Martinsburg.

I am indebted to the Maine Humanities Council and its associate director, Richard D'Abate, for making available to me a grant so that I could obtain the services of a researcher, Daphna L. Blair, to review papers in the Storer College collection at West Virginia University and have other research and photographic work done in South Carolina and West Virginia.

I am also indebted to the staff of the University Press of Virginia for recognizing the merit of Sarah Jane Foster's papers and for guiding me in developing them into a book that would be of interest to academic scholars as well as the general public.

Finally, my wife, Karen, has played an inestimable role. Her library, editorial, and typing skills, along with her personal understanding during some of the more arduous parts of this project, helped immeasurably. To her belongs a lion's share of the credit for the collecting and annotation of Sarah Jane Foster's papers.

ABBREVIATIONS USED IN NOTES

AMAA   American Missionary Association Archives, Amistad Research Center, Tulane University, New Orleans

BRFAL   Records of the Bureau of Refugees, Freedmen, and Abandoned Lands, Record Group 105, National Archives, Washington, D.C.

CSC   Collections of Storer College, Harpers Ferry National Historical Park, Harpers Ferry, W.Va.

HM   *Home Monthly* (Boston)

MS   *Morning Star* (Dover, N.H.)

NE   *New Era* (Martinsburg, W.Va.)

SJF   Sarah Jane Foster

WVH   *West Virginia History*

ZA   *Zion's Advocate* (Portland, Maine)

What historians have said about
Sarah Jane Foster: Teacher of the Freedmen

"Wayne E. Reilly's skillfully edited collection of his great-great aunt's diary entries and published letters to the Freewill Baptist *Zion's Advocate* reveals the religiously based social activism typical of white female missionary teachers during Reconstruction... Historians of women will find this volume valuable for its rendering of nineteenth-century teaching and the experiences of an unmarried woman working and living apart from her family." — Karen Trahan Leathem, *Mississippi Quarterly*

"[Sarah Jane Foster's] writings provide considerable insight into the motivations of a group of individuals who have been maligned by traditional historians of Reconstruction as carpetbaggers and glorified by revisionist historians as saints...[This] would be an excellent book to use in an undergraduate class in American History or Women's Studies." — Amy Thompson McCandless, *South Carolina Historical Magazine*

"Foster found herself both ostracized by and in occasional danger from southern whites who rejected the legitimacy of her goals and who were scandalized by her behavior. Her apparent rejection of convention was no more welcomed by her sponsors, who sent her to a remote plantation in South Carolina... By juxtaposing the private and public versions of Foster's experience, Reilly has added significantly to our ability to understand her." — Marli F. Weiner, *Journal of American History*

"This volume appears at first glance to be just another diary of a Yankee missionary-teacher in the postbellum South... But do not be deceived by appearances. Foster is more than simply another teacher of the freedmen." — M. Jennie McGuire, *The Journal of Southern History*

"This collection of letters and diaries is a valuable addition to the growing body of published primary accounts of the experiences and conditions under which teachers of ex-slaves and their students attempted the learning process... What sets this account apart from most others written by the white female teachers of freedpersons is the conflict within its author between her attraction to a man forbidden to her, a young black man, and her vision of marriage as a trap that she would not enter." — Carol Lemley Montgomery, *History of Education Quarterly*

INTRODUCTION

S arah Jane Foster was one of the hundreds of northerners who went South to teach the newly freed slaves during and after the Civil War. Their efforts have been documented extensively in books and scholarly articles, but autobiographical accounts by the teachers are rare. Foster's story, taken from her diary and newspaper writings, provides a unique picture of the public hopes and private hardships of one of those "soldiers of light and love."[1]

What is known of Sarah Jane Foster's life begins and ends primarily in her own writing. Between 1864 and her death in 1868 she produced at least two diaries, twenty-three published letters, and an assortment of short stories, poems, and essays. A small collection of private letters rounds out the available sources. The other twenty-five years of her life are mainly a blank. All that is known about her from official records can be summed up briefly. She grew up in the country town of Gray, Maine, a shoemaker's daughter, one of seven children surviving to adulthood. As early as 1860 she was working both as a domestic and as a schoolteacher. Her family belonged to the local Freewill Baptist Church, which no doubt was a bastion of abolitionist sympathies. Her father was a church official. Nothing more is known for certain about her education or anything else about her youth. Unlike her brother Samuel Howard, a private in the Union army, she left no military record with dates of battles fought and ills contracted. She never married. Even her death record was destroyed in a fire, so we know only by family tradition of the tropical disease that suddenly killed her at age twenty-eight. The granite marker in the cemetery behind the Gray fire station near the Maine Turnpike would be her only tangible remains today were it not for her writing, which until recently remained scattered and uncollected from Maine to New Orleans.

The dramatic critical point in her life was, as she referred to it, the "incident" in 1866 at Martinsburg, West Virginia, when the young woman from Maine confronted the bitter residue of the Civil War. It is detailed in the portion of her diary and fifteen of the travel letters originally published in *Zion's Advocate* included in this book. The impact of that crushing affair irrevocably shaped her future until the day she contracted the jungle disease in the swampy country on the outskirts of Charleston, South Carolina, where she had been exiled in her calling.

Beginnings

Jacqueline Jones's study of northern teachers in Georgia provides a benchmark against which to measure Sarah Jane Foster's background. Jones concluded the typical teacher was "the well-educated daughter of a farmer or professional and was highly conscious of her duty to God and country." Foster fits into the bottom end of the social scale of the teachers analyzed by Jones, who found only two shoemaker's children in her sample. Most had had some college or at least academy training. Many had been teachers, but only one had been a writer and none admitted to having done domestic work before going South.[2]

Born into an ambitious family on October 12, 1839, Foster was the daughter of Moses B. and Eliza A. Benson Foster. One of her brothers became a minister and another a doctor, while a sister became a nurse after her divorce and wrote a book on the care of babies.[3] Foster was aware of her siblings' high aspirations. On her older brother Caleb's twenty-ninth birthday, she wrote in her diary: "Oh how I wish that he were married and settled in life. I've been thinking that families that try to rise as we have seldom do marry."[4] Of the seven children, this analysis remained true for only her, perhaps making her one of those unmarried women whose numbers increased during the nineteenth century possibly because they saw spinsterhood as a means to accomplishing their goals outside of the constraints of marriage. However, such activism was "a double-edged experience." Women like Foster were deeply torn between the domestic role they were expected to fill and their desire for self-fulfillment.[5] The conflict was reflected in Foster's periods of depression when she was cleaning houses and caring for ailing people at the expense of her writing time. It is a theme reflected in the frustrations expressed by some of her female heroines in her short stories. This was the era of "The Cult of True Womanhood," as historians have conveniently labeled the complex of characteristics—piety, purity, domesticity, and submissiveness—embodied in the perfect ideal of womanhood.[6] While Foster sometimes promoted such virtues in her writing, her life strained to break the mold. Her strong religious convictions helped her in her struggle to be pure. But her domesticity quotient was low indeed. She suffered doing housework. As her experience in West Virginia plainly indicated, she was submissive only if it did not conflict with her convictions. Her motivating philosophy is better summed up in lines from one of her poems:

> Teach me that living is not life,
> If lived apart from noble strife,
>
> . . . . .
>
> Oh, teach me that life is to do and dare;
> That the glory of life is not to spare.[7]

Her life fits more comfortably within the boundaries of "the ideal of real womanhood" described by Francis B. Cogan in *All-American Girl: The Ideal of Real Womanhood in Mid-Nineteenth-Century America*. That "ideal" competed with the "cult" for acceptance in popular domestic fiction and advice books. It emphasized physical fitness, higher education, and the ability to earn a living if need be, as well as the astute selection of a husband for most women. It differed from feminism in that womanhood remained within "a separate sphere" in which females had a higher moral calling than men to maintain religious and family values.[8]

Foster admired her mother. Her admiration was revealed at the height of her troubles at Martinsburg when she wrote in her diary: "Today I have been fancying Mother in my place. She would defy the mob, board anywhere or nowhere and keep the school. I am at heart some like her."[9] Mrs. Foster may have been the model for the kind, nurturing mothers who appear in several of Foster's short shories. Like her character Alice in "From Twilight to Dawn,"

Foster believed she possessed "the quiet resolution which she had inherited from her gentle mother."[10]

She seldom spoke of her father. Once she described him as "cross, and then silly with kindness as he sometimes is." Another time she wrote, "Father lives without recreation always." He was not, however, an insensitive man. After viewing the damage done by the Portland fire in July 1866, he could not speak of it without tears.[11] But perhaps he was a model for the stern, humorless fathers portrayed in many of her stories. Her relationship with him may have approximated the relationship between the character Alice and her father. Alice overhears him state that he wishes his eldest child (Foster was second oldest in her family) were a boy to help him save the failing family farm. Cut to the quick by this comment, Alice shows what she is worth by earning $50 toward the mortgage with her skill in making pictures from moss, a pastime the Foster sisters enjoyed as well. When Alice's father asks what he can do to reward her, she responds, "Only be satisfied with me, dear father." The reader is informed that "Alice had proved what every true female heart longs to prove, that she was neither helpless nor altogether dependent."

This passage combined Foster's own longing for paternal acceptance with her lifelong struggle for independence and recognition. If she should fail, she was well aware of what happened to dependent, unmarried women without skills from the example of her friend Phi Haskell. In 1864 she had lived with Phi for a time to help her care for her sick husband and children. She recorded in her diary on July 4, "I hope that I shall never do as she has and throw away my life." After Phi's husband died, the Masons gave her a sewing machine. "Oh I am glad for her," wrote Foster. "I hope that she will do well because she is one of my most valued friends.[12]

A good marriage was a way to avoid dependence, but a bad marriage or a life of domestic drudgery was not for Foster. Upon visiting a cousin who lived in a neighborhood of weavers in a nearby town, she commented: "I wonder if I should be willing to be such a slave to work as those people all are. No I feel that I shall not. I could not marry for such a destiny. It can not be a duty. Yet all praise women who toil every moment and never spend an hour in self cultivation. I will never be such a drudge, however. Very likely I shall never marry at all."[13]

Home Duties

Until she went south, Foster lived a life little different from that of many young women. The expression "home duties" she used in a letter of application to the American Missionary Association in 1866 was a euphemism. She worked in many homes doing chores for relatives and acquaintances beginning at least as early as 1860 when she was listed in the U.S. Census as a domestic in the household of Mr. and Mrs. Frederick M. Cobb of Portland.[14] In the first three months of 1864 she was still working for the Cobbs. During that year her diary indicates she did chores and cared for sick and dying people in at least seven different homes in the communities of Portland, Gray, New Gloucester, and Raymond, Maine. In the summer of 1866 after she returned from West Virginia, she was sent by her family to care for, and sleep in the same bed with, her dying grandmother and other sick people. "I only keep cheerful by not thinking," she wrote in her diary during one such stint in a relative's home.[15]

The work was frequently backbreaking, and the people were not always congenial. Cobb was an easygoing railroad engineer, but his wife was a dour taskmistress who chided Foster for presenting "the appearance of evil" by writing letters on Sunday. She may have been a model for Mrs. Armitage in Foster's story "My Disappointment."[16] It is about an orphaned girl who lives as "a veritable prisoner" doing domestic chores for Mrs. Armitage, who is "one of those moral icebergs who can petrify all who come near them into serviceable automatons." Mrs. Armitage is preparing to move, just as the Cobbs had been preparing to do the year before, with Foster doing much of the work. The orphaned narrator in the story expresses Foster's own sense of repression in purple prose: "Denied all outward expression my hot passions were consuming my very heart. My icy reserve was but a surface crust. Beneath was a boiling crater into whose angry depths I dared not look, while sometimes conscience shrank back aghast at wild wishes that dared not shape themselves into deeds."

The story is also an expression of Foster's keen sense of class and gender consciousness, which occasionally appears in her diaries as well. In it, the orphan girl is helped to escape by a wealthy neighbor boy. "We were of an age; but he was the petted child of influential parents. He would be well educated. He would be able to move in the best society. Appreciation, approbation, success, awaited him everywhere. With *me* how different was life! Tied down to an irksome drudgery, kept back from all improvement, growing worse day by day,—whither was I tending?"

Writing

When she was not cleaning house, Foster was an avid disciple of self-improvement. Along with popular novels with titles like *Love and Secession* and *Herman or Young Knighthood,* she devoured Macaulay's histories, Poe's poetry, Shakespeare's plays, and Henry Ward Beecher's essays. She was also teaching herself French. After her experience in West Virginia, she took a special interest in books about black people, including *Uncle Tom's Cabin,* a biography of Toussaint L'Ouverture, and Livingstone's African explorations. One of her goals was to have enough money to own books.[17] Portland's stimulating cultural climate made up somewhat for the drudgery at the Cobbs, offering the country girl an expanded view of the world. During the first two-and-a-half months of 1864, Foster attended a dozen lectures by such luminaries as Beecher, Wendell Phillips, and Frederick Douglass.

Inspired by such a literary diet, she tried her hand at free-lance journalism with occasional edifying pieces for *Zion's Advocate,* the *Home Monthly,* and some other publications.[18] Her goal was financial independence and recognition. It was also to "do good." She wrote in her diary, "I am certain that I do not write for anything so much as the hope to being a help to some in the right way."[19]

Foster was one of a growing army of females writing sentimental and didactic novels and pieces for the dozens of women's magazines that appeared in the mid-nineteenth century. Their work was primarily concerned with the home and family virtues and the proper role of women. This was one of the few acceptable routes open to women who wished to enter the professions. The content of their work was intimately tied to advocacy of the moral values that women were supposed to be promoting in their own households.[20] This was certainly true of such Foster stories as "Silken Fetters."

The publisher and editor of *Zion's Advocate*, a newspaper affiliated with the Baptist church, was Dr. William Shailer, minister of the First Baptist Church in Portland.[21] Initially Foster was paid nothing for her work. But on February 24, 1864, she sent Shailer a note with her latest production, asking for some money. "I do not expect that he will. But I mean that he have to refuse," she noted shrewdly in her diary. After a long wait and a trip to Shailer's Portland office, she received $10 and an agreement for more money for future work. The arrangement with Shailer became her most fulfilling and lucrative outlet. Her obituary in *Zion's Advocate* stated that "thousands have read her articles with admiration."[22] Yet at that time she considered the paper only a temporary publisher. She wrote: "I mean to do so till I have a chance to do better. Then I will 'give them the slip'"[23]

Besides the religious essays in which she specialized, Foster was also writing instructive short stories with improbable plots and sentimental poems with edifying themes. On January 13, 1864, she "bought a book of a Mr. Pearson," striking up a potentially fruitful relationship. The Reverend Charles H. Pearson, who was the new owner of the *Home Monthly*, asked her for samples of her writing to show to the editor of another publication for which he was a columnist. "Thinks he can get me some pay," noted Foster. On June 3, Pearson accepted one of her stories for his magazine after Foster visited him in his Boston office with samples of her work.

"An excellent family fireside magazine, and cheap enough to come within the means of all," is the way an advertising blurb in *Hull's Journal of Health* described the *Home Monthly*. The *Lewiston Daily Journal* said, "As a high-toned family monthly, it is unsurpassed in the whole field of our periodical literature." Having gathered a stable of writers, Pearson announced: "More than fifty Authors and Magazinists whose pens are consecrated to noble aims will aid to make our Magazine varied, genial, fresh and homelike; useful, elevated, and unsurpassed in excellence." Foster was much impressed with her honor, but had she known how purely honorary it was to become she would have been sorely distressed.

Teaching

Foster is listed twice in the 1860 U.S. Census. Besides living in Portland with the Cobbs, she is also listed as living at home employed as a teacher in a common school.[24] The profession dominated by women in the nineteenth century was teaching, because it was socially acceptable and the pay was too low to attract men. Along with writing for the women's magazines, teaching was considered an extension of the True Woman's role as moral instructor of children. It was only a step further for an adventurous young woman infused with missionary zeal to join the teachers headed south to teach the freedmen where there were souls to convert and new material for the pen.[25]

Foster's level of education is unknown. She most likely attended school for a number of years. The Reverend Ebenezer Bean, minister of the Congregational church in Gray, described her as "well educated, a vigorous thinker as well as forcible writer" in a letter of recommendation he forwarded to her for the AMA.[26] Her sister Emma was still taking courses at the age of eighteen in 1864 at the schoolhouse located next to the Foster home on Church Street. High-school classes were sometimes conducted on its upper floor.[27] Perhaps Sarah Jane was merely well read. In a comment to her cousin Nelson Jordan, she wrote in her diary, "Nelson asked me 'where I got my education.' I told him I 'did not know.'"[28] The subject was sensitive. In an uncharacteristic burst of envy in her diary she wrote: "Delia Haskell was in to tea. She graduated at the Edward Little Institute at Auburn last week. Ah well such privileges are not for me and I must do as well as I can without them."[29]

Ample evidence of Foster's progressive teaching philosophy has been preserved in her short stories and in her letters from the South. Her teaching ideal was expressed in the character of Robert Cleveland in her story "Cast Down, but Not Destroyed."[30] The story's narrator, Ellen Vining, is an orphan, the daughter of an artist. Like so many of Foster's heroines, she is "a waif upon the cold world" and "a gloomy, morose girl-woman" whose childhood had been "enslaved" by unnamed oppressors. In school Ellen is considered academically inferior except in art, for which she is "sternly reproved for wasting time" by her teachers. Along comes Robert Cleveland who—in the space of two short pages—encourages her artistic talents, builds her self-confidence, finds a place for her to live in a kind, loving household, and then marries her. In another reflection of herself, Foster, through her narrator, tells us, "My life had been like the tree [sketched by Ellen], blown by adverse winds from its original symmetry and grace; but I could yet save and make it useful, even beautiful, by steady efforts to rise above low and unfavorable surroundings."

A story with a similar theme is "Appreciation."[31] Miss Winship encourages Johnnie, a presumed dullard, to develop his manual skills and build up his self-confidence. Johnnie builds a ventilator for the schoolroom and reroutes a mountain stream for a water supply. Another pupil, Susi, is a bookworm who wants to be a writer, but she is too bound up with her studies. Miss Winship encourages her to play games so that she will be fully rounded in her understanding of human nature. Johnnie grows up to be a successful inventor, and Susi writes a book. The secret of Miss Winship's success was that "all of the children were met upon their own ground, and felt sure of sympathy and encouragement."

Similar thoughts are expressed in other stories. In "Silken Fetters" and "Conquered," love and kindness are wielded by the heroines to tame the "vicious" streaks in young male characters. Foster found this technique did not always work, however, when she went south. Despite her personal repugnance for the practice but apparently under pressure from some parents, she decided she had to whip her students more often. On January 9, 1866, she recorded in her diary that her landlord had told her that "one of my large girls says I don't whip enough. I am not a brute and I won't be. I believe I am right." But on January 17, she wrote, "I see that I *must* whip in my school." By February 1 the technique had had its effect: "Got on well with the school today,. I begin to hope that I shall not have to trouble the scholars with the ruler much more." And the next day she wrote, "I mean now to try love on the boys who are trying to be good."[32]

She was less successful in quelling her impatience with stupidity. Ridicule became part of her classroom technique, although she apparently never felt comfortable using it. She informed her *Zion's Advocate* readers on May 2, "I sometimes use [students'] laughter as a sort of spur to dull scholars, letting them laugh at their blunders, and it works well, for they are sensitive to ridicule." Her ridicule may have gotten her into trouble with some students who complained, claiming she spent too much time preparing for her night classes. "They fret really because I ridicule their dullness sometimes," she surmised in her diary.[33]

Missionary Teacher

Nellie Stanwood, a crippled girl, wants desperately to be a missionary in India in Foster's story "Silken Fetters," published in 1865.[34] Nellie could be a missionary only in her imagination because of her physical handicap. While advising Nellie to settle for being a "home missionary" in the story, Foster determined to have the real thing. On November 13, 1864, she recorded a significant passage in her diary, around the same time she invented Nellie. "I've been reading about India today. Would that I could go there to carry the word of God. I long to work for him. May he open the way." Soon she was seized by the national spirit of altruism for the former slaves. A month later she sent off a letter of application to teach the freedmen to the Reverend Silas Curtis, corresponding secretary for the Freewill Baptist Home Mission Society in New Hampshire.[35] Foster's acceptance by the Baptists gave her a way to combine her ambition to write with accepted religious motives on a path toward her twin goals of independence and recognition.

Foster arrived in West Virginia in November 1865, one of a small contingent of Freewill Baptist teachers and ministers determined to aid the freedmen in several towns in the Shenandoah Valley. The Shenandoah Mission grew into Storer College, a normal school for blacks founded in 1867 at Harpers Ferry. Foster's tenure with the group lasted only one school year, however. What began as an inspirational adventure developed into the darkest period of her life when her actions, reflecting her belief in the equality of the races, drew fire from the local white population and the consternation of her supervisors. In April she was transferred from Martinsburg to Harpers Ferry under the closer supervision of her superiors, after her practice of walking in public with black men became the subject of barroom gossip and practical jokes and her school was repeatedly disrupted and vandalized.

Foster had come to West Virginia armed with a sincere desire to "do good," but her ambition blossomed into a full-scale ethical crisis.[35] Did "doing good" mean acting on her belief that black people should be treated as equals, or did it mean appeasing the local white population to satisfy her superiors that her presence was politically viable? The Reverend N. C. Brackett, her immediate supervisor, was under pressure from officers of the Freedmen's Bureau to remove her immediately after the series of escalating incidents at Martinsburg in January, but he did not yield until April vacation. She summed up her dilemma in a letter to *Zion's Advocate* on April 4: "I do not learn that anyone believes I have done wrong, but I have excited a prejudice that *they* think it best to favor a little." By then she had decided to "submit quietly" to the "powers that be" for the good of the cause as well as her own future.

But passages in her diary express the full depths of her outrage and despair provoked by those who, it seemed to her, were betraying the people they had come to help. The feelings of guilt, powerlessness, and loneliness, coupled with the fears that her reputation was endangered, caused her to go quietly. "I wish that I *could* be reconciled, but I never shall be I fear," she confided to her diary. On the same day, she wrote to *Zion's Advocate* expressing her willingness to submit quietly in the model of the good Christian woman of the time.

From Concord, New Hampshire, the Reverend Mr. Curtis wrote to Brackett: "I hope you will take occasion from this to give everyone of your teachers a *good, sound thorough lecture* on their *deportment;* and charge them to take an effectual warning from the affair at M. and shun the *very appearance of evil.* We cannot be at the expense of raising money, as it comes to pay traveling expenses, Board and Salary of teachers to go among the freedmen to bring reproach and disgrace upon the cause, and upon our denomination." Curtis then urged Brackett not to be too severe because Foster had not "intentionally committed any crime" and to keep the affair quiet so as not to injure her reputation. "State the cause and we must suffer on account of her indiscreetness. And I hope that others will learn to be more cautious and careful. They should remember that rebel eyes are constantly upon them seeking some occasion to injure them and retain or prevent our work of mercy among the Freedmen." [37]

The crisis at Martinsburg was not unique to the Shenandoah Mission. The issue of black and white fraternization surfaced often enough to become divisive in the freedmen's aid movement. At least one teacher asked for a transfer from her teaching assignment in Wilmington, North Carolina, rather than submit to an order to refrain from socializing with blacks outside of school. Martha L. Kellogg requested to be boarded with a black family. "I desire not to be identified with any policy that ignores or repudiates social equality, and I desire to be, where I can act freely in the matter, according to conscience and the gospel idea—to treat the colored people as I should whites in the same circumstances." [38]

Yet, Foster was not so naive as to believe that ostentatious displays of familiarity could suffice for real equality, a charge sometimes leveled at the northerners. "The colored people have a prejudice of color themselves. They do not know how to be treated as equals. In most cases an attempt to treat them so would result in the loss of their esteem, and do more harm than good. There are exceptions, but I speak of the mass. While all are trying to prejudice them against us, undue familiarity would tend to make them believe that we are, as they have been told, low and unworthy of respect." [39]

The treatment accorded to Foster by some of the citizens of Martinsburg was little different than that experienced by many other northern teachers in the South after the war. Conditions at Martinsburg were stressful for a young lady from the Maine countryside. Gunfire outside her school and harassment from drunken rowdies and practical jokers were standard fare. Only the presence of a contingent of soldiers and the earnest black men, sometimes armed, who occasionally walked her home at night guaranteed her safety and the stability of her school. Taunted with the title "nigger teacher" as she walked down the street, Foster roomed with "a most excellent Union family" who promptly evicted her when she became an object of controversy. Her next home was a rough log cabin with a gleam of daylight through the roof. But she was luckier than some of her colleagues in nearby towns who had to live alone in their schools because they could find no one who would provide room and board. Her successor at Martinsburg, Anne S. Dudley, had previously taught at Charles Town where she was escorted to town under an armed guard and felt obliged to keep a "good axe and six-shooter at the head of my bed at night, resolved to sell my life as dearly as possible—if need be."[40]

Even without Foster's personal problems, the working conditions in the freedmen's schools were abominable. She often worked night and day, so long, in fact, that her superiors ordered her to cut back the time she spent in the classroom. She was paid $15 a month and donated $5 back to the missionary association, so that she was unable to afford boots and other necessities.[41] The social price was high as well. Foster and other teachers usually were ostracized, or worse, at the hands of local white people, even in places like Martinsburg where large numbers of Union sympathizers lived. Some idealistic young women quickly retreated to their comfortable northern homes after a dose of culture shock and will-breaking work; a few died of tropical diseases as Foster did in 1868.[42]

Her school, described variously as "a small basement" and "uncommonly bad," was cramped and ill equipped. The classroom contained no blackboard or map of the United States and few textbooks. Attendance was more than fifty some days.[43] One of her chief reasons for writing pieces for *Zion's Advocate*, besides raising money to promote the cause, was to solicit Sunday school newspapers and books. Unable to afford the funds to provide her Charleston, South Carolina students with a picnic at the end of the term in 1868, she attempted to solicit the money from her readers with the promise of "specimens of atmospheric moss" by return mail. That raised only $4, and there was no picnic. Even to travel to South Carolina in

1867 she had felt obliged to raise some of her own support from black residents of Maine.[44]

Yet, despite the hardships, the spiritual incentives were great. At Martinsburg she made lasting friends in the black community, as evidenced especially by her strong emotional attachment to her teaching assistant John H. Brown and some of his siblings. The work fulfilled her lifelong need for accomplishment and self-sufficiency in a noble cause. Finally, the experience gave her interesting material to write about. During the depths of her troubles in Martinsburg, she summed up such rewards: "I never was in a work that so thoroughly aroused my whole being, and gave life such a zest."[45]

In July 1866, after she returned from West Virginia for the summer to her home in Gray, the Freewill Baptist Home Mission Society revoked her teaching commission for the next school term. Humiliated, Foster abandoned her writing in public journals and returned to her former career as a housekeeper and personal attendant in the homes of acquaintances and relatives. To make matters worse, Pearson, the publisher of her fiction and poetry, could not pay her.

Foster summed up her feelings in a letter to her two sisters, Emma and Lizzie.

> I lack sometimes hope for the future. Here I am past twenty-seven and what have I done as yet toward my great aim? God knows I've tried, and I should have succeeded if I had been fairly treated, for just pay for my last three years pen work would have made me able to write wholly and to publish one or more books. I feel thankful for what I have done, but now the way looks very dark to me. As to mill work I have thought of it, but I rather dislike the idea, and I would have to learn on woolen work. I can only go step by step. My present duty is clear and I am blessed with the strength to do it. Perhaps hard work is good for me, for I felt sick half the time home since I feared I was not going back to West Virginia. My mind and nerves always enslave my body, and I am always sick when I get low and despondent. Now I haven't time for that, and so I keep up which maybe I could not at home.[46]

Foster's "great aim" was to publish a book. She had written a manuscript for a novel, which is lost today. She had hoped to use the money from Pearson to pay for the printing of the book. Her life during this gloomy period remained dominated by an unremitting desire to "do good" through her writing or her teaching, or through domestic work if all else failed. When the letter to her sisters was written, her "duty" was to care for an invalid in Boston. The view from her window reinforced her gloomy outlook. She told her sisters, "Here my prospect front is a big chest factory, and in the rear the backside of a block of houses mostly peopled by Irish. Very inspiring isn't it? I do gain some amusement watching the children play."

Foster was engaged in more than self-pity at the time she wrote to her sisters. Three days before, she had written an application to the American Missionary Association for a teaching commission to replace the one that had been taken away by the Freewill Baptists. In it she expressed none of her bitterness and self-doubt, choosing instead to present herself in words designed to appeal to AMA missionaries searching for women of high virtue, boundless energy, and missionary zeal:

> "My name in full is Miss Sarah Jane Foster. I am twenty seven years of age. Being the eldest daughter of a large family I have been accustomed to the care and education of young children. I always succeeded well in securing respect and obedience. I have been for two or three years a regular correspondent of the Zion's Advocate and Home Monthly, which I may call my only settled occupation save last year's teaching aside from my home duties. I am *not* a singer, but in the elementary drilling which is so necessary in Freedmen's Schools I know that I excel. No pupil will pass over half learned tasks under my supervision. I have taken children from the Alphabet to three letter words in two or three weeks more than once. My health is excellent. I have not been confined to the bed by illness for over seventeen years, and I am not subject to any physical derangements that I know of. May I not hope for a commission ere long?"[47]

The only surviving candid assessment of Foster was provided when the ever-supportive Brackett wrote a recommendation for her application to the AMA late in 1866. His comments verified her self-appraisal with one important qualification. He wrote:

> Miss Foster is a remarkably healthy, zealous, enthusiastic missionary. She has the strength and the spirit to work day and night for the freedmen. She was unfortunate in not understanding the prejudices of the people, and in her zeal to do a great deal, exposed herself to scandal.
>
> Her weak point is in being a little rough in manners.
>
> I should think there are places, for instance, a plantation where Miss F. would do a good work, perhaps any where, except where she would come too much in contact with the white people. She is also able to do some service with her pen.[48]

Brackett's qualified recommendation of Foster was heeded at AMA headquarters. She was hired to teach in Charleston under the black educator and politician Francis L. Cardozo, but once there she was sent to an isolated, black-operated farm on rural Charleston Neck where she saw white people only once a week. No diaries have come to light from this period. The eight letters from *Zion's Advocate* reprinted here are the only record. It is clear from them that she fulfilled her wish to be a successful missionary teacher, although she never accomplished her "great aim" before she died.

Changing Perspectives

The movement of hundreds of Yankee schoolmarms and ministers to the South after the Civil War to teach the freedmen generated a heated debate. They were either criticized as meddlesome fanatics insensitive to southern mores and harmful to the interests of blacks or deified as God's army for black progress. The same issues have been debated by historians ever since.

At the turn of the century, for example, J. G. de Roulhac Hamilton in his history of Reconstruction in North Carolina concluded that the northern teachers "lacked moderation, tact, knowledge of the real condition of the needs of the negro, and, in far too many cases, that most priceless possession, common sense. They were free in their criticism of the South and frank in their expression of their dislike for Southern people. They were indiscreet in public speeches and persistently sought to antagonize the negroes against the white people of the South. . . . They lived often on terms of absolute equality with the negroes and complained that they were not received socially. Finally, in some instances, they were of bad character."[49]

At about the same time, W. E. B. Du Bois elevated the schoolmarms to saintly status: "The annals of this Ninth Crusade are yet to be written, the tale of a mission that seemed to our age far more quixotic than the quest of St. Louis seemed to his. Behind the mists of ruin and rapine waved the calico dresses of women who dared, and after the hoarse mouthings of the field guns rang the rhythm of the alphabet. Rich and poor they were, serious and curious. Bereaved now of father, now of brother, now of more than these, they came seeking a life work in planting New England schoolhouses among the white and black of the South. They did their work well."[50]

As late as 1941 Henry Lee Swint in a major study of the northern teachers in the South continued the debate in a predominantly negative vein. "The people of the South were not only sinners, but defeated sinners, who refused to be properly humble and abject, and who, worst of all, refused to repent of the error of their ways. Many of the teachers felt that everything which was, or had been, was wrong and must be uprooted and discarded." Nor did Swint approve of their teaching approach. "Given a group of zealous abolitionists and missionaries, fired with a desire to educate, convert and save, and well versed in the propagandist literature of the abolition crusade, stern in their righteous wrath against the people of an enemy section—given, in short, the self-appointed guardians of a nation's conscience—and it was to be expected that even the teaching of spelling and reading would be carried out with an eye to political effect."[51]

The civil rights upheavals of the last few decades have produced a new generation of historians with more sympathetic views. For example, Ronald E. Butchart found that the traditional interpretation of the northern teacher in the South had been "too narrow, too one-dimensional. It fails to point out that many educators went south to educate for freedom, or that such an effort might be needed to begin to compensate for two centuries of oppression. It fails to see the diversity of the teaching corps, the racism of many, the lack of commitment of some, the narrow ends and means of others. It fails to discover the humane ideals and human foibles of the movement." Much like Du Bois, Butchart emphasized the heroic stature of the movement: "They forsook comfort for the raw conditions of a war-ravaged country. They left friends for the malignity of a defeated people. Their courage often sprang from deep religious conviction but only occasional abolitionist ideology."[52]

Foster's writing reveals a person more complex than any of the stereotypes. She was unmarried and "no toady" by her own account, roughly approximating the image of the independent old maid, a stock character in the early literature of the freedmen's school movement. She did flout the social conventions of Martinsburg, but it was as much because of naiveté as conviction. She had not thought through the implications of her behavior in the tinderbox setting in which she worked. It is clear from her writing that she believed prejudice would evaporate in a short time. She was unprepared for the reaction of the white natives and of her superiors, and she lived to regret her behavior deeply. Her embarrassment in West Virginia stemmed from her initial uncertainty over how to deal with local white mores. "I have not yet visited any among the Freedmen, thinking it best to wait till the first prejudice of our opposers wore off. . . . I have not talked much as yet with the people, fearing that the white people might think I was searching out sensation items to their disadvantage. My silence and quietude has had the effect that I hoped, and all prejudice is slowly wearing out," she wrote to her readers in Zion's Advocate on January 1, 1866. Her private sentiments were the same. "I mean to act so that none can find fault with me about setting up the colored people above their place," she recorded in her diary on January 3. Within a few days, however, her ideals had taken control. After a black man was threatened for walking with her, she wrote in her diary on January 20: "I don't care. If he is not afraid to do it I am not. I shall treat all well who treat me well both black and white." And the next day she walked down the street with the same man "just to show that I did not mean to be driven off by the roughs. These men are good. Why shouldn't I treat them well."

Clearly, the mixed signals she received from her supervisors about the proper role as a teacher also contributed to the commotion that resulted in her transfer and dismissal. As a teacher she was expected to make official visits to the families of her students. Yet it was this very sort of fraternization that contributed to her downfall. Her problems had an immediate impact on her ability to carry out the goal, as reflected in the teacher reports she filed with the AMA. In January she recorded on her teacher report making fifteen visits to black families. By February her visits had dropped to only three as she struggled to repair the damage that had been done.[53] Faced with the controversy, she was hard-pressed to decide whether to accept personal invitations from her black friends or to attend their church services.

There is no evidence that she politicized her instruction. Her diaries and letters show her to be more moderate than radical in her politics. In a letter to the editor of the *Portland Daily Press* published on January 5, 1864, defending a speech in Portland by Anna E. Dickinson, she expressed support for equality for blacks "if it be possible," adding, "I care not how soon." Her grounds for opposing slavery were that it propped up "the unsightly edifice which we are trying to overthrow" and it degraded all workers whether black or white, southern or northern. On February 10, 1864, after hearing a speech by the radical abolitionist Wendell Phillips, whe wrote in her diary: "He is a good speaker but I think spoils his influence by going unnecessarily against the prejudices of the people." She was always a supporter of the war and interested in the movements of the Union as they pertained to her brother, Private Samuel Howard Foster of the 30th Maine, but comments about politics or the freedmen took up remarkably little space. One night she mentioned that a church elder had come collecting signatures on a petition to amend the constitution, but she did not tell to what purpose. During a stay with relatives in the nearby town of Raymond she expressed irritation at the Copperhead sentiments in town. Much more space is devoted to the kind of entries one would expect from a young woman

living far from the front, such as this one after a balmy spring day: "I
went Maying this morning with Emma and Avery as I planned. We
got some fine flowers and almost a quart of plums, . . . I have had
the headache all the rest of the day. But I have cleaned six windows
outside, made bread and fixed supper. I do not feel very plucky
now. Concluded to study my French lesson and did so an hour
or two." [54]

Besides being politically active abolitionists, segments of the
northern teaching delegation were labeled as bigots, feminists, and
temperance zealots. Foster does not fit into any of these categories.
She was intensely religious, but she was not a religious bigot like
her colleague who proclaimed of Harpers Ferry: "The only minister
here is a Catholic. It is a wicked place." [55] Upon visiting the Catholic
church in Martinsburg Foster found the service instructive and
commended the efforts of the Catholics to educate blacks. [56] And, far
from being a cultural bigot, she described with a fairly detached
eye the religious practices of blacks, including their spirituals,
"shouts," and other emotionally charged events that often offended
northerners. [57]

Nor was she a feminist. She did not believe in women's suffrage.
Instead she subscribed to the common notion that enshrined women
as the "Mothers of Civilization." [58] Her conclusion to an essay written in opposition to female suffrage is a good summation of the idea:
"A woman cannot share a man's public life while performing her private duties, and these duties cannot be neglected without endanger-
ing public morality. Woman may claim equality with man, but she
has been set apart to a holier and more silent work. Let man, as be-
fits their stronger frames, be the surgeons, doctors, lawyers, and
statesmen of our land, but let the women seek to be such wives,
mothers, and sisters as shall most purify and enoble these servants
of the public. [59] That she chafed under this perfect notion of womanhood is an irony that apparently escaped her.

Nor was she a fanatical temperance advocate. She might hand out
a temperance tract to a drunk on the street, but she was not averse
to a taste of homemade wine with friends. [60] Joe M. Richardson's
comment about the diversity of northern teachers serves as a fitting

benediction here. He wrote: "They were much the same as other
people: selfish and selfless, cowardly, courageous, understanding,
and arrogant. But whatever their human failings, they were as a
group far more sympathetic to blacks than was the country at large."[61]

Foster's bitter disappointment in West Virginia and her brief triumph in South Carolina make a uniquely American adventure story.
Her experience in the South was as much an intellectual as physical adventure. An inexperienced young woman full of fervor, she
learned firsthand what it was like to attempt to reform society. Her
principles were too politically inopportune to gain the support of either her superiors or even some in the black community.[62] Foster
tested her ideals against those of the world and found it lacking.
When she returned to work with the freedmen in South Carolina,
she was a wiser individual. Her initial goal in West Virginia of instill-
ing students with "English literature, hoping thus to elevate the
standard among them" had been tempered by concerns of a more
practical nature.[63] For example, two years later, upon her return to
the South, she noted: "The planters combine to keep down the farm
hands, and the people in the country are very poor. How can it be
otherwise when women have to work with heavy Southern hoes all
day for the paltry pittance of thirty cents? which is the usual rate of
pay now."[64] Her concern for poor black women, who attended her
schools in much smaller numbers than men, was also reflected in
her personal correspondence when she told an AMA official that she
should be paying her washerwoman "three or four dollars more."[65]

Integration could only fail in 1868 for most people unless they
lived like Foster on a black-run farm miles from the white community. Her fierce feelings about the conditions in which blacks lived
had deepened. "I only know that I never saw more sensitive children, and the longer I know them the more my soul revolts at the
tyranny which would fain deny them the right to all human feelings
and passions," she wrote.[66] Her rashness had not abated much either, although she now apparently exercised it only through her
pen, as when she rebuked a fellow Mainer, General O. O. Howard,
head of the Freedmen's Bureau, in print, much as she had done his
subordinates privately at Martinsburg and Harpers Ferry in 1866.

"The Charleston *Daily News* says that Gen. Howard thinks of aiding
planters with surplus funds in the Bureau. Can that be? God forbid!
It should all go to build school-houses," she told the readers of
Zion's Advocate.[67]

Early Death

Always a lover of nature, Foster described herself as having "a passion for rambling."[68] During these rambles through the quiet Maine
countryside or over the steep cliffs surrounding Harpers Ferry, she
often gathered armfuls of flowers, mosses, and other forest treasures. She described these walks and the vegetation she collected in
her diary and letters. The moss-hung trees along the old plantation
byways around Charleston especially attracted her attention. This
"atmospheric moss" was a sign of "malarial districts," she had been
told. "But, determined to defend what I so much admire, I always
suggest at the close of such information, that if it feeds and grows on
miasma it must be a benefit to the atmosphere after all by thus acting as a absorbent of malarial influences," she wrote in a letter to
Zion's Advocate on April 8, 1868. The moss was regarded as a malig-
nant sign by the locals. Even the devil might approach draped in
moss.[69] Taking the advice of her superiors, she planned to aban-
don her school a month earlier than the teachers in downtown
Charleston and head home to avoid the fever that plagued her district on the banks of the Ashley River. On May 8 she wrote to her
readers that "as yet I do not suffer from the heat, and though my
pupils have had fever spells, I have not had any, nor have I had any
illness at all."

A strange incident occurred in the final days of her school. "In the
afternoon a colored man from a remote district preached. His doctrine was excellent, but right in the midst of it he turned abruptly to
me and said with deep feeling:—'Taint likely that we'll ever meet
again in this world but I'll pray for you ma'am, I'll pray for you, and
God haint never refused me anything that I've asked in faith for
these thirty-six years.'"[70]

Foster was apparently shaken by the portentous words, for she
gave them a prominent display near the beginning of her last letter

to *Zion's Advocate*, written on June 19, 1868, after she had returned to Maine tired and with a severe cold. She was getting rested and recovering, she told readers. In a letter to the AMA the week before, she had noted her good health: "I am quite well rested and my friends think that mission life has agreed with me." On June 25 she died of yellow fever, the most dreaded scourge of the missionary teachers.[71]

Notes

1. Jacqueline Jones, *Soldiers of Light and Love: Northern Teachers and Georgia Blacks, 1865–1873* (Chapel Hill, N.C., 1980).

2. Ibid., 15, 210–21.

3. SJF was the second of seven brothers and sisters who survived infancy. The others were Rev. Caleb C. Foster (1837–1915), Samuel Howard Foster (1842–1908), Emma Ann Foster Thompson (1845–1924); Hannah Elizabeth Foster Gould (1848–1926), Dr. Avery M. Foster (1851–1929), and Eliza E. Foster Clark (1853–1924). Caleb received at least a year's education at the Maine State Seminary, the predecessor of Bates College in Lewiston. Avery was a graduate of the seminary and of Bowdoin Medical College. Samuel Howard, a private in the Union army, was a loom fixer in mills. Hannah Elizabeth's book was entitled *Science of Feeding Babies and Normal Care of the Growing Child* (New York, 1916). Emma Ann was trained as a milliner.

4. SJF, Diary, April 12, 1866.

5. Carl N. Degler, *At Odds: Women and the Family in America from the Revolution to the Present* (New York, 1980), 151–52, 159–60; Lee Chambers-Schiller, "The Single Woman: Family and Vocation among Nineteenth-Century Reformers," *Woman's Being, Woman's Place: Female Identity and Vocation in American History,* ed. Mary Kelley (Boston, 1979), 334.

6. Barbara Welter, "The Cult of True Womanhood, 1820–1860," *American Quarterly* 18 (Summer 1966): 151–74.

7. SJF, "Oh, Weave Me A Story," *HM*, Jan.–July 1865, 209 (reprinted below).

8. Frances B. Cogan, *All-American Girl: The Ideal of Real Womanhood in Mid-Nineteenth-Century America* (Athens, Ga., 1989).

9. SJF, Diary, Jan. 28, 1866.

10. *HM*, July–Dec. 1865, 23–28.

11. SJF, Diary, May 15, 1864, Sept. 22, July 6, 1866.

12. Ibid., Dec. 26, 1864.

13. Ibid., July 20, 1866.

14. National Archives, *Population Schedules of the Eighth Census of the United States, 1860,* Maine, vol. 3, Cumberland County.

15. SJF, Diary, Oct. 7, 1864.

16. *HM,* July–Dec. 1865, 179–83 (reprinted below).

17. SJF, Diary, April 21, 1866.

18. *Zion's Advocate* was a weekly newspaper published in Maine between 1828 and 1920; the *Home Monthly,* published between 1860 and 1908, "had a checkered career what with suspensions and moving to New York" (Frank Luther Mott, *A History of American Magazines,* 5 vols. [Cambridge, Mass., 1930–68], 2:65n, 59n).

19. SJF, Diary, March 31, 1864.

20. Degler, 377–79.

21. Henry S. Burrage, D.D., *History of the Baptists in Maine* (Portland, 1904), 265.

22. ZA, July 1, 1868 (reprinted below).

23. SJF, Diary, March 8, 1864.

24. National Archives, *Population Schedules of the Eighth Census of the United States, 1860,* Maine, vol. 4, Cumberland County.

25. Degler, 379–81.

26. Ebenezer Bean, unaddressed recommendation for SJF, Oct. 23, 1866, AMAA.

27. Emma Ann Foster Thompson, diary, 1864; George T. Hill, *History, Records, and Recollections of Gray, Maine* (Portland, 1978), 92, 104.

28. SJF, Diary, Sept. 19, 1864.

29. Ibid., July 27, 1866.

30. *HM,* July–Dec. 1864, 180–82.

31. Ibid., 111–13 (reprinted below).

32. Corporal punishment remained an issue for SJF in South Carolina. "I have not had to whip much, and have found that taking them by the hands for a kind and serious talk just after a whipping seems to astonish them into good behavior, for they appear to have been accustomed to threats rather than kindness, and have been driven to feel that anger rather

than love governed those who whipped them. One boy feelingly told me the other day that I was the best teacher he had ever had," (SJF to Rev. E. P. Smith, Jan. 3, 1868, AMAA).

33. SJF, Diary, Feb. 6, 1866.

34. *HM*, Jan.–July 1865, 13–19 (reprinted below).

35. SJF, Diary, Dec. 14, 1864.

36. "Doing good" was a popular expression of the day referring to the intentions of those people who wished to benefit society. SJF's desire to do good was recognized by Rev. Ebenezer Bean who wrote in a letter of recommendation that she was "a young lady of well cultivated mind, and Christian disposition; and is most earnestly desirous of doing good" (Bean, unaddressed recommendation for SJF, Oct. 23, 1866, AMAA).

37. Rev. Silas Curtis to Rev. N. C. Brackett, Feb. 8, 1866, CSC.

38. Leon F. Litwack, *Been in the Storm So Long: The Aftermath of Slavery* (New York, 1980), 491–92.

39. SJF, "Letter from Virginia," April 20, 1866, ZA, May 9, 1866.

40. Rev. Frederick L. Wiley, *Life and Influence of the Rev. Benjamin Randall, Founder of the Free Baptist Denomination* (Philadelphia, 1915), 276–77.

41. Rev. Silas Curtis to Rev. N. C. Brackett, Nov. 19, 1865, CSC.

42. Besides Jones's *Soldiers of Light and Love* and Litwack's *Been in the Storm So Long*, other books containing detailed descriptions of the northern teachers' experiences in the South include Henry Lee Swint, *The Northern Teacher in the South, 1862–1870* (New York, 1967), Robert C. Morris, *Reading, 'Riting, and Reconstruction: The Education of Freedmen in the South, 1861–1870* (Chicago, 1981), and Ronald E. Butchart, *Northern Schools, Southern Blacks, and Reconstruction: Freedmen's Education, 1862–1875* (Westport, Conn., 1980). Also useful, and of special pertinence to SJF's career, is Joe M. Richardson's *Christian Reconstruction: The American Missionary Association and Southern Blacks, 1861–1890* (Athens, Ga., 1986). Of great usefulness in understanding SJF's experiences in West Virginia are articles by John E. Stealey III in *WVH*: "The Freedmen's Bureau in West Virginia," 39 (Jan./April 1978): 99–142 and "Reports of Freedmen's Bureau Operations in West Virginia: Agents in the Eastern Panhandle," 42 (Fall 1980–Winter 1981): 94–129. Good background on the period in South Carolina is included in Martin Abbott, *The Freedmen's Bureau in South Carolina, 1865–1872* (Chapel Hill, N.C., 1967), Thomas Holt, *Black over White: Negro Political Leadership in South Carolina during Reconstruction* (Urbana, Ill., 1977), Willie Lee Rose, *Rehearsal for Reconstruction: The*

Port Royal Experiment (Indianapolis, 1964), and Joel Williamson, *After Slavery: The Negro in South Carolina during Reconstruction, 1861–1877* (Chapel Hill, N.C., 1965).

43. Rev. N. C. Brackett, Superintendent's Reports, February and March 1866, SJF, Teacher Monthly Reports, December–March 1866, AMAA; SJF, Diary, Feb. 5, 1866.

44. SJF agreed to write letters to a black Sunday school congregation in Portland, Maine, when its members decided to raise $50 toward her support (SJF to Rev. E. P. Smith, Aug. 18, 1867, AMAA).

45. SJF, "Letter from West Virginia," March 13, 1866, ZA, March 21, 1866.

46. SJF to Emma and Lizzie Foster, Nov. 2, 1866.

47. SJF to Rev. Samuel Hunt, Oct. 31, 1866, AMAA.

48. N. C. Brackett to Rev. E. P. Smith, Dec. 29, 1866, ibid. SJF was well aware of this appraisal of herself. After losing her teaching commission in 1866 she wrote, "I have decided to be frank and tell everyone just how I am circumstanced for I do not feel to blame, and no one can say ought that is against me save that I am a little unpolished and no toady" (Diary, July 24, 1866).

49. J. G. de Roulhac Hamilton, *Reconstruction in North Carolina*, Columbia University Studies in History, Economics, and Public Law (1914; rept. Gloucester, Mass., 1964), 318–19.

50. W. E. Burghardt Du Bois, "The Freedmen's Bureau," *Atlantic Monthly* 88 (March 1901): 358.

51. Swint, 56, 92–93.

52. Butchart, 134.

53. SJF, Teacher Monthly Reports, December–March 1866, AMAA.

54. SJF, Diary, April 29, 1864.

55. "From Mr. W. W. Wheeler," *American Missionary*, July 1864, 175.

56. SJF, "Letter from West Virginia," Jan. 1, 1866, ZA, Jan. 10, 1866.

57. Litwack, 458–60.

58. Mary P. Ryan, *Womanhood in America from Colonial Times to the Present* (New York, 1975), 137–91.

59. SJF, "Musings by the Way," ZA, Aug. 21, 1867.

60. SJF, Diary, March 10, 1866.

61. Richardson, *Christian Reconstruction*, 163.

62. "I'm too radical even to suit the blacks I think. So I keep still and listen" (SJF, Diary, May 18, 1866).

63. SJF, "Letter from Virginia," April 20, 1866, ZA, May 9, 1866.

64. SJF, "Letter from the South," April 8, 1868, ibid., April 22, 1868.

65. SJF to Rev. George Whipple, Feb. 28, 1868, AMAA.

66. SJF, "Letter from the South," April 8, 1868, ZA, April 22, 1868.

67. SJF, "Letter from the South," Jan. 9, 1868, ibid., Jan. 22, 1868.

68. SJF, Diary, May 7, 1866.

69. SJF, "A Charleston Letter," ZA, Feb. 12, 1868.

70. SJF, "Our Charleston Letter," June 19, 1868, ibid., June 24, 1868.

71. Minna J. Thompson, personal communication; Richardson, *Christian Reconstruction*, 176–77.

WEST VIRGINIA, 1865–66

Letter from West Virginia

Martinsburg, West Va., Nov. 27th, 1865 [Dec. 13]

Dear Advocate:—It is now nearly two weeks since I left home to come here as Mission Teacher to the Freedmen.[1] Quite unexpectedly to myself I met with two other teachers on the boat who were going, like myself, to report to Rev. N. C. Brackett[2] at Harper's Ferry. There were also others, two going to Savannah and one returning to Wilmington, N.C.

I shall always retain very pleasant recollections of the Chesapeake and its gentlemanly commander. We not only had a free passage, but also subsistence on the same terms, which last was no trifle, as none of our party were seasick. Dr. Graham,[3] of Casco Street Church, was so positive that we should be that he gave us each a lemon to use for that purpose. We brought them safely through and I for one have therewith celebrated my triumph over Neptune.

A heavy fog delayed our arrival in New York, and we did not get to the pier till dusk, Friday night. Dr. Graham had given us the address of a gentleman whose office was very near. But he had closed it and gone. Captain Sherwood kindly invited us to stay on board all night, therefore, which we did. On reporting to the proper officers the next morning at the rooms of the American Missionary Association, we were advised to stop in New York until Monday night at seven, which would bring us to Baltimore Tuesday morning and to Harper's Ferry at noon or shortly after. Of course, we complied. Our party had received an addition of one, and we now numbered four. viz., Miss Annie S. Dudley of Lewiston,[4] Miss Sabrina L. Gibbs of Wells, Miss Anna A. Wright of Montpelier, Vt., and myself. Saturday afternoon we devoted to sightseeing in part, and in part to Central Park. Saturday evening we attended a Quaker meeting at the Friend's meeting house on Twentieth St. It was a new experience to me. The Spirit was there, and the prayers and exhortations were beautiful and excellent. Hereafter I shall make it a point to look under all Quaker bonnets to see if they do not frame faces of rare purity and delicacy. Sabbath day we went twice to the Freewill Baptist Church. The afternoon service was a prayer-meeting largely attended and blessed richly with the Spirit and power of God. Our errand was introduced by a friend. We were made special subjects of prayer and felt more than repaid for our delay. Evening we went to hear Dr. Cheever.[*] He preached a stirring discourse on the duty of Congress to the blacks. His subject was "Naboth's Vineyard."[6] and he dwelt upon the importance on the North's being aroused lest the Southerners should ruin the black race, manufacturing crimes to rob them of their rights as did Ahab to steal Naboth's Vineyard. He said that the amended Constitution permitted slavery as a *punishment for crime.* Each state might make a black code whose violation would be a *crime,* and whose observance would be nothing less than slavery. I wished that all the North could hear his trumpet-tones, for the heart that he could not reach must be buried deep in prejudices and selfishness.

Monday night, as was planned, we started for Baltimore. It was very dark and soon began to rain, but the lady's car was very comfortable and we slept as well as the conductor and the venders of eggs, sandwiches and apples would permit. From three in the morning till past eight we had to wait in the Baltimore and Ohio depot. It was still raining when we left for Harper's Ferry, but even rain could not prevent us from enjoying the wild and romantic scenery along the route.—That enjoyment reached its culmination when we arrived at Harper's Ferry. There Mr. Brackett met and welcomed us, conducting us at once to his domicile, an old Government building on Camp Hill.[7] We were charmed with the view of Maryland and Loudon Heights, and the junction of the rivers below,[8] especially as it ceased raining and the sun peeked out at us driving the mists, like stealthy creeping ghosts, off over the mountain tops. True, it soon clouded up again, and has been cold, raw and dull much of the time since,—rather a cool welcome to the "Sunny South."

It was decided to send Miss Wright and me here, retaining for the present, Miss Dudley and Miss Gibbs at Harper's Ferry. The thought of being removed 20 miles from our new found friends made us feel almost homesick, but we said not a word. Last Thursday we came here accompanied by Lieut. Smith,[9] agent of the Bureau of this subdistrict, and Mr. Brackett, our Superintendent. They found all things favorable, and decided that we should begin our labors today, which we accordingly have done. The colored people here have subscribed fifty dollars per month for the support of the school, and a very smart and intelligent committee have charge of the affairs of the one school room already open, and are to secure us another, for we hope soon to have scholars enough to require more than one.[10] We hold one session of four hours daily, and shall have one evening session three times a week. Of course it is too early to give more than a mere outline as yet. The colored people, old and young, seem much interested. There were but sixteen out to day, but we hear of many more who want to come, and the evening school will doubtless be fuller than the other. There has been no school here, yet most have some little notion of reading. Several read very well, and one smart little girl already has begun arithmetic. It is an interesting field of labor, but we shall constantly need the prayers of home friends. All seem willing and anxious to buy their books, and will do so as fast as they can. After Christmas many now at service will be free to come. All things considered I am glad that I came and that I am here.[11]

This place is intensely Union. A rebel is worse off here than farther North. I learned that the Mayor[12] favors our educational work, I think that very few oppose. We are boarding with a most excellent Union family named Hoke.[13] I give the name because their devoted loyalty throughout our great struggle for right, is worthy of a more enduring record than I can give. I never weary of hearing them tell of the varied scenes of the past four years. It seems strange to realize that I am where war was so long a dread and actual presence, and I am sure that those who were all the while faithful, merit immortality, if earthly fame can bestow it.

The town here has suffered much, as have all places in the vicinity.[14] I can but own that our army practiced more vandalism than was necessary or excusable. Yet I hear no real complaint. Northern loyalty is put to the blush by their conduct. Now the place is terribly crowded. All classes seem flocking in. Rents are scarce and high. No one seems able even to estimate the number of the population at present.

Outside of this family we know, as yet, nothing of the people save the blacks. They all seem to know us as if by intuition and welcome us very warmly, but always with due respect.

Wednesday evening we were in a colored prayer-meeting at Harper's Ferry. It was a solemn and interesting service. The prayer of one woman was unequaled for its simple child-like confidence, appropriateness, and a certain touching, poetic beauty that words would fail to reproduce. She would say,—"Dear Father didn't you

promise?" or "didn't you say, so and so?" with the most perfect freedom of address, and each petition ended in a sort of chanted rhyth-
mical "Jesus if it be thy will." One petition I will try to quote. It was
this,— Dear Father we has good reasons to know that you's been
quartered here at Harper's Ferry, an, now we wants you to come
agin, Jesus if it be thy will, an, please don't ride, way off roun, but
jist come right here an take a gentle ride roun, amongst us, Jesus if it
be thy will." But words would fail to convey to another the impres-
sion that it made upon my mind. At the close Mr. Brackett asked
those who had a hope in the Savior to rise. A number remained
seated. Then he asked those who wished to obtain such a hope to
rise. Somehow I half expected that all the remainder would rise like
so many puppets; but they did not. One after another, three arose,
and I could not doubt that they were in earnest. I will not weary
your patience by writing more now. After a little more experience in
our school I will write a report of it. Till then I remain,

Yours in Christian Bonds,
Sarah Jane Foster

Letter from West Virginia

Martinsburg, West Va., Dec. 16th, 1865 [Dec. 27]

Dear Advocate:—Three weeks of our school have passed away very
pleasantly indeed. For the last week I have been alone. Miss Dudley having been sent to open a school in Charlestown,[15] Mr. Brackett
was forced to recall Miss Wright to Harper's Ferry, for awhile at
least. Their day school there numbers about eighty, and is necessarily divided into two parts. After the holidays ours will be largely
increased, and we anticipate a like division, though our day school
now numbers but forty-five. At Harper's Ferry they have but about
that number in their evening school, while ours numbers already
sixty, and is rapidly increasing. I have found the latter branch of our
school much the most interesting. It pays principal and interest as
one goes along. They are eager to learn, and some even come in several miles from the country, nights. One evening weekly is set apart
for instruction in writing, which many need and earnestly desire. I
make efforts to teach them that reading and spelling are only the
beginnings of a good education, and get all who can to take up Arith-

metic and Geography. Nearly all are doing well. In the day school, where all save two are under eighteen, there is of course a spirit of mischief to control, and many are disposed to be inattentive to their books, but no more so than any children. Of the night scholars thirty-six are over twenty years old, one being sixty-two, and, feeling as they do the importance of time, it is a pleasure to teach them.

Some have picked up a great deal of knowledge without ever having been to school. One young man named John Brown,[16] one of our outside committee, is really very intelligent. He showed me one evening a page of his own composition, in which the language was quite well chosen, and nearly every word correctly spelled. Capitals were used rather promiscuously, and there was of course no attempt at punctuation; but it was a very creditable performance. I at once loaned him my best and favorite Grammar. Since Miss Wright has left me alone I could not have done justice to the evening school without his aid. He has proved an invaluable assistant in the school, though very diffident of his own powers. Seeing my dilemma he quietly and unobtrusively took charge of several of the lower classes to the neglect of his own books, but I tried on the evening of the writing school to make him amends, asking him to bring in his books for that purpose.

A brother-in-law of his has come into the school who would pass for a white man anywhere. In fact Mr. Brown is partially white, his hair being simply curly and his features not African, though he is dark. But color I find is no test of ability. I have encountered but three, out of more than a hundred in both schools, who could justly be called stupid. I certainly expected to meet more low, animalized natures among them then I have found.[17]

My Northern friends need not think that I have any difficulty in recognizing my flock. There is as much individuality among them as among white people. Some of the children are really pretty. One little boy has straight hair and no visible trace of negro blood. One young woman has greyish blue eyes, but, though light and pretty, the hair marks her race. One of my day scholars, though quite dark, has hair as straight as my own, while others far lighter have the crisp wool of the African. A slight admixture of the races seems almost universal.

The "New Era," an opposition paper here, week before last contained a slight fling at us and our work. The editor of the Berkeley

Union very kindly admitted a reply made in our interest.[18] There is
really no opposition worth naming here. I sometimes hear myself
pointed out as a "nigger teacher," and people, especially children,
stare in on passing the school-room, but we are as yet entirely un-
disturbed, and likely to remain so.

Last Sabbath our Sabbath school was opened. There were about
fifty present, and we shall find no difficulty in providing the requi-
site number of teachers from among themselves, so that I shall only
be one of nine or ten teachers. Our plan embraces, first, a general
oral lesson in Bible history after singing and prayer of course. Next
the classes and then singing again. Their devotional music seems peculiar to themselves, and therefore I do not feel the lack of musical
ability as much as I feared I might. I am making an effort to raise
some papers for them,[19] and hope to make our Sabbath school very
interesting, and also profitable.

At first in the day school I found slight falsehoods continually told,
evidently from habit, to avoid punishment or blame. I talked to
them earnestly on the subject, and endeavored to impress upon
their minds the fact that I regarded lying one of the worst of vices,
and also the Biblical view of its enormity. Since then three instances
of frank acknowledgement when an offender was inquired after,
have proved that my words were not unheeded. In each case, while
blaming the misdemeanor, I praised the honesty, I hope with good
effect. But I must close. Ere long you may hear again from

Sarah J. Foster

Letter from West Virginia

Martinsburg, West Va., Jan. 1st, 1866 [Jan. 10]

Dear Advocate:—The old year has flown, and my first salutation
must be "Happy New Year," and in my heart I cordially wish that
the new year may be both happy and prosperous. In my last I omitted to tell you that I have begun to teach *four* evenings per week.
Thursday night they have a prayer meeting. I design to attend myself and make it a permanent institution.

I have not yet visited any among the Freedmen, thinking it best
to wait till the first prejudice of our opposers wore off.[20] I think now
that that time has come, and shall begin to-morrow if the weather is

fair to make the personal acquaintance of my scholars at their homes. I have not talked much as yet with the people, fearing that the white people might think I was searching out sensation items to their disadvantage.[21] My silence and quietude has had the effect that I hoped, and all prejudice is slowly wearing out. Several with whom I have talked admit that Education must and should follow Freedom. Soon I am sure that no one will regard their instruction as degrading to the instructor.

I cannot report much change in the school since my last, for our Holidays began Dec. 22nd and only close with to-day. Christmas week seems to be a season of great leisure and dissipation here. The people, both black and white, indulged heavily in liquor, and Christmas noon, when I went to the depot to take the cars for Harper's Ferry, I should not have cared to go through Queen St. alone. Arrived at Harper's Ferry I found the same scene of dissipation and consequent quarreling being enacted there also. It was sad to see Christ's birth-day thus celebrated by anybody. The weather sadly interfered with our programme for the week, but we had nevertheless a very pleasant week. Our party numbered six, for we all went there together, and Mrs. Brackett[22] has now come out. Lieut. Smith dined with us, and we enjoyed our dinner much. Most of the viands were contributed by the Freedmen and were excellent.

The day before Christmas I went with a friend, Capt. H——, to the Catholic church.[23] I had never entered one before and was very much interested. Much of the ceremony seemed senseless, but I was charmed with the attentive devotion of the entire audience, and began to question whether the almost total lack of formality in our common church service did not allow too wide a limit for wandering thoughts. The officiating Priest really delivered an excellent discourse. He distinctly showed that the "birth of Christ in the heart" was essential to salvation, and though bidding them "do penance for sin," he insisted upon the necessity of a thorough heart-work. Several colored persons sat near me in the Church. I think that the Catholic church has acquired considerable influence over them here from the fact that Catholic families began to instruct their servants while others neglected their education.

We had planned various excursions in our week of leisure, and were somewhat disappointed by the weather which forbade our going out at all till Thursday. Then we merely rambled about a

grave-yard near the Lockwood House.[24] For a burial place it was
more sadly dilapidated than any that I ever saw. The gates were off,
the walls in many places broken down, and hogs and cows roamed
through it unmolested. It is not unused, for there were several new
graves, but Nature alone seems to care for the mounds that dot its
surface. Over some of them she has tangled a rich profusion of the
finest myrtle, but the evidences of human neglect and war's vandalism were saddening.

Friday morning, before breakfast, I visited Jefferson Rock[25] which
was nearby, and climbed over and around it finding it an excellent
sharpener for the appetite. I found myself trying to take all sorts of
impossible steps, for the ponderous masses of rock around me made
three and four feet seem insiginficant distances. Miss Dudley tells
me that one of her little pupils defined mountains to be "rocks and
hills piled up." Applied to the scenery from Camp Hill the description is highly expressive. Friday forenoon our entire party visited
the cave where it is asserted John Brown stored his pikes.[26] Mr.
Brackett would only permit us to penetrate its gloomy depths some
three or four hundred feet, and in truth it was curiosity and not the
beauty of the spot that had attractions for us. It is simply a wild,
rugged passage for the distance that we went, presenting no stalac-
tites and no beautiful incrustations. The presence of iron appears to
have changed the latter to a dingy, mottled yellow. Here and there
the effect of candle-light on the walls was pretty, but only the story
about John Brown made the place interesting. Mrs. Stowe in her
"Sunny Memories"[27] tells of sentimentalizing over the poet Gray in
the *wrong graveyard,* and we may have committed a like mistake
for I have since been told that John Brown had nothing to do with
that cave.—Though generally received the story is doubtful. But we
did not know it then, and such as our party that could sing sent the
thrilling "John Brown Chorus" echoing through the cavern. If he did
not store his weapons there he ought to have done so. The place
seems the very abode of secrecy, and ought, if it is not, to be
romantic.

Leaving the cave, we climbed up the hill which roofs it, and kept
on over Bolivar Heights, skirting along the breastworks thrown up
by our army, where Miss Dudley picked up three minnie balls.
Thence we had a fine view of the broad and lovely Shenandoah valley. Looking, I thought of Sheridan and his brave men, and in fancy

saw the broad fields curtained with the smoke of burning houses. Everywhere we meet ruined houses, and lonely chimneys like specters guarding the desolation. But I must close. I have only time to say that Miss Wright goes to Shepherdstown Tuesday to open a school.

Yours,
Sarah J. Foster

Diary, 1866

Monday, January 1

Rose quite early this morning, and wrote till breakfast time. Sent off this morning letters to four of the Cobb children,[28] and to Lizzie[29] enclosing a reply for Mattie and Frannie. I also wrote to Miss Rogers and sent reports to the A.M.A. and to Rev. Silas Curtis.[30] After dinner I began a sketch to please Binnie, and Kittie as they all call Miss Wright. I got letters at night from Lizzie and Abbie Humphrey. The latter was difficult to read, but I made it out as well as I could, losing but little, and at once sat down to reply. Lizzie gave me leave to write to Buffalo about Jule, and I do so. She writes that Howard[31] still tries them. May God perfect his work. I have been reading a History of France tonight. I am much interested, but alas through what seas of blood have all nations waded up to civilization.

Tuesday, January 2

My school reopened today. I had thirty present. They were studious and reasonably quiet. A young man, who said he was chaplain of a New York Regt., came in and stopped an hour or so. He seemed very much interested in the school and scholars. I had one scholar fifty five years old. At noon I called on the family over my schoolroom to see about a girl who talked of coming to school. Saw, when I came to my dinner, Mr. O'Connell moving his books to the office, and told him that I hoped he was not going away. It was truth I am sure.

Tonight bad and snowy, had nineteen at school, some of them new ones. Got through tonight without Mr. Brown's aid, and helped him some besides. Two boys annoyed me by mischief, and a foolish young fellow yet more by laughing at them. Sent off my letters. Got none at all.

Wednesday, January 3

My list made up to forty one scholars. The weather yet holds very muddy. Fannie Lee's grandmother has come in. She is learning fast. She bought a book. Tonight I had in a few more scholars. They were very quiet indeed. Only two had copies set. I attended to the lessons of the rest. Three ladies came in. I treated them politely and they seemed well enough. I mean to act so that none can find fault with me about setting up the colored people above their place. I cannot help liking them. Even the wildest are always polite and civil when spoken to. Got a letter from Emma[32] today. She has been too busy and too tired to write. She did not have so good times Thanksgiving and Christmas I think as I had. I hope that I shall be able to reply tomorrow morning. I am well. I do like out here very much.

Thursday, January 4

The coldest day so far. I was unavoidably kept very late at school this afternoon. I must plan to come out at noon and go in again. It will be better all round. After my dinner I went out and called on two colored families—those of Fannie Lee, and Emmie Bacy. This morning I wrote to Mr. Pearson[33] again, and most of a letter to Emma also. This afternoon Mr. Hoke had an ill time at the shop and was thought to be dying. Littleton had to get the doctor at the shop and after a long time they brought him home in a carriage. He will not live long I am sure. Had an excellent prayer meeting tonight. Mr. Hopewell[34] was in and came home with me. Mr. Brown was there too. I shall enjoy the meetings very much. Mr. O'Connell is gone to the country, I think to get a school. I shall miss him much if he goes off.

Friday, January 5

Still very cold, too cold to make any calls at all. I was doubtful today whether it was best to whip two boys or not. Did not decide to do it. A new scholar who hails from Charleston seems to belong to a different race of beings. I like him though he is slow to learn. He is politeness itself. Tonight at school one young man, whose foolish laughing has greatly annoyed me, was very insulting to an old man who reproved him. I rebuked his ill manners sharply. He says he shall

not come any more. Well I am sure I done right. It may be better for
the school that he should not. Only got my Home Monthly for mail
today. No word from Mr. Pearson as yet. Wrote again yesterday. A
piece of mine in the Monthly. Florence liked it very much.

Saturday, January 6

Oh Lord I will praise thee. Mr. Brown is seeking the Lord. Mr.
Brackett came up today, and tonight we had a little meeting. For a
week I have longed to talk to Mr. Brown about his soul. Tonight I
did so, and found that he had really started on the good way. I am
glad that I gave him an encouraging word. May God lead him. Mr.
Brackett has been urging him to go to Lewiston, Maine to school.[35] I
wish that he would though I should be sorry to miss him here. Mr.
Brackett has brought me up some clothing to distribute among my
pupils here. Oh may I be led in the right way. Guard my heart and
my tongue that I may not injure thy cause oh Lord. I am *so* happy
tonight.

Sunday, January 7

Staid at home and wrote to Lizzie and to the Mission sister this
morning. This afternoon I went to the Methodist church where Mr.
Brackett addressed the colored people especially the children. He
was followed by an clergyman who was there and then Mr. Matthews, the mayor's brother made a few excellent remarks, and
avowed himself a firm friend of the blacks. This evening I have been
to the Methodist church with Mr. Brackett and Mr. Canby. The sermon was very good indeed. I never felt to pray more for the blessing
of God on my work. I do have great hope that He will work with us
here. As to Mr. Brown my prayer is "Give me *this* soul for my hire"
and may the Lord hear an answer.

Monday, January 8

This has been a terribly cold day. My school was much interrupted
by the weather, and not near all were in. Mr. Brackett was in for an
hour or so. Seemed much pleased. I meant to have begun two sessions today but had not a chance as it was too cold to send the children home. As cold as it was I had nineteen in tonight. Mr. Brown

was not in. Charlie Howk told me that his sister's child was dead. Today Mr. Hopewell came in and got the watch that I borrowed last week as the man wanted it and let me have another.

I wonder why Mr. Pearson does not write or send me the money. I hardly know what to do. I ought not to have to send home, but must ere many days unless I get some elsewhere.

Tuesday, January 9

Still awful cold. Water froze very thick in my room. The streets were full of ice carts all day as it will soon thaw. I began two sessions, but didn't get through til past four in the afternoon. Mr. William Hoke says that one of my large girls says I don't whip enough. I am not a brute and I won't be. I believe I am right. I mean to be certainly. Tonight Mr. Knapp was in to school. He seemed much pleased. By the aid of some of the larger boys and Mr. Brown I got through at nine and had time for Mr. Brown too. Did not get a chance to talk with him any alone. But I can pray for him. I don't forget his case at all. Yesterday I heard from home and Geo. Cobb, also from Buffalo. Today I got no mail. Have form letters to send to Miss Wright soon. I am nicely but some tired.

Wednesday, January 10

Just a bit warmer but yet very cold. I have felt this cold snap as bad as I ever felt the cold in New England. I have at last made out to get my fire into good hands, and now have a warm room mornings. Had a very pleasant though rather long school today. Must manage to hasten matters. At writing school tonight a number wrote, and many more were in too, but I got thro at a quarter past nine by having help. Got a word with Mr. Brown. He seems to hold on his course. Some of the boys annoyed us all tonight. Shall have to punish Robert Jackson. He is too bad altogether. Wrote to George Cobb and sent it today. Have drawn up my bill on the Mission Society, and I must get money to buy me some boots.

Thursday, January 11

Rose at seven and wrote till breakfast time. At school I felt a little faint this morning. Got nearly over it though. This afternoon Harvey

Davis stayed out of school for fear I would punish him because he had run against a lady who complained of it. He is a little rude, and I had intended to deprive him of recess or something of the kind. Meant to whip him for truancy, but saw him while calling at Mrs. Bacy's to see Emma who is sick and talked with him and decided to let him off as he seemed touched.

On my way home heard Mary Hopewell tell his father that he was out of school. Hurried on and overtook him and asked him not to whip him this time, and to tell Harvey that I had asked him to try the effect of that method. Had a very excellent prayer meeting tonight as Mr. Thompson was in—very smart and intelligent. Also Mr. Brown's father is much the same. Mr. Hopewell of course was in. Mr. Brown has not yet found peace. A little boy is also seeking the Savior.

Friday, January 12

Mr. O'Connell has come and gone for good to Jefferson County. Got somewhat tried today in school. Elisha Brown came in, and I almost love the little fellow who *is* a rogue. One of the boys tried to pick a fuss with him in school and they tried to have a fight about it at noon. Another was rude and noisy in the street, and led on in a fuss with some white boys. After school though it was raining a little I called on one Colored family. Found great need of clothing. Tonight should have had a pleasant school, only my omnipresent brother Robert Jackson forced me to whip him. I had not a suitable stick and so fear that I done him no good by it. Walked home with Mr. Brown as usual. Oh how glad I shall be to hear him praise God for deliverance. Got a letter from Lizzie tonight. She says that Caleb[36] heard that Jule was a good fellow from a member of his Regiment. I hope he is.

Saturday, January 13

This has been a day as pleasant and warm as April. Though it was muddy I have been going about among the Colored people considerable today. I have called on Mr. Sam Hopewell's family, a Mrs. Leyton's, and Andy MacDaniel's. Also Mr. Brown's and Mr. Howard's. Owing to the sickness and death of his little girl the latter has not of late been to school, but he will soon come in now and a cousin

with him. I find Mr. Brown to be one of a family of twelve, of whom
Mrs. Howard only is married. They all live right together in good
style too. Have enjoyed my calls very much indeed. Got only my
papers tonight   my Advocate and S.S. papers.

Wrote letters all this evening, but I am sleepy and must now retire. Mr. Lamb has come in and when he is through work, it is time
that other folks were through likewise. So I must to bed. Oh why
don't Mr. Pearson send me that money or write. I have sent my bill
to Elder Curtis. I hope he will be more prompt. Am sure he will.

Sunday, January 14

This morning I stayed out of church, bathed myself and wrote letters. This afternoon I went to S. school, and organized them for the
year. Forty-two were in. Six or seven were competent to aid me.
Uncle Andy suggested that I appoint a prayer meeting tonight, I did
so. Have just come from it. The house was full to overflowing and a
good meeting was held. John Brown has not yet found peace. I have
lent him my Advocate and can but pray that God may bless its words
to his soul's best good. There is deep feeling here. Oh Lord dawn
into John Brown's heart. He seems so penitent, so humble that I can
but hope he will find light soon. Oh what can I do? My Howard was
in.[37] I talked family to him. He says he will come Thursday night. I
hope to get him too on our side. Oh for grace.

Letter from West Virginia

Martinsburg, West Va., Jan. 14th, 1866 [Jan. 24]

Dear Advocate:—This week we have had an experience of one of
the peculiarities of this Virginian climate. Monday and Tuesday
were excessively cold, and the cold came on so suddenly that I do
not remember ever to have felt it more sensibly at the North, though
of course the thermometer was not nearly as low as I have known it.
I have observed that the colored children feel the cold much more
than the whites. Several of the little ones were so cold those cold
mornings that I had to take their hands in mine to warm them before they could bear to approach the fire. Some of them come long
distances, and many from localities where the streets are rough,
muddy and unpaved. Since ascertaining where some of them live I

wonder that they come at all this cold weather. I know of a number
of new scholars that will come in the spring. Yesterday was a very
warm day. It being a leisure day with me I called on five different
colored families. Since writing you last I have made ten calls among
them. Mr. Brackett has received a quantity of clothing for distribution among the freedmen, and I have a portion of it with me with
the privilege of sending for more. I had directions to sell at low
prices to those who could buy, and only to give to the utterly destitute. I begin to think that there are more of those than I had sus-
pected. Some who have fitted out their children to go to school have
almost nothing to wear themselves.—Rents are extremely high.
They have to pay often as high as ten dollars per month for wretched
little shanties of not more than two rooms. I fancy that colored
people are oppressed by exorbitant rents, but am told that rents are
extremely scarce and high throughout the town.[38] The first call that I
made yesterday was upon the family of a Mr. Hopewell, one of our
committee. He is a very smart, intelligent man and the only reason
that I have not named him before is that he does not, like Mr.
Brown, come to the school, his business keeping him away. Some of
his children come to the day school. We have had two Thursday evening prayer-meetings, and there he is an invaluable aid. At the first
but few were in, but all who were Christians took part, and I was so
much interested that I very gladly appointed another for the following Thursday night. Saturday night Mr. Brackett had a meeting at
the school room. To my great joy I found that my faithful ally, Mr.
Brown, was seeking the Savior. He certainly will do much good as a
disciple of Christ. He has not at this date found peace, but I feel
sure that he will persevere. Sunday afternoon Mr. Brackett secured
the Methodist Church here to address the colored people. He was
followed in a few excellent remarks by the clergyman who had supplied the desk for the day. Then Mr. William Matthew, brother of
the Mayor, avowed himself a warm friend of the colored race in a
few words of the kindest interest.

Thursday night I attended our second prayer meeting. Twenty
eight were present, and it was very good. The father of my assistant
John Brown was present. He is a good Christian, and in intelligence, a worthy father of such a son. Mr. Hopewell was in at each
meeting. There was also a Mr. Thompson, whom I had never met
before, in at our last meeting. He is the best educated colored man
that I have met with. A man with a white skin might well be proud

of being so thoroughly well read as he is, or seems to be. I do not name these instances of superior intelligence because they are all the worthy ones that I know, but in their cases Freedom had aided the development of natural capacity, while others, of perhaps equal ability, were tramelled by Slavery. To-day forty two were present at Sunday school.—Out of that number six were competent to act as teachers, and several more who were not in, may reasonably be depended upon.—With quite a number Sunday school affords their only chance to read. So we have to give regular reading lessons, which makes it seem odd to me. I try to add some biblical instruction as well as I can. Often I am led to feel my own weakness, especially now that I can see and feel the dawning of a religious interest among the people. I feel that I need the earnest prayers of all God's people at home that I may get good and do good in this place.

I have never attended better prayer-meetings than since being here. Few as were the worshippers the spirit of God was in their midst, and there is a genuine, unaffected earnestness in their devotion which charms me. There is no emotional extravagance. It is simply a natural expression of strong spiritual feeling. Their language is terse and expressive, often striking out involuntary poetic images like sparks from a flint.

I knew a good man in Maine who, on the Sabbath after President Lincoln's assassination, opened the singing in a prayer meeting by striking up in a high and jubilant key:

"The morning light is breaking."

That man might learn a lesson here. The hymns chosen are singularly appropriate to the peculiar shade of feeling to that part of the service when they are read. They sing many pieces of which the words are familiar to me, but give them with variations by repetitions and choruses that make them almost new again.

Since New Year my day school had been daily increasing. I have had to begin two sessions a day. I devote the entire morning to the lower classes, dismiss them at twelve, and then attend to the more advanced pupils after dinner. I thus have many hours' work a day, but thus far never enjoyed better health than since being here.

Miss Wright has written me two letters since going to Shepherdstown. She has about forty pupils I believe by day, and has begun a night school.[39] Affairs at the Ferry are going on much as usual. Their day school is large, but my night school I think exceeds theirs in good weather. The more intelligent here assist me now, and I no longer depend solely for aid on Mr. Brown. I must now close, and go to a prayer-meeting at the school room.

Yours Truly,
Sarah J. Foster

Diary, 1866

Monday, January 15

Stormy tonight. I have had no school. Have written a long letter to the Star,[40] as Mr. Brackett requested me to do so. Mr. Campbell, a colored man, was in school today. Mr. Hopewell came in just at noon to see about some coal, and John Brown at night to fix a bench lower for the scholars. Just before he came in Mr. McKenzie,[41] whom I had met with Lieut. Smith at Harper's Ferry, came in and was there then. I longed to introduce my best helper but, to excuse the introduction, must have wounded John's modesty by a long valuation of his services. So I let his fine, intelligent face tell its own story.

Elisha is a darling little rogue. I do hope I'll never have to whip him. It would hurt me worse than it would him. I kept David [   ] standing all day for his fighting. As he is laziness itself I think it will do better than a whipping would.

Tuesday, January 16

Whipped Mary Smith today. A very thin school til after dinner owing to the bad walking. Had quite a full night school though. Robert Jackson and another boy disturbed the family over the school-room. I was going to whip them both but Bob ran off hatless. Charlie Howk hid his hat and when he ever gets it he will remember me. I gave the other a severe flogging. Guess he'll not forget.

I tremble now from exertion. I dreaded it terribly when I knew that I had got it to do.

Mr. Brown is not yet at peace. Oh for the dawn to rise in his heart. I have prayed for him earnestly and somehow feel more at rest about him. I know that he is determined to keep on. He will not be deceived either, but I long to hear him praise God for deliverance from sin.

Wednesday, January 17

I have had a very pleasant day today except a little brush with John Hopewell. His father saw me and said he would whip him. I see that I *must* whip in my school. Well I mean that once a [   ] shall suit them as far as I go. I do hope that I shall not have to whip my favorite Elisha, but the rogue will be very likely to need it ere long, and I must not *act* partially. My feelings I cannot help.

Had eleven writers tonight. Isaac Brown takes hold nicely. Most of the men are awkward, and some of the women too. Got a nice letter from Geo. Cobb tonight. Have before tea and since school, written him a reply. Mr. McKenzie was in just a moment this afternoon to leave me some bills and a blank to fill for him. He may come here to board. I hope that he will. I shall then be all right about the boys if they disturb my school. Dave's fight has made the other boys some trouble about the [   ].

Thursday, January 18

Mr. or rather Capt. McKenzie has come here to board. Had some new grown up scholars tonight or rather late this afternoon. They'll come to both schools now. Had an excellent meeting tonight. Rev. Mr. Osborne preached from the text "Blessed is that people whose God is the Lord." The room was crowded. A slight disturbance was made outside. Hope we have gotten the neck of the one who made it.

Mr. Brown yet in the dark. A lady who came in with Mr. Osborne was struck with his appearance and asked who he was. Mr. Osborne talked with him a little, but it all seems to do no good. Lizzie wanted to know in a letter if she might write him a note. I shall say yes praying that it may do good. Joseph Suecors is seeking God. I talked with him and Isaac Brown tonight. Nat Wood had been drinking today. Tonight I gave him a tract on Rum's Doings.

Friday, January 19

Nat Wood had been drinking yesterday but is not a habitual drinker. I like him very much.

Muddy again. Snow nearly all gone. Got a letter tonight from Emma. Yeterday heard from Caleb, Lizzie and Miss Rogers. Had to whip Harvey Davis today quite severely. After school tonight went upstairs and wrote two letters for the girls. Am to have two new scholars from them. At the school tonight Robert Jackson tried to get me to say that I would excuse him if he would not do so again. I told the boys to bring me no more messages for I should not change. Joseph Suecors was the skittest of all tonight. Some rascals broke down our door about nine. I think that the men were afraid for me for the Browns and Mr. Howard and several others came over with me. Perry Brown has come to school. Jake[42] cut my hair today. Elisha brought me in a splendid apple. Guess I've won him to goodness. Because the work of God has started here, Satan has begun to show his power. Oh Lord conquer him for me.

Saturday, January 20

Went over to see if the rowdies got into our schoolroom last night. Called in above. Heard that Mr. Hopewell had been threatened because he walked through Queen St. with me the other day. I don't care. If he is not afraid to do it I am not. I shall treat all well who treat me well both black and white. She said some talked of watching for Mr. Brown too. Passing Jake's shop I saw him and stopped to talk, in part to show the street groups that I did not care for them. Sent letters to Caleb, Lizzie, Emma and Miss Rogers today. So I have been very busy writing. At meeting tonight Mr. Brown Sr. was there. John had a cold and was not out. Someone opened our door. Joseph Suecors and Charlie Ford were mourners tonight. May God bless both. Maybe I have,—I *have* been limiting God's grace in feeling as if John Brown was a necessary aid here and *must* come first. Work thine own way Father, but [   ] him too.

Sunday, January 21

Staid at home this morning and read "Theodosia Ernest" a work on Baptism, loaned me by Mr. Canby, and also have written, during the day, a long letter to Abbie Humphrey. Afternoon had forty-nine into Sabbath School eight of whom were assistants. Mr. Hopewell and Mr. Thompson were in, each for the first time.

Gave the latter charge of the Bible class which is large. Then I had enough to do. Joseph and Charlie were in S. School, and quite sober. They are in earnest I think. Mr. Brown showed me a very kind letter that Mr. Brackett had sent to him. I told him of Lizzie's proposal to write to him. He seemed touched at our interest. How little he knows his own worth. Mr. Hopewell thought that we had better have no meeting tonight. So I am at leisure. I walked through the street all the way with Mr. Hopewell, just to show that I did not mean to be driven off by the roughs. These men are good. Why shouldn't I treat them well?

Monday, January 22

Mr. Hoke seriously advised me to stay away from school tonight. He says that the roughs are terribly exasperated because I walked with Mr. Hopewell. Capt. McKenzie has volunteered to protect me to and from the school house, and did so tonight. Mr. Hopewell and Mr. Brown stood guard by turns and we were not disturbed, though, coming around in the evening Capt. McKenzie saw indications that led him to go and get his pistol before coming around for me. But it was not needed. I hope now that I know what the fuss is it will blow over. Mr. Hoke's folks were really alarmed because I had done so for fear they might be mobbed. Even they too are not free from negrophobia. Well I must ere submit.

Thursday, January 23

Dull and inclined to snow some all day, but I had quite a full school. Got on very pleasantly all but one thing. I kept three boys at noon for not studying, among them Elisha Brown, and he showed me that he could be as obstinate as he is roguish. I really dared not begin to punish him unless his folks were present for fear I should injure him for life or have to stop for fear of killing him. So I managed to wait and tonight I have told John about it, and either he or his father will be in to see about the affair, and then I can punish the little mischief as he deserves with no fear of consequences. But anyway, I hate to hurt the torment. I do like him twice as well as he deserves and I can't help it either. Perhaps he may cure me now.

Wednesday, January 24

A stormy day. Three men were in, Adam Howard among them. Mr. Brown did not come in. Elisha ran out of doors when I tried to whip

him, but finally came back of his own accord on my telling Adam
Howard that I would not have anyone else present when I whipped
him if he would come in.

The boys laughing was what galled him at first. But he showed
himself a man at last, took his whipping and talked civilly about it
afterward. I believe I love him better than ever. I am thankful to
have got through it so well. Joseph Suecors annoyed me again tonight. I can't understand him. Got a letter from John Breey, also a
half illegible one from Henry Wellington, one of my scholars that
has gone to Pa.

Thursday, January 25

I tremble now with excietment. Our meeting was disturbed and
some of the Colored people fired a pistol after the intruders, and
gave chase and caught two. They have the names of two more. Capt.
McKenzie was sent for and took them to jail. John Brown says that
he thinks it is his cross to stay here and stand or fall with those of his
color. He is noble. God help him. I misunderstood the firing and
caught his hand to hold him back lest he should be shot. I could not
help it.[43] Adam Howard was in school again today. Had to whip a
large boy for ill conduct. Heard tonight that he whipped the in-
former. Well—must see to that.

Never felt so much like staying here as now. May I be led aright is
my constant prayer. I am glad that the disturbance came tonight. A
business meeting had called out the best men. Joseph Suecors is still
seeking. He means well.

Friday, January 26

Another week's work completed. Have decided not to have any
meeting tomorrow night. John Brown will fix the shutters for us to
open only from within before we go there again. Did not have to
punish anyone today. Only talked to Jim Haynes, for he told Nat
that my ferule gave him the "hardest licks that he ever got." Capt.
McKenzie is gone to Winchester[44] to see what to do about the case
of last night. The fellows gave bail and are now out. Got a letter from
George Cobb tonight. Got him a business card at Honnett's where I
took a watch today.[45] Shall write to them tomorrow. Our school was

not disturbed tonight. George Layton and John Campbell stood guard outside which doubtless kept them off. Ellen Wood gave me a lot of hickory nuts tonight. Mr. Osborne called at the school—called me out and gave me a friendly warning about strict conduct toward the colored people. I shall have to take it. Met a man with a wounded hand tonight who told me to get out of the way of the flood. I was alone too.

Saturday, January 27

I am in trouble tonight. I have been slandered by the mob til Mrs. Hoke dares not board me. I can hardly blame her and yet it cuts me deeply. Mr. Brackett has come up to see about it. They say that I have walked night after night arm in arm with Colored men. It is a lie, and yet how can I prove it. God help me. Got a good letter from Miss Small, our old traveling companion, tonight. She has a good chance. She is not alone. Rode out with Mary Hopewell tonight on the Winchester pike and around town a little. Could not help it. Said "yes" without thought when she asked me and then felt I must go. Called at Mr. Brown's and three other Colored families today. Elisha went to show me one of them. I somehow begin to renew my faith. God is at work here. Oh Father let me stay. I cannot give it up now.

Sunday, January 28

Awoke feeling very unhappy, but went to church and found a measure of peace. Have concluded "Theodosia Ernest."[46] May I here emulate her faith. Today I have been fancying Mother in my place. She would defy the mob, board anywhere or nowhere and keep the school. I am at heart some like her.

This afternoon sixty-three were in Sunday School—eleven able to help me. Did not require all. Mr. Thomson took charge of a Bible class as before. Tonight we have had a most excellent meeting. Joseph Suecors seemed to find peace. John Brown gave his first testimony and three of his brothers seemed to be seeking. Two pledged themselves to me. Another arose with nine or ten more. I think that more yet feel. May God touch many hearts. I *must not* leave here. I cannot. Oh may God guide me. The wounded man that I had met the other night had been shot at for disrupting a party to which he was not invited. Oh what a place.

Monday, January 29

Well, I have changed my boarding place. I now board with Mrs.
Adam Bayles. She and her husband and two children, a nephew and
a niece constitute the family. Mrs. Bayles is not afraid much of public scorn, having once taught the blacks here herself.[47] She assisted
me in the school tonight. Bob Jackson came in and took his flogging.
I gave him a severe one. I hope that I shall now be led so that I may
remain. I do love my school, and cannot bear to think of giving it up.
   I classified the school over again but they won't stay so I know
long. Got letters from Caleb and Lizzie tonight. The latter enclosed
one for John Brown. I gave it to him. He can show it to his brothers.
He does not need it now. Mr. Bayles came home with me.

Tuesday, January 30

Got along well in school today, only I had to whip four or five boys
for ill behaviour at noon. Bob was again in the mess and again ran
out of doors. I hope he will never come again. Tonight Joseph
Suecors was very annoying. I had to talk hardly to him for the good
of the school. He is either foolish or crazy. But what can I do?
   I like my boarding place much. It is a little Virginian log house,
and I can almost see out through the roof, but I believe that makes
me like it. I am well yet, but got tired today with whipping so many.
Wrote to Caleb and Lizzie tonight. I hope that John Brown will send
a note to Lizzie. He was not in tonight. Now I must close.

Wednesday, January 31

This forenoon I hastened through with all the juveniles, and then
after dinner had a regular spelling contest. Just as we began Mr.
Brackett, and Mr. Cowan, Superintendent of the Valley Schools,
came in.[48] They seemed much pleased with the exercise. Mr. Cowan
insists that I am laboring too hard and must cut short my hours. I
must try, but don't see how to begin any way. I want to do *more*
rather than less. I feel willing to wear out. I am in earnest. Mr.
Cowan addressed the school tonight instead of the usual writing
school. He is a good speaker, both to children and adults. I know
that he done John Brown good by his talk tonight. It was so sensible
and far reaching. I got no letters today nor yesterday. I was annoyed

this morning by the stealing of a knife. A book has been stolen too. I strongly suspect the thief too.

Letter from West Virginia

Martinsburg, West Va., Feb. 1st, 1866 [Feb. 7]

Dear Advocate:—I should have written several days ago, but my school had been disturbed, and I waited to see what came of it. I now think that it will die out. The ostensible reason was my having twice by day walked along the street in company with Mr. Hopewell, when he was going in the same direction, and having had some of my older pupils walk around home with me since I have been alone. The latter was regarded as merely a just and necessary protection, but it proved otherwise. One night the door was broken down in school hours, and twice a meeting was disturbed. On the latter occasion two arrests were made, and since, by close watching, all has been kept quiet. Capt. McKenzie has opened an office of the Freedman's Bureau here at the Court House, and he now has here a small guard of soldiers, on whom I can call on an escort when I need one. I have just returned from a good prayer-meeting at the school room. I have been much interested for the people here. Nine or ten manifest a good religious interest. I have talked personally with each that I could approach. At our last two meetings I must confess that there has been some emotional extravagance, but yet it bears evidence beyond a question of being genuine, and I hope that God will give me grace not to regard it with contempt.

John Brown has found peace, developing into a firm and consistent Christian. Several others have likewise come from darkness into light, and still the work goes on.

Since writing you last I have changed my boarding place. I now board with a family named Bales. I have a longer walk, but the part of the town is pleasanter than where I boarded before. The lady of the house has even taught some of them here before I came.

Yesterday we had a genuine spelling-school for an hour or two, for I have really some very fine spellers. In the midst of it Mr. Brackett came in, accompanied by Mr. Cowan, superintendent of the Valley Schools. He talked kindly to the scholars and they all seemed to like him. In the evening he addressed the people instead of my usual writing school.—He talked with earnest zeal, and I am sure that all who heard him were interested. He has placed a veto on my long days' works, but really I see so much to do that I know not where to stop. I am enduring it well, and, were I not, I would willingly wear out in the work. I often meet with discouragements, and yet earnest devotion to the cause bears me up. I am in no danger, I think, of wanting to desert the field while circumstances will allow me to stay. As far as I know all the other schools are coming on well. I see great progress in many of my scholars, and the vicious seem to be becoming tractable. Some of the most troublesome are now seeking Christ. But I must close. Christians pray for us here. God is at work. I need grace to help me in what I have to do.

In haste yours,
Sarah J. Foster

Diary, 1866

Thursday, February 1

Got on well with the school today. I begin to hope that I shall not have to trouble the scholars with the ruler much more. Mr. Brackett went off at noon. This evening I have been to a prayer meeting. God helped me wonderfully in prayer and speaking. I know that I touched many hearts. Many are seeking, among them Willoughby Fairfax and Isaac Brown. Elisha too and Harvey Davis seemed touched. One boy found peace. I hope God will give me grace not to feel contempt for their emotional extravagances. I talked personally with nine or ten, and sent word to John Brown's brother George that on account of his ill health I was going to make him a special subject of prayer. God grant it may do him good. Since meeting I have written to the Advocate. I have a bad cold now, but must not get sick. Got letters from Susan and Emma. Glad to hear from them.

Friday, February 2

Candlemas day bright, clear and not over warm. My boys are really trying to be better I hope. I stopped at noon and talked to Elisha Brown and Fannie Lee about plans for their benefit. Wanted to give Will Fairfax a good word but he was nowhere alone. I hope that he will keep on his way. I mean now to try love on the boys who are trying to be good. Tonight I have had a good school. Two of the

guard came in. One of them came home with me. Got a letter from
Eld. Purkis tonight. He was slow to write but is good when it comes.

Some scholars annoyed me by stupidity, but John Brown's map
lesson atoned for all. It was *perfect*. Oh, how I wish that he had a
white man's chance. I long to help the family rise. I am not tired
tonight. Shall have to whip one boy next week for truancy. Oh how
hard that is for me.

Saturday, February 3

This has been a good day. I have spent it in resting, and in writing
letters. I have written to Eld. Purkis, Mrs. Cole, Susan Jordan[49] and
Emma. Then I got a letter from Miss Wright and answered that and
one from Geo. Cobb which I have begun to answer. William Bowman
took my letters to the office and brought down George's. Mary
Hopewell brought in Kittie's. Her father had been to Shepherdstown, and had seen Kittie. She has got a good school in a church.

Sunday, February 4

This morning I went to the Methodist Church. Then after dinner I
had my Sabbath School. Fifty-three were present. This evening we
have had a full and good meeting. Two more have found peace.
Others yet are seeking. I talked with several. Was annoyed some by
thoughtless laughing. I must try and be patient. I cannot name my
trials for no one sympathizes with them.

I know that God is at work here and am not going to cast off his
children for ignorance and mistakes. May God lead me aright. I was
glad to see that Isaac Brown yet held on. God help him.

Monday, February 5

Had quite a full school today, and had no trouble either. Tonight I
had a young gentleman visit in school. I know not who. He helped
me and seemed interested and then walked home with me. Forty
seven were present. Some object cards have been added to our
room's furnishing. By whom I know not. Now a blackboard, and
then a map of the United States and I shall be all right. I do feel
interested in my school. I long to do there all good now in haste. I
cannot wait. Oh help me Father to have patience. I mean to do all I
can to make the folks learn fast. Some need no urging.

Tuesday, February 6

Had a very good and quiet school today though fifty-two were in.
Some need driving to learn. Well I must drive. At teatime Mary
Hopewell came to tell me that the young man who was in last night
was thought to be the one who beat down our door. I don't believe
it, but of course his motive was only curiosity. He appeared well
though. Mr. Hopewell sent me the pencilled address of a Mr.
Vosburgh, with the statement that I had more friends than I knew
of.[50] Uncle Andy tells me that some of the scholars are finding fault
because I spend my time for the long classes at night. Can't they be
more sensible? They fret really because I ridicule their dullness
sometimes.

Wednesday, February 7

Capt. McKenzie had Bob Jackson and Jim Haynes arrested this
morning. Bob had stolen some money and Jim had charge of a part
of it. Another boy was partially implicated but got clear. It disturbed
the school some, for the soldiers, having kept four or five boys hunting up the delinquents an hour in the morning then came to get Jim
who was in school. Tonight I had twenty-seven in school—twelve to
write though it has been raining and sleeting some. Got a chance to
have a few words with Isaac Brown. He yet holds on his way. May
God soon give him peace. I know he will be a good Christian. I long
to hear him praise God. But, like John, he will never be vehement,
only good and quiet.

Thursday, February 8

A wet slippery day but I had a full school. Have tried ridicule when
other efforts failed on some of my slow scholars and it seems to
work well.

Had to punish two boys today. One does not mean to be bad at
all. Tonight Rev. Mr. Osborne preached to the people. He preached
well but he ought to have waited to have talked to the mourners
afterward which he did not. I talked with three or four. I feel deeply
for them. I will do my duty by them. I long to hear them praise God
for deliverance. Heaven help me to guide them aright. I have at
least my heart in the work. Who *can* hesitate as to duty in such a
case. Certainly not I.

Friday, February 9

Had a nice quiet school today. I think that I have got them disci-
plined into good order at last. Had a talk with my pet at noon. He
ought to have a better chance than this place affords to develop his
abilities. Tonight John handed me a note in reply to Lizzie's. It was
excellent—just as modest and unaffected as the writer. It ought to
charm our home friends. I have written to Lizzie. Shall enclose the
note, and see what will come of it. I hope that Caleb will set the ball
rolling to send John to Lewiston. I know that it ought to be so. I am
unselfish, for if he should go I should lose my best help in the
school. May God bring his purposes to pass is my only prayer.

Saturday, February 10

This morning I darned stockings and knit a little. After dinner I carried some clothing to a little girl that was needy. Then to see what
the meaning was of Mr. Vosburgh's address sent by Mr. Hopewell, I
called over at Adam Howard's and Mr. Brown's. The Vosburgh's are
Northern people, and are really desirous of seeing me. So I told
Mary Brown that, if it was fair, I would go over there next Saturday.
Mary will tell her. Mrs. V. said that if she knew Mrs. Bales she
would call on me. Tonight I have been reading to and with Rosa and
helping Billie with Geography, besides knitting to fill up the time. I
met Adam Howard's mother and two of her sisters—one of them the
mother of Will Fairfax. They all look smart.

Sunday, February 11

This morning I went to the Catholic Church. The priest read the
address of the Bishop and the Regulations of Lent. A special dispen-
sation has been granted to them this year to omit some of the usual
observances, but the priest did not think the indulgence needed
here. The address was good in part—in fact mostly for it lashed social vices with an unsparing hand. Had a good S. School this afternoon. Sixty present—not the usual number of helpers, but I got on
well. Tonight Will Bowman went up to our meeting. It was wretchedly crowded but very good—save one man's performance. Bell
Hopewell and another girl fainted away. Isaac Brown had not yet
found peace, but he is in earnest, and may God soon help him to
grace and glory.

Letter from West Virginia

Martinsburg, West Va., Feb. 11th, 1866 [Feb. 21]

Dear Advocate:—It is about nine, Sabbath eve. I have just returned from a prayer-meeting at the school-room. It was, as all our meetings here are, emphatically a prayer-meeting, for there was but one exhortation, and that short, though nearly two hours were spent in the exercises with hardly a lost moment. The room was literally packed. Many went away unable to gain admittance, and so it is each Sabbath night. On Thursday nights the attendance is never so full, yet there is no lack of interest. There is, in fact, a deep and widely spread interest. Five conversions have already occurred, and a number more are seeking to find the Savior. Our Sabbath school, too, is on the increase. Upwards of fifty were present to-day, though the walking is wretched, and, in some locations, the mud almost impassable. We have now quite a large Bible class. Mr. Thomson takes care of that, that I may have leisure to manage the rest of the school. For so large a school it is very orderly indeed, and I find the superintendence a pleasant task.

My day school, too, is growing larger. Its list is now seventy, while the night list approaches fifty. By the aid of the older scholars I have succeeded in cutting off about an hour and a half from my daily labors, but, even then, I spend not less than forty-two hours per week in the school-room, counting my Sabbath school and the meetings that I attend. Yet I am wonderfully sustained.—With all the changefulness of the climate and the humidity of the air, I find the place healthy, and never enjoyed better health anywhere. There has been no further disturbance, and I now walk home alone though the soldiers are yet in town, for I think it better to show no distrust. I understand that it was reported in the Baltimore American that our school was disturbed by returned rebel soldiers. I am not aware that such was in any instance the case, and think it but just to say I anticipate no trouble from them.[51]

I spoke of good spelling in my last letter. Week before last a boy of sixteen, named Willoughby Fairfax, who chanced to recite alone, spelled seventy-five long words and only missed *two*. At the beginning of the year he was in words of four letters. He is one of my best pupils but not the best in spelling as good as he is. A girl of thirteen bears off the palm in that branch.

I now have several who are making creditable progress in cyphering, not to mention the boys who do easy sums on their slates, which I set to relieve the tedium of study. I have also several very good pupils in Geography, and actually hear some as good map lessons as I could expect to at home. Quite a number are learning fast to write. A great many are in Mental Arithmetic. I even have one small class in the night school who recite in the old but good Colburn's Arithmetic, which quite carries me back to my early school-days again. I have met with two copies each of Webster's and Town's spelling Books. Those most common are Comly's, which are not so good as either of the above. But, in spite of all the disadvantages, the scholars are bound to prove their capacity to learn. They are usually fond of school, and punctual in attendance, and, as a class, orderly on the street.

I daily become more and more interested in the school, and in all that concerns the welfare of the colored people here. One thing I particularly need, and that is a supply of papers. I have a monthly supply of Freedmen[52] and Banners, but, the three intervening Sabbaths, I depend on supplies from other places. Papers are needed and highly valued. Cannot the Sabbath school scholars who read the *Advocate* remember the colored children of Martinsburg? Will they not save their papers and send them to me? Each little Sabbath school paper may thus do two-fold good. Parents get your children to act in this matter. And, could any Sabbath school spare an old library, it would be worth its weight in gold. Will not some school send one along?

But I must close for now.

Sarah J. Foster

Diary, 1866

Monday, February 12

This has been a dull bad day but yet I have had a good school. Will Fairfax has come back to school. I was very glad to see him again.

Tonight I got letters from Lizzie, Avery,[53] Geo. Cobb, and Mr. Brackett. Lizzie has dropped J.D.R. He is found out to be a wretch at last.

This evening in school Joseph Suecors annoyed me so much that I had half a mind to send for Capt. McKenzie to come and put him in jail. But finally he begged pardon and I let it go for once. He is both foolish and crazy but what can I do?

Isaac Brown I think feels better. His face indicates as much. I hope it is so. John was not in. How I miss him when he stays out. He is my firmest support in the school. I long to see him educated to help his race.

Tuesday, February 13

I had a good and quiet school today though many were in. I got a wretched Valentine today about Slander. It was a hit on somebody else but me for I have been slandered but have not slandered any one.

Joseph Suecors remembered his destiny if he didn't be still and was very quiet though he acted foolishly with a Valentine that he had for a pretty yellow girl. Forty-one were in. Coming home I felt afraid that a man who was after me on the street was meaning harm, but it was one of my scholars. I made a misstep, and he spoke to me. I was greatly relieved to hear his voice. I am not far away from the men who come over this way any time. So I hope to be safe from harm. I am not very timid but others fear for me.

Wednesday, February 14

This has been a rainy, sloppy day but I had a full school. Joe Suecors was in the school after dinner and he acted so badly, cutting up and making the boys laugh, that I ordered him out of the school. He went but had to be sent out the second time. He was very angry and was around early at night and got in swearing and scolding badly. After I came in he was still save preaching in pantomime half of the evening. But on the street he came down this way as crazy as he could be, cursing and swearing awfully and declaring that he didn't know where he was. I should have been afraid if he had been able to get very near me, but he could not seem to walk fast and others were between. I heard tonight that I was going to marry John Brown. What next? Well let the fools talk. Can't they have wit enough to let me alone? I like the Browns of course but have given no cause for talk.

Thursday, February 15

Very cold indeed, but bright and I have had a very full school today and have made out to get my classes reduced in number so that I can

get through earlier and attend to more of them myself. Joe Suecors
came in again and I again ordered him out. Tonight we had an excellent meeting. Five were seeking the Savior. One at least found him
ere the meeting closed. Joe Suecors was in cutting up and acting like
a fool. Uncle Andy says he will have him attended to if he don't
do better.

Tonight I got a good letter from Emma Rogers. She is visiting in
Winthrop Me. Had a few minutes talk with John Brown. He has
heard too of the story that is out. Well, I have done no harm. Neither has he, and people may talk. The scholars know that I am clear
of blame.

Friday, February 16

A very cold day, but not so cold as yesterday was. I had not so many
quite in school though. Uncle Andy came in to say that Joe S. prom-
ises to do better if he may come at night. Well he may try. Tonight
he did do better any way. I took too many Bronchial Troches and felt
sick, but had a pleasant school. I got a good, kind, sisterly letter
from a stranger lady in Sumner Me. asking, after many expressions
of sympathy, what she could do for the school. I have already written a reply in part, and tonight I took the liberty to read the letter in
school. The scholars were touched and pleased at the interest felt
for them by strangers at the North. A kind allusion to my aid here
pleased me much. The letter was most excellent. It has done me a
world of good. I have just mixed the buckwheat cakes. Ellen went
off and forgot them.

Saturday, February 17

I have made out to have the most pleasant day yet. I wrote and
sewed till noon, and then went over and got Mary Brown to go to
Mrs. Vosburgh's with me. Had a very pleasant call on Mary then a
most agreeable visit at Mrs. V's. Shall go there again I am sure. She
invites me every Saturday till I make other friends. Out there it has
been told that I was part colored and was *married* to *Geo. Brown*—
whom I have only seen three times—ha, ha. A neighbor asked Mrs.
V. if I wasn't "half nigger." Dropped in on my way back to see Mrs.
Adam Howard's new baby. A dear little boy, not a week old. Then
Mrs. V. and a young Mrs. Webster came over home with me. I
found Mrs. Bales in a "state of mind." Ellen had not been smart and
was summarily dismissed while anger seemed to rule my hostess.

Sunday, February 18

A bad, cold stormy day. I did not go out this morning, but I did go to Sabbath school. Over forty were present and we had a good school. Tonight, fearing it might not look well, I have not gone to meeting— though I wanted to very much. I have been talking and reading, and have passed quite a pleasant day and evening. I miss confidential friends though. Oh if Lizzie were here. I am not homesick but I am in want of a confidante. It never can be anyone here that I shall choose.

Monday, February 19

Got letters from Lizzie and Mrs. Hutchison. Still quite cold, but clear. I have had a nice school. I hope that I have about done whipping. Some of the dullest are beginning to learn. Found Nat Wood reading my Bible Reader, and agreed to give it to him when school was done. Caleb will let me I know.

Isaac Brown I am sure has found peace. I gave him a cheering word tonight. John has gone to Hancock for a day or two, and judging by Elisha's mischievous looks, the public need not marry him to *me* just yet. Mrs. Bales is now doing her own work. She is pleasanter than when vexed by a servant. Ellen was at school as usual after dinner, but I said nothing of course. Well I must off to bed now. I hope that I shall sleep. I have not felt quite well. Took some paregoric at noon.

Tuesday, February 20

A little warmer, but yet cold. I find the school going on well, and hope that I shall have them in order without more whipping. At noon Mr. Hopewell was in. He has given me the author of a story that is around and leave to expose it, and I think that I shall do so. Tonight had a full school, and was late though but took an opportunity to talk before several of the school, about the yarns that are around. I addressed John Brown, but all heard me. I know that I shall have to demonstrate some or lose my best pupils. I am not going to do that.

I wrote a letter to Lizzie today, but got none from anywhere. A letter from Marion Higgins is gone somewhere—the postmaster thinks to Martinsburg, Pa. Hope I shall soon get it. I am well again today. Only dull from the effect of a heavy dose of paregoric yesterday. Was a little tired in consequence.

Wednesday, February 21

A splendid day—not too muddy nor too cold. I had two men in school besides my usual number of scholars. One is a good scholar, but not so superior in mind as some others that I know here. Well I must take people as I find them. Some of the boys are learning to write well, and in Arithmetic and spelling they do well too.

Tonight I had about a dozen to write, and was pretty busy, but I like to do it, for I contemplate having some nice letters from some of my present pupils after I get home. I am well again. I hope to feel well now all the time. My cough is all gone. I wish all nights were as bright as this. Someone said "There goes 'Miss Foster' tonight. Before it has been "the nigger teacher." I felt glad to hear the difference. Hope it will last. I certainly offend no one now, and don't mean to.

Thursday, February 22

Got letters from Abbie Coombs and Geo. Cobb tonight. Another magnificent day. As the other schools had a holiday, I had a spelling contest by choice of sides after recess. They all liked it so much that I held it by vote of theirs till nearly five. Mr. Brackett looked in just a moment in the afternoon and was in to our meeting tonight though he came late. We had a crowded, excellent prayer meeting. Mrs. Vosburgh and Mrs. Webster were in, and were very much interested. Mr. B. thought that there were a number of white people in. Some of my pupils were so light colored or "bright" as they say out here. Mr. John Hoke is very ill, will hardly live long. May God prepare him for what awaits him. I asked Mr. Wm. Hoke how he was this morning. I swallowed my pride and feel better.

Friday, February 23

A little overcast but yet a beautiful day. Still I fear it will rain tomorrow, and I promised Mrs. Vosburgh that if it was decent I'd go over there. I am to have the two men who have been in for day scholars. I like the idea of advanced scholars, but Mr. Christie is something of a pedant. I like George Harris best for he is unassuming, and means to be a good scholar. Tonight had twenty-eight in school. Mr. Brackett says that I have the largest night school in his circuit. I have

hopes that N. G. will send a teacher out here. Mr. B. hopes so too. I
have carried out a wayward purpose tonight. I hope that it will do no
harm. I believe I was right, but hardly dare trust even my diary with
the secret.

Saturday, February 24

As I feared it has been a dull rainy day. I have written to Geo. Cobb,
Mrs. Hodsdon, and to Miss Fletcher to tell her *not* to send a box
here, also a letter for Mary Hopewell's mother. Then I have sewed
since I got through writing. It held up long enough to allow me to go
to the post office and to get some trifles that I needed. I have felt
disappointed at not having been able to go out today. I wanted to
see Mrs. Vosburgh, and to pet that dear little babe again. I feel so
much better since last night. Nature made me wayward and independent, and I must act myself. God knows I mean well, and I believe that He will guide me aright. I feel to trust all to Him now.
Tomorrow will tell whether I have done well or ill in my wayward-
ness. I think all is for the best.

Sunday, February 25

A beautiful day. I did not however go out any where till afternoon. I
then went to Sabbath School. I felt anxious to hear what came of my
freak, but felt well prepared for what came. I am relieved and yet
more ensnared than ever. God has charge of all things and I shall
only have to trust *him*. We had a very good prayer meeting. A white
man came in. I don't know who he was. Charlie Ford and I think one
other found peace tonight. Isaac Brown yet mourns. Uncle Andy
McDaniell and I have talked to him. May God bless our words. I
talked to Geo. Phenix too, and hope it will do him good. I am going
by prayer and self denial to strive harder than ever to save souls.
Maybe that will keep me from sad and discouraging fancies. I must
work all that I can.

Monday, February 26

Began the week well, I hope to get on nicely. I receive often gratify-
ing tokens of love from the scholars. Today the reported author of
the story about me and Mr. Hopewell came and denied it. She was

in tonight at school. I am rather late home, but hope to be through earlier soon. I love my work as well as ever.

Got a letter from Miss Gibbs tonight. I was glad to hear from her. She is good and lively.

I was pleased to learn that Mr. Brackett thinks I'm doing well. I certainly try to do all that I can. I have to be busy too, and to hurry all the while, but I feel better to be active than to be idle—especially now. Ah well I am a strange piece of humanity any way. My life is bound to run in strange channels. Where will I go, and what will I do next?

Tuesday, February 27

The same as ever in school all day. Mary Hopewell, having been to Shepherdstown, brought me a letter from Kittie. Then at night I got one from Mr. Brackett enclosing blanks from my reports. Tonight I have made out my figures. It is late and I must go to bed. My last ink is so poor that I can't use it—O what a place this is.

Wednesday, February 28

Had a quiet pleasant day in school. Hope that the worst of the trouble is over. Mr. Bales says that they say in some of the barrooms up town that I went out and stayed some time alone with this white man who was in one meeting. Pooh. They haven't wit enough to lie straightly and sensibly out here.

Got packages of papers from Portland, New Castle and Sumner tonight sent by readers of the Advocate who had read my call for them.

Had a good meeting tonight. Mr. Osborne preached. A colored man present made the best prayer that I ever heard or read. It was grand. Then such singing. Next Wednesday they mean to see about starting to organize a church.

Letter from West Virginia

Martinsburg, W. Va., Feb. 28th, 1866 [March 7]

Dear Advocate:—Again I snatch a few minutes to pen a short report of my school and its affairs. We are having now I judge about the fullest school that we shall have at all. The weather of late has been such as to allow the small children to come, and young men and women, who will soon be out at service for the summer, are now improving the time to come to school for a while. Even now the schools begin to change a little. The day school for a week or two has diminished a little, and the other has proportionately increased. One after another they come to me with the remark "Miss Jenny, I can't come to day-school anymore, I'm going to work, but I'll come at night," and they do so all that they can. The boy to whose spelling I alluded in my last will not be able to come any more than this week, for his father has bought a farm in the country and has work for him now: I regret to lose so good a scholar, but he will not fail to do well anywhere. The religious interest yet continues good, and one or two more conversions have occurred. Our two last prayer-meetings were among the best that we have had, and the room was full, the door wide open part of the time and a group outside. The men who are busy when meeting opens come crowding in at its close, content to get a standing place in or near the doorway to hear maybe a single prayer or hymn for their pains. Their interest shames our home lukewarmness. I am so fond of the meeting myself that I have missed but one—a very rainy Sabbath night. But even then the room was full and the meeting good.

The Sabbath School too is large. Over sixty were in last Sabbath, and week before last, though very rainy, forty were out, and yet I have not half of the time any papers for them and no books at all. Since writing you last I have had two pleasant surprises. A lady reader of your paper in Sumner Maine, who only knew of me through your columns, sent me a cheering word. Her kind, sisterly letter touched my inmost soul. It came to me like a cool refreshing spring in a desert. To her offer to collect a box of clothing for this place I felt compelled to respond in the negative. So liberal have been the contributions sent to Mr. Brackett that he has been obliged to cry "Hold—enough," and I am now fully supplied from Harper's Ferry. But I do want a S. S. Library, and I want papers. We need more copies now of the Banner and Freedman, and even they leave three weeks of each month unsupplied. Old papers or money to get new ones, will help the good cause along. We will not stop you then. One hundred and fifty papers this month did not half meet the demand.

But I spoke of two pleasant surprises. The last was the discovery of Northern friends in town, or rather my being discovered by them. They are a family from New York by the name of Vosburgh, and

seem most excellent people. They sought an introduction, invited
me to their house, and I have passed one very pleasant Saturday
afternoon there, and have a standing invitation for many more. Mrs.
Vosburgh has attended since one of our meetings and professed herself much interested in the exercises. The cognomen of "nigger
teacher" seems to have died out, and I occasionally hear my own
name as I pass in the street, or, more frequently some person is noti-
fied that "there goes the Freedmen's Bureau." I have not met with
any annoyance on the street but once, and then a white man addressed an insolent remark to me as I was going into the school-
room door. I don't mind such things at all. Report has married or
engaged me several times to men connected with the school, and,
Mrs. Vosburgh was actually asked by a neighbor the day I was there
"if I was not part nigger." I hope they will believe it, for then surely
they could not complain of my teaching the people of my own race.
But Rev. Mr. Osborne preaches at our school room tonight, and I
must prepare to go.

In haste, Sarah J. Foster

Diary, 1866

Thursday, March 1

I have enjoyed today very much, for the air has been mild and
springlike. People are working their gardens. My school glides along
smoothly too. Tonight Mary Brown came in to school to see me.
Waited half an hour to talk with me afterward. We did not walk together on the street but she came after me and stopped at the shop
window to call out Isaac. A lady(?) called out "Is that a 'nigger' or a
white woman?" just as I passed her referring to Mary at the shop.

Got no mail tonight at all. Had my writing school. John Brown
favors the idea of a F. W. B. church here. He will help.[54]

Friday, March 2

A springlike overcast day. I fear it will rain tomorrow. My day and
evening in school were as usual pleasant. Will Fairfax has done coming for now. He must work. I gave him a nice book. He seemed glad of
it. I also gave him my last Advocate letter in which I had praised him.

Tonight two white men came in to school for about twenty minutes. They were civil, but will doubtless go off and be as hard as they can.

Got papers tonight from Skowhegan and Minot. Counting on my monthly supply I have now enough for two Sabbaths. I am glad that I thought to ask after them. I shall now have enough.

Saturday, March 3

Overcast this morning, and I feared a rain, but it cleared up and was the sweetest possible weather before noon. While I was mending a young man came who manufactured an errand. He staid an unconscionable while and finally invited me to the Stereopticon now here. He claims to be from the North—five years out here. I think his cheeky invitation was his errand under the form of a barroom bet, and that he was heartily ashamed of it too, for he acted as if he was. Afternoon went to Mrs. Vosburgh's—dropped in to see the baby at Mrs. Howard's and also a while to see Mary Brown. Got a letter from Emma today and a few papers from North Fayette.

Sunday, March 4

A delicious day. I had sixty-seven scholars in S. School. I gave away sixty-nine papers. Mr. Campbell was in and had the school singing before I got there. A young Mr. Geo. Christie—a very good scholar, was in. He lined off the hymns and then, by his and Mr. Campbell's help, the scholars after school sung some fine S. S. pieces very nicely indeed. I talked with Mr. Christie about getting a thorough education on account of helping his race. Hope he will think of it. I certainly want somebody to do so. Tonight had a real good meeting, but it wound up with a "shout."[55] Isaac Brown is yet far from peace, but very much in earnest. I mean to pray particularly for him. Moses Hole too seemed in earnest in wanting to be a Christian. Mary and Amos Brown were in. Geo. is not so well they say.

Monday, March 5

A cold, windy day. I had not so large a school as usual today. Only thirty-five were in. I got through early. I got letters from Lizzie, a circular from N.Y. and a letter from a Mr. Hathaway regarding some books for one S. School and some papers too. I have written a letter

to the Advocate and one to Mr. Hathaway mostly. Tonight I began
to call classes out on the floor and to compel them to learn more
than they have for a while past. I was busy till nearly ten, and very
likely shall be so now, for I can't well do otherwise. I hope that Mr.
Brackett won't find it out for he would hardly like it and indeed I
can't help it. I hear that there is a complaint that I attend to the light
colored ones to the neglect of the rest. It is a *lie*, and the author
knows it. I don't make any differences at all.

Letter from West Virginia

Martinsburg, West Va., March 5th, 1866 [March 14]

Dear Advocate: I write this hasty note to acknowledge the receipt of
parcels of papers from New Castle, Minot, Sumner, Skowhegan,
Portland, and North Fayette, in all more than seventy-five papers.[56]
I distributed *nineteen* of these in addition to my *monthly supply*,
from which you may see that they were needed. Emma G. Donnell,
Hattie A. Chase, Cora L. Dodge, and Abbie Sturtevant may be sure
that I shall not forget their names. I would send personal thanks
could I find time. I also noticed a pencilled name on one paper—
Eddie Waters. I was reminded of a dear little Eddie whose soul long
since went home to heaven, for, if he were living, he too would do all
that he could for the Freedmen, his heart being full of love to all the
world. But he sleeps in Mount Auburn, and I shall love to think that
somewhere there is another Eddie trying to do good in the world.

The religious interest yet continues, and there is the best evidence of genuine heart work. True, I have been disappointed in
some, but even Christ's little church had a Judas, and therefore I
know that I ought not to be discouraged, for indeed there is not
much of spurious religious emotion here. On Wednesday night last,
Rev. Mr. Osborne preached to us at the school-room, his text being,
"So run that ye may obtain." His discourse was excellent, and was
heard by all who could possibly crowd into the room, with the clos-
est attention. A colored man from Hancock, formerly a resident of
this place, was in. He made the best prayer that I ever heard, and I
was surprised to learn that he was not a clergyman. After services
were over, the visitor and some of his old friends gathered in a
group and sung several impressive hymns and choruses with thrilling effect. It did *me* good if no others were benefited.

A colored man named John Campbell has begun to instruct the children in singing Sabbath school hymns. Already they do credit to him and to themselves, though he does not know how to read music. A young man named George Christie was in our Sunday school yesterday for the first time. He is a very good scholar apparently, and bids fair to be a valuable help.

The colored people here are very anxious to get a church of their own, and I have hopes that they will succeed. Should they ever build one, they will probably build it with a basement for vestry and school-room. Their burying ground here is very much dilapidated, and they must first get that in order, which they mean soon to do. As fast as they can they are buying property and in all possible ways striving to care for themselves. Very few indeed seem to lack the ability to do so when they have a good chance. The good weather has put the men to work on the land, and my school to-day only numbered thirty-five. But I can be busy enough, and then, as the day school decreases the other enlarges. In fact, with the little ones that are soon to begin coming, my day's list will hardly diminish much for more than a week or two at this present time. Very soon I will write again. Now I must close.

Yours, &c
Sarah J. Foster

P.S. Should any one contemplate sending S.S. Library books, a letter before sending would oblige

S.J.F.

Diary, 1866

Tuesday, March 6

Not quite so cool, but yet cool and windy. Think my school is to be smaller now for a while. I can get through half an hour earlier easily. I have had a cold today, but feel better than I thought I should. Tonight I had a contest with a troublesome scholar. I did not mean to be too severe and did not think that I was either. I am well enough to stand quite a battle but yet I am tired. I had a good full school and so I had to hold late, but then if I have done any good by my fight I shall be glad.

I trust that I shall not allow even the knowledge of slander to make me make any differences in my treatment of the colored

people. I mean to be just and generous to all. No wonder they are
jealous and ill tempered often.

Wednesday, March 7

This morning when I went to school I found Elisha Brown with his
head badly cut. Nat Wood pushed him out of the room and he fell
and hurt him on a stone. Mrs. Weldon was sick and Nat *ordered* him
out. He was nettled and was saucy. The wound was not intentional.
I washed his head and face. Meanwhile Jake came over and took him
to the shop to dress his head. He did not pity Elisha much. Had
several new scholars. Mrs. Campbell was in and sung with the school
a while. Got a paper from Portland and a letter from Mr. Perkins
and also one from Phi Haskell[57] for mail tonight. Was glad to hear
from both. We have had a most excellent class meeting. They have
chosen a leader—Mr. Perry Brown, and they feel strongly interested in getting a church built. I hope that they will succeed. I am
sorry that they cannot feel to be F. W. Baptists. John Brown is inclined to be. The rest are not.[58]

Thursday, March 8

Yet cold and windy. I wrote letters this morning till school time. I
am glad that the mud is dried up, for now my walk is pleasant.
Elisha Brown came to writing school tonight. There were thirteen
writers—one new one. I felt easily fretted in school today, but ought
not to complain for I have few such days. It was in *me* I dare say, and
I am glad I whipped no one. Tonight for mail I got letters from
Joanne Leavitt, Susan Jordan and a Mr. Whitney of Thorndike. *He*
was the sender of my Advocate extra I take it. Well I shall reply with
thanks, for he wrote a good letter. He is a good scholar too, and old I
judge. Ah well. Maybe I shall make a good friend in Maine by coming here. I can't love anybody though. "[   ]."

Friday, March 9

I felt better and the school machinery worked well today. I had no
trouble with what would have fretted me yesterday. I got no mail
today. I had time therefore to mostly answer my back mail. Tonight
I had a spelling school. I expected the Vosburgh's in but they did not

come. We had a fine time. Nat Wood and Mr. Willis chose sides.
Nat's side got all of the other, captain and all twice, and then weren't
they glad? Some day scholars were in among them—Elisha Brown.
He has some way made up with Nat, and was fast by his side all the
time. He can forgive quick I see. Well I like him more and more
daily. May God make him a good man. I had Mrs. Cook and Mrs.
Lewis home with me. They would come. Said they could not bear to
see me coming home so lonesome. I could not refuse them this
chance to be kind. Well we'll see.

Saturday, March 10

I wrote to Phi, Susan and Kittie this morning. Then after dinner I
went over to Mrs. Vosburgh's, She had a headache, and refining
some maple sugar had almost made her sick, but she was better
after I had rubbed her head a little while. Mrs. Webster came in
while I was there. She brought in some wine. By some mistake Mr.
W. had sent some in just before. We all tasted it a little. Mrs. W.
wants me to go there. I mean to. In my vacation I am not going to
slight my new friends. They shall have half if they choose. Saw my
baby too. It notices more. Its mother is proud and likes my attention. Was in at the Brown's a moment or two. George is worse. I
wanted to talk about his soul, but I could not find a chance that
looked suitable. At least I hesitated to do so. I can pray but if he dies
unsaved I can't feel clear not to have said a word. I must speak. I
gave Mrs. H. my handsomest ring. She was delighted with it. Mary
B. invites me there to meet Miss Ransom in three weeks—shall go.
Got a letter from Mrs. L. H. Coombs and my paper.

Sunday, March 11

Dull—almost rainy this morning. Did rain before daylight. I feared
that it might create talk if I went out to a colored gathering twice on
a wet day. So I did not go to the class, but stayed at home, and wrote
a long letter to Mrs. L. H. Coombs. We had a good S. S. School a
little hurried by a funeral that was to be held after it. I had papers too
—enough of them. Tonight we had the German Reformed Church
and a white man from Baltimore preached to us. He was good. He
appoints a meeting for tomorrow night—a class meeting. They had
some splendid singing. Bill and Rosa were with me. I am sure that

they like the services much. They could not have helped it. The music was so good and deep.

Monday, March 12

A delicious day—only misty, very warm and Springlike. The sun got out too at night. I have got some a–b–c scholars in who can *spell*. So irritating to drill such ones. I got tired and vexed. Hattie Davis is twenty-nine years old today. I'd like to see her. Wonder whether I'll ever hear again from the careless creature. Tonight our minister disappointed us and so we had a small but good prayer meeting. How long Isaac Brown is in the dark! I long to hear him praise God. The meeting closed in a "shout" and, it being payday on the railroad,[59] that drew some drunken rowdies around. One caught me by the arm as I went out. I got away, and put the colored folks between us in a hurry. Some pistol shots were fired near our meeting time. But we did not mind them at all.

Tuesday, March 13

A magnificent day. I had to work hard though in school, for I feel to hurry on some slow scholars, but then the most are doing well. I need to pray for patience. I've found a "dunce's bench" to work well. I make them *stand* there while getting their lessons over.

Tonight had only twenty-two in school, but, owing to the mulish dullness of some, got on slowly and did not get fairly through at ten. Then too many were in late. I must do as well as I can. I am not expected to do impossibilities. I feel so anxious to get on though that I can't bear dullness. I got vexed but the prayers of my *best friend* calmed me. There was *one* poor lesson that I know how to account for and did not chide. I am a perfect thermometer. I *feel* the mental atmosphere about me. I cannot help it either.

Letter from West Virginia

Martinsburg, West Va., March 13th, 1866 [March 21]

Dear Advocate:—It is a delicious spring morning. The air is really life-inspiring, and the season seems at least a month in advance of our's at home. We are still going on the even tenor of our way. I have had some new scholars, and, the removals not having changed much the organizations of the classes, I have been compelled to labor more hours for a few days past, as the new children are in the alphabet or small syllables, while I had none so far back.

Last Wednesday night the colored people met at the school-room, and organized a class meeting, to meet Sabbath mornings, choosing the father of John Brown for a leader, with a unanimity that proved the high estimation in which he is held. The meeting was most excellent. Four of the recent converts were there, and testified to what God had done for them, and three out of four seekers present expressed their fixed determination to seek God's favor till it was found to the joy of their souls. I was not present at the meeting Sabbath morning, but doubt not it was good. Our Sabbath school was quite full and very good, though a little hurried in its exercises, on account of the funeral of a colored girl at an hour earlier than our usual time of closing. We have now a juvenile class in the Bible besides our large class. Mr. Christie was in again, and, in singing, proved himself an invaluable aid, and both he and his brother aided in our school. Instead of our usual prayer-meeting, we had the use of the German Reformers' church, and were addressed by a clergyman from Baltimore. He left an appointment for last night, but was compelled to leave in the afternoon. Yet we had a good meeting. Six present were seeking the Savior. Among them is a younger brother of John Brown, who has now been in the dark more than a month, but is yet in earnest, and pledges himself never to give up till he shall find Jesus. He bids fair to be as good and reliable in the cause of Christ as his father and brother John. Last night our meeting terminated in a "shout." The noise drew some outside attention. Whether to disturb us or not, I cannot say, several pistol shots were fired near by, and when I came out I encountered a few young white men at the door, one of whom caught me by the arm. I paid no attention to his rudeness, slipped away from his grasp, and soon placed several groups of my pupils between us, coming home without further annoyance.

The subject of building a church is in serious contemplation, and will, I think, be brought to a successful issue during the summer. Thursday night the colored people are to have the Methodist church, and, after preaching, they will circulate a subscription paper for the purpose of building the church. Some white people here will doubtless aid them. In fact, it is not the refined and wealthy who are the

most bitter, but the lower classes,—those who in habits and education are but little, if any superior to them. As one of my pupils remarked: "T'aint them that used to own servants that's so hard on us,
but them that never had none. My observation inclines me to his
opinion, but yet I feel that the cause will move on. The black race
will not again be enslaved, though years may lapse before they can
take their rightful place. Just now education is their aim, and nothing is suffered to hinder them in its pursuit. As I look back I am
astonished at the progress that some of my scholars have made.
True, some need driving to learn. Others need strict discipline,
which is difficult in a crowded room, but yet I see progress, and
mean, God helping me, to persevere till Providence shall close the
door now open for me here. I never was in a work that so thoroughly
aroused my whole being, and gave life such a zest. And never did I
feel so ready to work with, and for, God.

                                                    Sarah J. Foster

Diary, 1866

Wednesday, March 14

A warm day—delicious only the air in my schoolroom was hot and
dense. I had a good day though. Oh I wish I could take the school
here a year. I don't want to leave it in July at all. I want Lizzie too.
So do the scholars, for they have heard me speak of her. This afternoon Mr. Brackett came. Tonight he was in to school with a colored
man from Harper's Ferry. I had but few in—twenty or so—8 to
write—two new ones—one my best speller. Mr. B. has engaged a
better room for April—Thank God for that.[60] I had a talk about the
stories with Mr. Brackett. He laughed at the "half nigger" story.
Said he hoped they'd think so. I am well and don't mean to stop
night school till I have to on account of lack of scholars and want of
time. I am in love with my work.

Thursday, March 15

Another sweet warm day. I had a pleasant day in school. Several incidents showed the good feeling of my scholars toward me. Tonight
Mr. Mark [   ] preached at the Methodist Church to the Colored

people. It rained the first of the evening and not many were out, but they took the names of some who wanted to join the church when organized and are to have another meeting in two weeks when they will have found out what the expense of a church will be, and will start a regular subscription paper. I long to see the work go on. Mr. Matthews and Mr. Snyder[61] came and spoke to me. I never *looked* at them till they did so. Some of the colored people felt nicely about it. I overheard them talking. They saw and liked my independence. Well I know it is right to do so.

Friday, March 16

Cooler, and not uncomfortable. This afternoon I had a spelling school. Elisha Brown and Washington DeVane chose sides being elected by the scholars. Elisha's side whipped the other twice when Washington backed out and John Hopewell took his side and got whipped over once more. At night I had a contest in school with a girl and boy who were mulishly dull. The girl made me very angry indeed, but I kept myself calm. I did not get through till late, and then had to come home with no one near me at all, for all had scattered off that come this way. I never go with them but do like to hear them behind. Well I am not going to be dismayed yet. All will be as God ordains.

Saturday, March 17

A windy March day. I wrote to Lizzie and Emma. Then Frannie Lee's grandmother got me to go in there and write two letters for them. After dinner I went over to Mrs. Vosburgh's. Of course I had to pet little Lewie on the way and I took the opportunity also to do a solemn duty that has long lain on my mind. May God bless the result. Now I can only pray.

I had a pleasant time but came home early. Mrs. V. puzzled me a little by something that she said about Mr. Brackett. She seemed vexed with him, but she says that he thinks I'm a great worker— earnest and faithful. My own conscience bearing me witness, I enjoy the praise and hope always to merit it. I long to get rid of passing through town as I do now. Ah well I shall get settled in good time. I must learn patience.

Sunday, March 18

All my trials meet me for Sunday I believe. This morning Mrs. Bales began to talk with me about leaving here. She seemed vexed and inclined to find fault, but who can keep *ex post facto* laws? She says Mr. B. indicated an intention to exchange me to some other place. What can he mean? *He* ought to be honorable with me. I don't know what to make of it. I went this morn to the Methodist Church and got a lesson from the life of Christ that did me good. After noon I had Sabbath School—over fifty-six. Others have heard of the rumor of my removal. I shall write to Mr. Brackett. I am as innocent as a babe unborn and I cannot bear to think of a change. No one else would feel as I do about this school. I *must* know who has been wronging me. Another would done no better and I might fare worse in a strange place because of the change. Oh Lord lead me right.

Monday, March 19

A dull day. I have written to Mr. Brackett. I must know what the story means. I am not going to let it worry me. Tonight I got letters from Lizzie and from Mary Bradbury—the latter to solicit a correspondence I replied, for I cannot write to Lizzie now till I know what the story about removal means. At school tonight I only had eighteen in—only sixteen pupils yet I found enough to do for now I attend to all myself. Mary Ann Cook and Susan Claiborne and Mary Ann's husband I think kept close behind me over the bridge. I was glad for I met a group of men on the bridge and a drunken crew were around the streets singing early in the evening. I mean to be careful and not get molested lest that should hasten my removal, just when danger is over.

Tuesday, March 20

Yet dull, and rainy since dinner. I had however a full school, and it was pleasant too. I see good progress in many. I hope to get leave to stay and harvest my seed sowing. I have tried so hard to do good that I must not be blamed for wanting all the credit myself. At noon Belle Hopewell brought me a letter from Kittie—short but good. She is hurried but lives in hopes to meet us all soon at Harper's

Ferry. So do I hope so too. Tonight it rained and, as I had so thin a school last night, I had none at all. So I am at leisure, and am going to bed early for a rare luxury. I got some papers from Portland, Maine, and have been reading select pieces to Rosa. I got a Portland Star from Mary Bradbury. It looked good and I read the very advertisements for home's sake, yet I am not at all homesick.

Wednesday, March 21

Dull, but the sun got out just at night. I had as full a school as usual however. Tonight I got a reply from Mr. Brackett. He says that I am to be in Mrs. B.'s school at Harper's Ferry. He has on his own responsibility delayed my exchange as long as he could when all the bureau officers urged it upon him and thought it even best for me. Well I hope it *is* for the best, and that I shall see it so. In my writing school I had hard work to govern my feelings for I knew that it was the last time, and could not bring myself to say so either. Seventeen were in—eleven to write and I was busy which kept me calm outwardly. I cannot feel willing to leave now when the way is just cleared. I've had this hard school and now another will take the best chance. Well God knows my heart. I've done right as far as I knew what was best.

Thursday, March 22

Got up early and wrote to Lizzie. I was too sad to do it last night. Now I feel calmer. I have gained nothing by silence. It is in the school that I shall leave, and I had to own it to them. I think that they will remember me with kind regard. I know I shall try to keep up with some of them an acquaintance after this. I guess I've made arrangements to get a photograph of the building where our school now is. I sent the errand. I want it and some scholars in view if I know when it is taken. I got a lot of papers tonight, and a letter from a Miss Chapman of Newport, Maine. I shall have to answer that for I fear that I shall get into hot water if any books come here with freight to pay. I am not going to be here and can't [   ] matters. Well I'll write and refer her to Mr. Brackett and *he* may do as he likes. I'm not going to let them blame me for extra bills. A good goodbye meeting tonight.

Friday, March 23

Had a nice school today. At noon got a photograph of the school-
room and a group in front. John Brown superintended the affair. I
am to have six copies of it. I could get them for a trifle more than one
would cost. I had an Arithmetic review to try for a prize. Only two
competed. Elisha Brown and Fannie Lee. I had bought for both.
Only Elisha got it. He came off bravely on it and I gave him a nice
book. Gave my Bible Reader to Nat Wood. He seemed to want it
and I gave it to him. I wish that I had a chance to pay him for the
care he has taken of the room for three months. I will if I can. It was
raining tonight and yet I felt that I ought to come in to school.
29 were in. John Brown helped me get through. The scholars feel
sad to have me go. I have agreed to stop over Sunday. I wish that I
could go home.

Saturday, March 24

Katie Wood has given me a present—a Pocket Ladies Companion.
    This morn I packed my trunks and got ready to come over to Mrs.
Vosburgh's. I got a letter from some hateful puppy or more likely
[   ] purporting to be from a young man who in order to make my
acquaintance wanted me to meet him at the school house Saturday
eve before Easter. Oh Lord help me.
    Not finding Mrs. V. at home I went over to Mr. Brown's. I had a
very pleasant time, but the more I hear of the Colored people's attachment to me the more I hate to leave here. All up here are very
indignant, and I am not less so, but I cannot help myself and what
shall I do? Oh if I only had what Mr. Pearson owes me, I could be
able to start now. I can't bear to stay when I am so ill treated. I know
that I have done my duty and I want to feel as if others know it.

Sunday, March 25

A cold, raw day. I read and fussed about till afternoon, but was not
able on account of a squall, to go to Sabbath School. I went down to
a meeting with Mrs. Vosburgh, and had a good meeting, but I can't
bear to think of being turned out of the school as I have been here. I
know that I have done all that anyone can do for this school, and
now if I'm taken off so they can say that Mr. B. believed what has

been said. And I am so powerless that I cannot bear to think of home at all. I long to write to the Advocate but cannot feel calm enough yet. I see that I shall have the love of my school always and they shall always have my prayers. I never can love another school as well as I do this one.

Monday, March 26

I have been reading "Alone" today.[62] Oh *I* can write what "alone" means, only I can't half express it either. I went over this afternoon and petted Mrs. Howard's dear baby, and, of course had a pleasant call on Mary and Ann Brown. Emma has sent me an embroidered necktie in a roll of papers and Elisha Brown had brought up my Photographs. So I had something not quite so sad to think of, and I have not cried much today. I gave George some tracts that Emma also sent. I don't know how to open talk. I fear he yet thinks he shall live. Annie Leavers sent me a collar by her father. He says she has cried all day about my going off. I have felt as if I could not go for myself. These tokens of love make it harder yet.

Tuesday, March 27

I am yet at Mrs. Vosburgh's. I cannot feel like going to Harper's Ferry for I am so sad and so vexed at Mr. B. that I cannot bear to meet him. I have told Mrs. V. how I feel, and had a good confidential cry before her and Mrs. Webster. I tried to write my Advocate letter and found out that even there I had an attack of the blues. Tonight I got a few papers and a letter from Caleb, and one from Mr. Hathaway about the books he was to send. He has sent a box and sent me a dollar to pay the Express bill. I went over and gave the matter in charge to John Brown. He walked home with me. I am glad to have had one more talk with him. I have bade *him* goodbye now. I must not give in. Have wanted to leave but daresay that resignation is better than rebellion. Talked with Mrs. V. tonight. She is in trial and needs Christ. God help her to find him.

Wednesday, March 28

Yet here. I still feel homesick, but not as bad as I did yesterday. This morning I went in to Mrs. Webster's and had a pleasant call. She is a

nice woman. After dinner I went in to Mr. Brown's. Then, though it
snowed, I went downstreet and bought some nice apples and an
orange for Geo. Brown. Mrs. Vosburgh and I are going to bake these
apples with sugar in them. I have finished "Alone." It is a nice book.
I got a letter from an S. A. Dodge of Seal Cove, Maine and some few
books and some tracts and papers. I have decided that I had better
go to Harper's Ferry and be quiet about it. Well, I hope that I shall
like them. I don't feel now as if I should. Mary Brown has given
me some cuffs, a collar and a velvet bow. Dear good girl. Heaven
bless her.

Thursday, March 29

This morning I fixed the apples for Geo. Brown. Annie was in and
in a skylarking mood tied my hands behind me. Afterwards when I
was over to fetch the apples for George, I caught a chance to salt
her coffee. To pay for it, she chased me into Margaret's and beat me
well. I came into Margaret's after dinner calling by the way at Mrs.
Webster's. I noticed then where there was a shell came down through
the house. I got letters from Mr. and Mrs. Cole, Kittie and Miss
Fletcher, the latter sending a dollar to do good here. I set some
copies for Mrs. Howard and wrote down, to order, all the family
names. Was glad to meet Will Fairfax for I was afraid I should not
see him again. I feel badly to think that the school would be hurt,
but fear it may.

Friday, March 30

Was sober enough all the forenoon, for I meant to go away. After
dinner, Mrs. Vosburgh went with me to bid my friends goodbye. At
Mrs. Webster's I got to crying in spite of myself. She is very kind. I
kissed all hands for goodbye, Mrs. Howard, her children, the Brown
girls and Elisha, but I missed the train. I got a letter from a Miss
Dodge. I have got to wait so late that very likely I'll miss the talked
of excursion to Antietam that Kittie tried to bait me with, and now I
shall not try to go till Monday. I shall feel better to stay here. This
afternoon Mrs. V. and Frankie and I went out to their house lot to
see what it was like. They'll have a fine house, only a lot of hateful
"shingle palous" are going up near it.

Saturday, March 31

Today has not been fair enough to admit of going anywhere, and I have got fatigued by lounging away the day. I wonder if G. S. W. is waiting at the school house. Hope he'll have a good time. It is a beautiful thundershower out—not much rain. Mr. Cage and Nannie have come in and Mr. Cage and Mr. Vosburgh are playing cards. I feel dull and shall excuse myself and go to bed at once. Got a letter tonight from a Miss Batchelder of Hartland, Maine—very good, also from the Tract Society—a dunning letter for periodicals. Well I'm glad I got them, and hope that they'll do good. There is a Colored clergyman at Mr. Brown's. He came here yesterday. He ought to be ashamed to stay there when George is so sick.

Sunday, April 1

We laid in bed late, and then I lounged about an hour or so, but finally I went into Mrs. Brown's. I staid there to dinner and till nearly three when I went into Mrs. Vosburgh's again. I had a pleasant time. Mr. Bowman says that Mr. Brackett is not to blame, and that there are several changes to be made and that none of them seem suited. I hope that they are all pouting at the ferry. Tonight Mrs. Vosburgh and I went out to go to church. We found no service at several and the Methodist too full. So we went to the schoolroom, where they had a good meeting. John Brown made a most affecting prayer for George. The bench where I sat fairly shook with the sobs of those who sat on it. *He* could hardly speak for tears. He is *so* good—*so* noble. Oh Lord answer thou my prayers.

Monday, April 2

Tonight finds me at Harper's Ferry and rather tired too. I got here just in time to go up Maryland Heights with the party. A lot of colored people were over in the morning from Charlestown. Mr. Cowan was here then, but he was gone before I came. I did not want to see him. We had a fine time on the Heights. A Mr. Given[63] and a Mrs. Smith[64] and Miss Libby[65] have been added to our party since I was last here. We make a pleasant party. I got some bits of stone from the Heights and some Laurel leaves. I shall never forget the view.

One can afford to be tired for such a treat, for many such cannot
come in a lifetime. All the rest seem happy. I am sad whenever I get
to thinking. I wonder if I am doing wrong. Mrs. V. and Frank came
to the cars. Harry Webster bade me goodbye too. Elisha and other
scholars were there. I had to bid a quiet goodbye then.

Tuesday, April 3

This has been an interesting day. We have been to the Antietam
battle ground.[66] A Mr. Ames, a Mrs. Clemmer and her daughter,
and a Mr. Keyes (colored)[67] were with our party. We had a U.S.
Wagon and five horses and we attracted more notice than a caravan
would up our way. We lunched near Burnside's bridge[68] and then
went over the ground near the school house, and to Bloody Lane.[69]
We got water at a house where the lady said eight thousand had
been buried on their farm. They had been cultivated over. Horrible—I wish the ghosts could rise and haunt them. We came home
through Shepherdstown. Didn't they stare? We enjoyed the day.
I'm glad that I came. I've missed Loudon Heights but then I'm not
so sad as I should have been last week—blue enough though.

Wednesday, April 4

We breakfasted about half past ten and I have been writing most of
the time since. I wrote a letter to the Advocate. I am a little bluer
today than yesterday. I talked with Miss Gibbs and *she* says that Mr.
Brackett is not to blame and has been satisfied with me. But talking
got me to crying. I am wrong maybe, but I think not. I got letters
from Caleb and Emma. We've had a good meeting tonight, but it
made me homesick because I did not know the people. They sang
two or three new hymns, among them "Go Down Moses." I wish
that I *could* be reconciled, but I never shall be I fear. We went out
and had some pistol shooting once this afternoon. We all stand our
exemsioning very well indeed.

The Freedmen

Harper's Ferry, April 4th, 1866. [April 18]

Dear Advocate:—After a longer delay than common, I again "take
my pen in hand," and you will perceive that I date from a different

locality. Our Spring vacation began March 24th, and, with the term, my connection with the Martinsburg school closed. I believe that I am to be retained here in this school. I need not say that the change is not of my own choosing, nor that I was sad to leave the place where I had toiled and borne so much for four months. But thus the "powers that be" have decided. I believe that the change is not wise, and that time will prove it so, but of course I submit quietly. Ever since the disturbance at Martinsburg many have thought that the school would be benefitted by a change of teachers. Mr. Brackett did not think so, and to him I owe my stay until vacation. Now he has yielded to the outside pressure. I do not learn that anyone believes I have done wrong, but I have excited a prejudice that *they* think it best to favor a little. Aside from the progress of my school and the religious interest among the people, a prospective change of schoolrooms and the prospect of the teachers boarding at Mr. Vosburghs made my removal particularly hard to bear. I endeavored to get away without a farewell, but could not, as the story got about, and on the eve of March 22nd we had an affecting good-bye. I had intended that that should be my last meeting, but, as I spent a week with Mrs. Vosburgh, I attended two more in company with her. There are yet some who seek the Savior, and they have pledged themselves to me to persevere till they find a peace. I hope that the change of rooms will not affect the religious interest, but the old room is dismantled and the other not yet ready for occupancy, and the meetings will of necessity be interrupted somewhat.

Our Sabbath Schools become each week more interesting. I left with them over two hundred papers that I had received, and hope that the supply will yet continue. I have kept a list of the names of those who forwarded papers, as far as I could ascertain them, but not having it now at hand—as my baggage is yet at the station, down in the village—I am unable to return particular thanks.—All may be sure of my gratitude, and the colored people of Martinsburg are grateful too. Should I neglect to answer some of the kind, sympathetic letters that come to me from readers of the *Advocate*, the writers may know that only lack of time prevents due acknowledgement. Words cannot express the good that they have done. I shall ever gratefully remember those who cheered me on when toiling far from home and friends.—Though I have left the school, papers are yet needed there; and, to those who have written to ask if old *Advocates* and Sabbath school papers would be acceptable, I here reply that they will, and I would desire to have them sent to Martinsburg,

as I have got them in the way of expecting papers. I know not who
will succeed me in the school, but parcels may be sent by mail to
Mr. Samuel Hopewell or to Mr. John H. Brown. Either will care for
and distribute them. A small box of books, freight prepaid, has been
received from Mr. Hathaway of Waterville, Me. Others may "go
and do likewise," but, unless the freight *is* paid the matter must
now be referred to Rev. N. C. Brackett. To those who have sent
smaller parcels, my absent baggage must be my apology for want of
acknowledgement here. Miss R. R. Fletcher, of Sumner has my
thanks for the dollar sent to me. I gave it to John Brown to aid in
fitting up the new schoolroom, as he and his father have the repairs
in charge. Whatever I receive will doubtless be sent there as I feel
inclined to do all that is possible for my first field of labor.

Perhaps I ought not to complain. Several other changes are to be
made, and in no case I believe because either teacher or pupils are
dissatisfied with present arrangements. I only came down here two
days ago. Just before my arrival a large delegation of Miss Dudley's
school had unexpectedly appeared at the Ferry to vote for her,
having been told by some white people at Charlestown that their
doing so would insure her return. I was not present at the "surprise
party" but Mr. Cowan was, and after addresses, refreshment and
singing, the people left in good humor I believe. I did not meet Mr.
Cowan, for he left just prior to my arrival. A. M. Given[70] is here
with us, recently come from the North to labor, I believe, as a sort of
itinerant missionary among all the schools of this section. Our family
of lady teachers has received an addition or two of late, a Mrs. Smith
and Miss Libby, who have been teaching some time in Eastern Virginia. We make a pleasant party, and, though very sad last week, I
find that the gloom exhales a little in the sunny atmosphere of our
mission "Home."

The wild scenery here suits and charms me. I am often reminded
of the remark of one of my adult pupils. He said: "Harper's Ferry's
the last place that ever was made, and it wasn't finished. They just
piled in what they had left."

Before I came, the party, tired of awaiting my coming, had ascended Loudon Heights, repeated our excursion to John Brown's
cave and over Bolivar besides other rambles. But I was just in time
for Maryland Heights, going up the very afternoon of my arrival.
The day was beautiful, and, turn which way we would, a soft smoky
haze—not enough to obscure the landscape—supplied that sort of
dream inspiring, languid beauty which is the charm of many pic-

tures. It was something never to be repeated, and we all drank in eagerly deep, soul satisfying draughts of beauty. I think the most quietly beautiful scene was Pleasant Valley on the Maryland side. It was not so vast, and the eye could compass it all, while the broad and beautiful Shenandoah Valley wearies eye and mind as one sees its surface spread out like a map, and thinks of its boundless re-sources and of the beauties and wonders that nature has bestowed on it so lavishly. Nor were we denied a glimpse of Loudon Valley— just enough to suggest its unseen beauties. We visited the storm fort, peopled again in fancy the deserted village of soldiers' huts near by, and found shells, exploded and unexploded, to aid us in bringing up past scenes. Both ascent and descent were wearisome, the latter especially so, but we felt amply repaid. We met on our ascent a horseback party—descending, and learned subsequently that they were a wedding party—the marriage having been solem-nized on the Bridge—as runaway matches often are hereabouts— the river belonging to Maryland. After the bridal they had ridden up the Heights.

Yesterday we made up a party for the Antietam battle-ground. We had a sky blue U.S. wagon, with a black oil-cloth cover that would roll up at the sides. That was filled and the rest of the party went on horseback. The party included Mr. and Mrs. Brackett, Mr. Given, the Misses Dudley, Wright, Gibbs and Libby, Mrs. Smith and my-self, besides a Mr. Ames formerly of Massachusetts—now trading here, and a Mrs. Clemmen [71] and her daughter also from Massachu-setts, a young colored man named Keyes, invited to go as a friend and to point out localities, and our sable driver. Mr. Ames and Mr. and Mrs. Brackett rode horseback all the way, and Miss Clemmen nearly all, while Mr. Given and Mr. Keyes alternated with each other. We made a merry party, and seemed to attract a great deal of attention. We first visited the Burnside bridge near which we lunched on the grass, drinking from a cold spring that has doubtless slaked the thirst of many a wounded and dying soldier. Then we moved over to the place where the Irish Brigade fought. [73]—Dis-mounting we walked about among the trees which bore many scars of shot and shell—bits of shell yet remaining in some of them. Mr. Keyes got our party some water at a house not far beyond the battle field. They inquired where we were from. He told them from New England, and that we came to visit the battle ground. They seemed to think us a long way from home, and he did not correct the impres-sion that we came on purpose to see Antietam. The lady of the house said that eight thousand dead bodies were interred on her farm, and previously Mr. Keyes had pointed out a large field, once filled with graves, now cultivated over. The lady spoke of it without seeming conscious of the horrible sacrilege of thus utilizing a nation's hallowed ground. We soon turned back from the plough polluted graveyard, and, coming to Bloody Lane, drove up it a little way, trying to fancy what it must have been when piled with reeking corpses, but the horror of the field beyond yet clung to us and no one alighted to search for relics. The place seemed too awful for tarrying.

On our return we passed through Shepherdstown. A menagerie with all its trappings might have made the tour of a New England village without exciting half the attention that our party aroused wherever we went, but Shepherdstown in particular made a general turnout to view us. They probably thought, as a Harper's Ferry loafer remarked one day, that we were "Freedmen's Bureau—a whole heap." We could but observe the improved appearance of everything in Maryland. The barns looked nice and comfortable, and the houses had a more homelike look than the majority of Virginian farm-houses, but the chimneys were almost universally turned out of doors, reminding us that we were not in New England. There seemed some point in the suggestion of Mrs. Smith, that "out here they first build a chimney and try and see if it will draw well, and if it does, they build a house to it." Some New England chimneys that I know of would never have graced a house had that experiment been tried; but however useful, I cannot say that I like the looks of the thing.

To-day we are resting, for our journey could not have been less than twenty-five miles yesterday, and the rockiest New England pasture would fail to convey an idea of a part of the road. Coming back, we had a better road but we were well jolted, and to-day finds us all somewhat lamed by our two days of rustication. But a home letter awaits my perusal, and I must close very soon this letter, which I fear will exhaust your patience.

Yours, Sarah J. Foster

Diary, 1866

Thursday, April 5

I finished up a lot of letters and then took them down to the post office with me. I had to get me a pair of boots. I sent five dollars to

the Tract House to pay for Martinsburg papers. I have sent letters to
Mrs. Vosburgh, Mary Brown, Emma, and several others. I had a
talk for half an hour or so with Mr. Brackett. He certainly has felt
kindly and has thought that he was doing right. I was rash the other
day and Capt. McKenzie feels hurt some. I met him at the cars and
was rough, not to say rude. Mr. Brackett was sorry for that. So am I.
I am willing to say I'm sorry and did not mean it. I wish that I was
not so rough. Major Welles[73] is here tonight and may stay. I hope
that I shall get over my hard feelings. I avoided an introduction, but
did go to the table. If he stays I can't help it though I had much
rather not do any such thing. But I must conquer self at once.

Friday, April 6

Wrote, read, mended and lounged this forenoon, and till four in the
afternoon. Then we all went and spent the rest of the time till nearly
ten at Mr. Ames. As I conjectured he is the husband of Mrs. Mary
Clemmer Ames. She was not at home. They have tasty, cozy rooms
and all things indicate taste and real goodness. Maybe I shall feel
better here after I get at work. Got a letter from Lizzie and also from
Geo. and Lizzie Cobb. Poor Lizzie Cobb is sick. I fear she will not
live long. I hope that I shall see her alive though for I should be sad
to have her die now while I'm gone. She wants me to write to her. I
must do so soon. I'm glad that I've got her picture. She is a nice
little girl and I've always loved her much. But I must off to bed. Our
circle breaks tomorrow morning. I wish I was going.

Saturday, April 7

Mrs. Smith and Miss Libby went off this morning in company with
Mr. Brackett. They went to Charlestown. Mr. B. came back at noon
and went with Kittie,[74] who seemed not well, to her school at Shepherdstown. We had to hurry Mr. Given off with housekeeping articles for the Charlestown teachers who had not found a boarding
place. He has just come back leaving them in high spirits. Major
Welles is really boarding here, and I hope that I shall have grace to
act as a Christian should. He seems a good Christian man and I
daresay that he acted conscientiously, but I feel sad yet at the decision that takes me away from my school in the time when I could
just begin to do it justice. There has been an important bill on civil

rights passed over Johnson's veto in the senate.[75] Thank God for that.
Now for rest and sleep.

Sunday, April 8

Wild, windy, snowy in the morning. But Binnie[76] had fifteen in her
Sabbath School. Miss Dudley and I did not go in there being so
few of them. I wrote letters to Mrs. Howard and Mrs. Vosburgh.
We had preaching at half past two. Afterward a class meeting.
Miss Dudley and I were in. It was good. This evening Mr. Given
preached again. Mr. Ames, Mr. and Mrs. Clemmer and Fannie
came up and went in. Mr. Ames and Major Welles had a bit of a
theologic sparring match before meeting. I felt to agree with the
Major. After meeting, to interest Fannie, Mrs. Brackett got Keyes
to lead off in singing some peculiar hymns. They sung well, and interested us all. They sung "Beautiful Star" varied to an excellent
hymn. It does me good to hear them.

Monday, April 9

I opened school here today. I only had fifteen in. I almost felt provoked at the small number by which I had to keep busy. At noon
Miss Dudley went off. I felt homesick then for I wanted to go too. I
have been telling her about my classes some what. I hope that I shall
have grace to wish the school well under her charge. I got a letter
from Phi tonight. I have written a reply. Major Welles has proved
himself good company tonight. He is a good talker. I hope and pray
that I may yet be vindicated by him. I know he must see that I am
not what some have tried to prove. I don't believe that Miss Dudley
will be contented at Martinsburg. I know she never would bear
what I have. She is not that kind of stuff. Oh Lord give me grace
here and now.

Tuesday, April 10

This has been, as yesterday was, a cold raw day. I only had eighteen
scholars in. Mr. Brackett came at noon bringing me a good letter
from Mrs. Vosburgh and a paper and a Magazine. I was glad to hear

from Martinsburg. Miss Dudley had very few pupils indeed. Kittie came in and astonished us at night having ridden over with Mr. Ames. She too began small. So I hope for more. I shall be sorry to have so small a school. That alone would make me homesick. I am well, but I miss the night school and feel oddly here as if I were not one of the family. I can't get over it. God help me to do right and feel right. I can't wish my old school well. Uncle Andy is dead. Our loss is his gain. None ought to mourn.

Wednesday, April 11

Avery's birthday. He is fifteen. It don't seem possible. It was a little warmer, but, as my fire bothered me, it was not warm in school. I've only had nineteen in today. I can keep busy, but not contented because I want to have all I can do just as I have. Tonight I got a letter from Mary Bradbury. I wrote at once to her and to Mrs. Vosburgh. I feel very gloomy; have wanted to cry all the time since school. We had a good meeting here tonight. It has done me some good. Maria has gone. Laura Keyes has taken her place. She is here in our room now. But I am tired and must to bed. Mr. Keyes made a splendid prayer tonight. It was perfect almost in language and sentiment. He is good, but not so grand and noble as J. H. B.

Thursday, April 12

Caleb's birthday. He is twenty-nine. Oh how I wish that he were married and settled in life. I've been thinking that families that try to rise as we have seldom do marry. Maybe we shall not many of us. Lizzie may, for she has now another correspondent. I hope she will. As for me, God only knows. *I* know what I hope, and I must "wait and see." I have some faith too at times.

I had twenty in school today. I had some new ones but still the number is no larger. I am doing well though, and if they are suited I am. Only I don't—can't like my scholars so well as I do my old ones at M. Johnny Parker is twice as handsome as Elisha Brown, but he will never fill *his* place in this world. Tonight I got a nice letter from Lizzie. A glass of flowering mountain moss and another of wild flowers fill our room with fragrance. A girl brought them to Miss

Gibbs. I've been reading Macaulay's England and resting with Swiss Family Robinson.

Friday, April 13

A warm nice day, but yet I only had fifteen scholars in. I had hard work to keep my patience with them. I felt all day just as if I could scold and cry or any thing else of the kind. I am foolish to feel so, but I cannot get reconciled to the change. If I had a full school maybe I could. I gave an oral lesson in Geography to my scholars and they seemed to do well and to like it. I felt sad to think that I was not to have the good scholars that I had got started at Martinsburg to drill with maps. After school Binnie and I went down to the Ferry and called on Maria. She looked neat and cozy. Coming up through the graveyard we got some myrtle blossoms and other trifles to add to our bouquet. I got too many and they are withering on the table. Major Welles seemed inclined to be sportive at my gloom tonight. I could have cried all the time.

Saturday, April 14

One year ago today our dearly beloved President was killed. Now we have I fear a traitor at the helm. Heaven save us all. This morn I helped rearrange some things in our room and done some mending. Mr. Brackett had some company. A Mr. Morrell and Mr. Garrison from Washington. He and his lady ascended Maryland Heights with them. While they were gone I went on some errands down to the Ferry. I met Mr. O'Connell with great pleasure. He seemed glad to meet me too. After dinner the party of exemsionists started for Charlestown, but a heavy shower arose suddenly and drove them back. We all had a good time together. Mr. Morrell staying to tea. He vaccinated Mrs. B. and me. Got a letter from a Miss Donnell of Newcastle tonight. I have been reading in Macaulay's History. I must read all that I can of useful matter. Now it is a good chance for me to do it.

Sunday, April 15

This morning the Sabbath School was reorganized and our classes assigned to us. I have one, but don't know a member of it. Mr.

Bowman preached from the text "Ye must be born again." He
preaches well but is very prolix. Then they had some very noisy
classes. I went in at the close of the last one. After it Keyes went up
with us to Mrs. Brackett's room and Mrs. B. read aloud "The Grandmother's Apology" and "The May Queen" besides other pieces
mostly from Tennyson.[77] Keyes seemed to appreciate them well.
Then we had some biblical reading, and now this evening Mr.
Bowman preached again. As usual his discourse was good but too
long. My eyes ache terribly and Binnie has a severe headache. A day
when one reads and lounges so much is hard to get through with.
Oh for work like that I have had.

Monday, April 16

A wild, rainy day. I had two new scholars in but only eleven after all.
I paid extra attention to those however and filled up my time easily.
I think that I would have had a good number had the weather been
fair. I feel somehow better. The Sabbath School needs me and I
hope the day school soon will. I am not going to worry myself at all.
I got no letters at all today. I want to hear from Mary Brown. I hope
to get some pictures soon for them. I must write soon to Elisha. A
letter will do him good. I am yet reading Macauley. I am now however so sleepy from drinking milk at tea time that I shall have to
retire. Binnie and Laura are not at all inclined to go to bed yet, but I
must. Mr. and Mrs. Brackett were just downstairs a few minutes. I
like them both, but yet feel sad at being put here nolens volens.

Tuesday, April 17

It is stormy yet, but I had twenty in school today. I had enough to do
for I am taking very great pains to learn the little ones. I got no mail
today. One boy tried me much, but I think that firmness and patience have begun to conquer him. After school though there was a
very heavy mist flying. Binnie and I went out to an old ruin on the
other side of the hill, then to the brow of some grand cliffs over the
Potomac. We got some moss and saxifrage from the rocks. Then we
went down and got some myrtle and yarrow in the burying ground.
We have got our table profusely decorated with our spoils. Mr. and
Mrs. Brackett have just been down. Laura is here as normal studying. I have been reading in Macaulay. I am much interested. I must

not fail to read all that I can of such books now. Wish I had O'Connell's books to go to now or him to talk to.

Wednesday, April 18

Yet a heavy fog all around. I had only thirteen in school today. A boy who has been in once or twice has acted very badly. He was not in this afternoon. I am glad to see this room small as my school is. Major Welles wife and their children have come for a short visit. Binnie and I have given up our room to them, and have taken one half filled with bands and boxes of clothing. Tonight I got letters from Mrs. Vosburgh, Mary Brown and Lizzie. Lizzie sent me her picture—a good one I think. Also from Geo. Cobb. Poor Lizzie is dead. She died a dear little Christian. They sent me a leaf that came from the flowers on her coffin. Geo. Brown is near his end. Fannie Ransom has been there. Elisha has gone to live in the country. Mrs. Vosburgh has met and talked with Geo. Rhenn. He sent me word that he was still seeking. God help him. Mr. Brackett asked me if I would be willing to open a school at Smithfield. I would, in case they do not come in better here. The Gray churches talk of sending me another year under the National Freedmen's Association.[78] Then I should not be in the valley I suppose but I might [   ] somewhere. I pray for grace and strength to help me daily.

Thursday, April 19

This morning the sun came out and made a fairy world for us a while by brightening up the mist and at length conquered it all. I had nineteen in school. Had to whip my troublesome boy. He acted badly. I got Mr. Brackett to talk with him. He put his further attendance on the condition of his good behavior. He done very well in the afternoon. I hope he will not be so bad. After school Binnie and I started to go to the Catholic graveyard in Bolivar. We then rambled on and finally brought up at Keyes' house. He was not at home. Then we came home by the Charlestown Pike. We missed the path up back of the Hill and came all the way to Shenandoah St. before we knew it, and had to come up the steps by the Catholic church. We are tired but have got some splendid heartsease, violets and other little flowers. I've written to Mary Brown and Mrs. Vosburgh letters to send tomorrow. I sent one home this morn that I wrote yesterday. Mr. Brackett goes to Smithfield tomorrow. Now for bed.

Friday, April 20

I had twenty in school today. I have got the classes drilled to call and leave by the bell, and today they all done very well. Even David Artemous, my torment, tried to do right, and I tried to feel kindly. Had two new scholars. I hope to be able to do well by my school. I got a letter from Dr. Shailer tonight. He sent me ten dollars. I went down to the Ferry and bought me a gingham dress and the trimmings. It was just about a good walk for us. Binnie had the headache till this evening from her walk. We were weighed. She weighed 108 lbs. I 123. I never was so heavy before by 5½ lbs. I am glad that I am so well. I have written to George Cobb tonight. I did not feel like it before. I hope that I shall have comforted them somewhat. I mourn with them I am sure. The Major's folks went up the Heights today.

Letter from Virginia

Harper's Ferry, April 20th, 1866 [May 9]

Dear Advocate:—It is now two weeks since I opened school here. Miss Gibbs retains the school that she has had from the first, except that a few of the poorest scholars have been put in the other department. So she has a fine school, while mine are yet in the earliest stages of reading, or else unable to read at all. The colored people here are scattered, and many of them in very destitute circumstances. They do not now come into school so well as they did last term. The older ones are gone out at service, and smaller ones, who have long distances to come, fear to do so without protection; for the white boys will molest them when they find an opportunity. The boys of both races seem rather pugilistic about here. They have had several battles for the possession of this hill as a playground. The weapons were stones, and both parties were in earnest. My scholars at Martinsburg, though not destitute of spirit and courage, had the good sense to avoid collisions with the white boys, who often played marbles before the door. Jefferson County is much more aristocratic than Berkeley, and, as a consequence, the colored people seem much more degraded as a class here than they are there. Here is a field for

much mission labor. In Berkeley County there are more of the blacks
who are competent to care for the interests of their race. But they
are not dull here. Several children, who two weeks ago did not
know the alphabet, are now reading in words of three letters. In the
short time that we have taught out here, many, who did not know a
letter, have learned to read in the Testament, and to spell well. The
united testimony from all our schools is, that color is no barrier to
progress.

I have four boys in my school who are so white that I should not
suspect their lineage elsewhere. One has straight, light hair, and all
are fine looking. Miss Gibbs has several little girls who are even
whiter, or "brighter," as they call it here. One in particular, very
appropriately named Lillie, has flaxen hair and grey blue eyes. One
white boy comes to my school. His brother lives in the chambers
here, and very wisely discards prejudice that he may have the benefit of a free school.

Last Sabbath our Sabbath school was reorganized here, some colored teachers being appointed; as Mr. Brackett wishes to get them
prepared to continue the school after we go home in hot weather.
Each of us takes a class. I do not know personally a member of mine,
but hope to get acquainted soon. When we go North, the people
here will lose one of the best of their number; for Mr. Keyes will
accompany us to perfect his education in Lewiston. But we hope
that they will not let the Sabbath school die out. I feel confident that
the one at Martinsburg will thrive under the management of those
who will have charge of it, and, though indications are less favorable
here, there is much interest in the maintenance of the school in this
place. A number of conversions have taken place since Mr. Brackett
came here, and the converts seem to be sincere and straightfor-
ward. We have good meetings each Wednesday night, and also Sabbath afternoon and evening. A colored preacher addressed the audience last Sabbath. He is a man of excellent abilities, though without
much education. He now preaches on a circuit comprising all the
places where our schools are located. As Mr. Given also takes the
same circuit, they will have preaching quite often.

We daily expect the arrival of the Misses Stuart,[79] transferred
from Eastern Virginia. They design to open a school at Front Royal.
They have been long in the field and are excellent teachers. Should
our school not increase here, one of us will be at liberty, and start a
school at Smithfield, five miles from Charlestown. It is Mr. Brack-

ett's design to open as many schools as possible, for we expect a larger force in the autumn, and wish to occupy as much of the Valley as we can. A better superintendent than Mr. Brackett could not be obtained. Since talking with him, I feel much more reconciled to my change of schools. Miss Dudley has taken my former place. The school there too is much reduced from its size last term, but will doubtless be hard enough for warm weather work. Miss Wright returned to Shepherdstown, and Mrs. Smith and Miss Libby took the school at Charlestown. If either of us change again, I shall be likely to go to Smithfield. Mr. Brackett has asked me if I would be willing to do so. I think that I would, but find this a very pleasant place. It is easy to take long rambles here. The other day after school Miss Gibbs and I started with a basket to search for wild flowers. We visited a small Catholic burying ground over toward Bolivar Heights, beautifully situated in a grove of pines and cedars, and covered with myrtle in blossom. It was unenclosed. Nor was another that we saw on the same ramble at all protected from the hogs and cattle that roam at large. The soldiers' burying ground, not far from here, has a slight protection; but hogs have intruded upon it and have rooted out some of the head boards already.

We found a plenty of violets, a few anemones, and some flowers very much like our garden pansy covered a whole hillside with their velvety blue and purple blossoms. Some other unfamiliar flowers made up a choice collection, to obtain which, however, we strolled at least two miles from home. On our return we skirted the cliffs that hang over the Shenandoah, designing to ascend by some steps before reaching Camp Hill. But we unwillingly passed a long distance by the place of ascent, and, coming around through the Ferry, and mounting the steps in front of the hill, we could not have made much less than five miles for an afternoon walk over rocks, hills, and rough roads. I felt as well as ever though the next morning, and weigh now five or six pounds more than I ever did at home. I have a passion for scrambling over rocks and exploring wild places, which will insure an abundance of out door exercise should I stay here. And in a new place the necessary missionary explorations would have the same effect.

A few days since I had a pleasing evidence that the religious interest in my old school still goes on. A lady told one of my larger school boys that she was going to write to me, and asked what message he would send. Said he, with starting tears: "Tell Miss Jane that I'm

still trying to find the way to heaven." I hope I may meet him and
many others for whom I have labored and prayed, in that home
above. I seem now to appreciate the feeling of Rutherford when
he said:

> "Oh, if one soul from Anworth
> Meet me at God's right hand,
> My heaven will be two heavens
> In Emmanuel's land."

Oh it is sweet to labor with and for the Lord thus, and the un-
avoidable interest in one's work prevents all weariness and lassi-
tude. There is very much to be done. Years of bondage leave traces
that only time can efface. The colored people have a prejudice of
color themselves. They do not know how to be treated as equals. In
most cases an attempt to treat them so would result in the loss of
their esteem, and do more harm than good. There are exceptions,
but I speak of the mass. While all are trying to prejudice them
against us, undue familiarity would tend to make them believe that
we are, as they have been told, low and unworthy of respect. With
the children lies the hope of the race, and there indeed then is
hope. There is need of inspiring them with loftier ideas of education. To be able to read and write seems now a great deal to them.
We hope, however, to induce a few, such as Mr. Keyes and John
Brown, to acquire a thorough knowledge of English literature, hoping thus to elevate the standard among them. I am satisfied that
there is no lack of mental ability.

I hear that several more packages of papers have been sent to
Martinsburg. I ordered that such parcels should not be remailed to
me. Many thanks to the donors. With all your giving, give us your
prayers, and, God helping us, we will do all that we can.

Yours,
Sarah J. Foster

Diary, 1866

Saturday, April 21

This afternoon, having got through with my mending and such work,
I have been reading Macaulay and Shakespeare. How I wish I could
own books. I finished Macaulay's first volume. I've read also "The

Tempest" and "Two Gentlemen of Verona" in part. I've likewise written to the Advocate. It is a stormy day. But Mr. Brackett has been to Winchester and Front Royal, and has got back tired enough. This evening we spent in our [   ] apartment with Major Welles' family. A man from Eastern Va. called today to get some clothing and to inquire about the schools. Some families may soon remove to this place that will send children. The man could read and seemed intelligent. I liked his manner very much indeed.

Sunday, April 22

This has been a lovely day. But now it is showering. We had a good beginning for our Sabbath School—not half as good as my old one at M, but better than I expected. My class only turned out three but one was Mr. Poles, brother-in-law to Keyes. Mrs. Poles has had a triumphant exercise of the "Civil Rights Bill." This afternoon the people had some Classes. Binnie and I went in. Tonight Mr. Ames preached. Mr. and Mrs. Clemmer were up and a young man besides. It seems so at the close of service that they had to come up and wait the shower over. Have been glancing over Cheever's "American Poets"[80] and reading the "Fourth Annual Report of the Christian Commission." Mr. Brackett gets honorable mention in several places.[81] He was a Field Agent. He is good for such a place.

Monday, April 23

Mr. and Mrs. Brackett have been to Charlestown and back again. A rainy, cold day. I only had nineteen in school. But I managed to keep busy with that number. I have quite a class in the Alphabet, and I also have a number just beginning to read. I therefore have work that is capable of indefinite expansion. I feel to like the work yet, but the children here are not as good as they are in other places. They are the fag ends of their race mostly.

I shall like a few but shall not soon if ever replace my Martinsburg pets. Some large boys have neither manners nor decency about behavior. David Artemous does better than he did. A James Piper would be unendurable if he did not seem like Fred Cobb. He acts like him too, but is *not* disposed to behavior with decorum in school. I really think that he must be a son of Eben Cobb. I mean to ask him if he was raised in Texas or find out somehow.

Tuesday, April 24

Cold and windy all day. I've had twenty-three in school, I may count
on most of them constantly I hope. A Lizzie King is a great trouble
though smart and intelligent. I hope to get her interested in learning soon however. Today I've had to punish her twice a little.

Those large boys and another with them laughed and acted so
badly that I sent them out in a body. I will not be bothered with
them so. I would not hear them recite. I never will again unless they
act decently. They only act a trifle rude, but it makes the little ones
laugh and then they laugh at that. I cannot bear them. They are my
torment here. Why won't they see that we are here for their good? I
had no such plagues at Martinsburg except Joe Suecors. I expect I'll
stay here. I almost wish I might not have to, for I do not think it is as
good a school as I ought to have after my trials.

Wednesday, April 25

My scholars really begin to come in quite freely, but I cannot look
on them as I do on my other pupils. They are ruder and rougher. Yet
they are learning order well. I make them learn too. I hope to get
them on very fast. If the Stuart girls, who are expected to come from
East Virginia to open a school at Front Royal, don't come soon they
might as well not come at all. I would not want a school for less than
three months I am sure. Well I did want to go to Smithfield, but that
was when I had no school at all here. Now I do not feel so at all. I
shall have no pets here to love I am sure. I had to guard myself not
to be partial at M. Here I do not feel near to anyone in particular.
Oh for a Will Fairfax or an Elisha Brown to feel attached to. I've no
such *nice* large scholars here as I had at M. I miss my grand spelling classes.

Thursday, April 26

Cold yet, but I had thirty-three scholars in. Those large boys came
up the hill and made a noise outside, but only one came in. He sat
down and acted well. Mr. Brackett went out and talked to the rest. I
think frightened them some, for they came in soon and were quite
still. I had thirteen in the Alphabet today. I've worked hard. Binnie
and I took a walk. I scrambled down a very long steep descent and
got some dogwood blossoms. I can run over rocks like a goat. A

lovely little island in the Potomac is a splendid picture now. I got a nice long letter from Emma tonight. I also got one from a Mrs. Corthill in Montville Center, Maine. She is a clergyman's wife and claims an Advocate acquaintance. I've written replies. May God bless all my Maine friends, and *nearer* ones too. Oh Lord thou knowest my heart.

Friday, April 27

Not as cold as yesterday but yet the wind was chilly. I had nearly as large a school today, and I hear of more to come Monday. Mr. Brackett has been to Shepherdstown and back. Binnie has gone to Charlestown to stay till Monday. I shall go to Martinsburg in the same way some time. I must. Major Welles' family left today. They very kindly invited us all to come to Washington. I do hope that we may get there ere going home. I've had a very orderly school today. I could get John Parker in time to love as far as looks go if I could dress him up and fix his fine glossy hair properly. I mean to try and get his pride worked up a little. He is not my best old Jet and never will be, but is handsome and not so roguish. I've got my old quarters tonight—roomy enough for one alone. Now I must off. I've been reading Shakespeare. I must make some extracts tomorrow.

Saturday, April 28

Oh grand—grand. It has been the most magnificent thundershower. The sky was filled at each flash with broad sheets of flame and the heights were lit up by chains and wreaths of vivid fire that contrasted fearfully with the darkness that followed. It is hardly gone yet, but my window has ceased to command the view. I have sewed and read today. Got a letter from Mr. Perkins. He wrote about visiting Lizzie Cobb. She died in the triumphs of faith, a dear little Christian. Oh God be with George Brown. I daily pray for him. I want to feel the weight of souls more. Let me mourn and pray till Zion be refreshed.

Sunday, April 29

A splendid day. The air has been delicious after our shower. Our Sabbath School had eighty-eight in. God guard and increase it. I do begin to love my work. We had a good sermon this afternoon and

again tonight. At class meeting one woman got the "power" enough
to repeat things generally. Mr. and Mrs. Clemmer, Fannie and Mr.
Ames and a young man besides a Mr. Hall were up from the Ferry.
Before service Mr. Ames baptised Mr. Cook's child by the name of
Samantha Rosalind. Oh dear—a Miss Lee (colored) sang like a night-
ingale tonight. She ought to have suitable cultivation. She would be
another Black Swan.[82] I hope that she can some time get a chance.

Monday, April 30

A cool day but yet fair! We had a removal this morning. They moved
Binnie's school into the room back of mine. She got home at noon.
They are getting on well at Charlestown. I had a good school today.
Thirty-three were in. They really do well in keeping order, and I
hope not to have to be very severe. I have quite a cold, but I am far
from sick. I've sent off letters to Mrs. Corthill and Mr. Perkins and
have written to Lizzie. She will be glad to hear and I must "do as I
would be done by." They feel a desire to hear all the little things and
I must gratify them. I have some headache and I must now go to
bed. I have not read any at all today. I must each day. I did not feel
like it what time I had a chance. I do not somehow feel so much like
special prayer as I did all last week. I must not neglect it, however.

Wednesday, May 1

Nellie's birthday.[83] I wish that I had some gift to send her, but I have
none. May God keep her pure in heart and keep her in His love.
    This has been a dull stormy day but I've had twenty-seven in
school. They do nicely. One boy and a young woman vexed me by
dullness, but I ought not to get fretted. I must daily pray for patience. Miss Wright and Miss Dudley sent in their reports tonight.
Miss Dudley writes that Geo. Brown died happy a few days since.
He and a Mr. Henderson were buried Sunday. A little girl has recently died and a son of John Campbell's is near his end. I see now
how I lost my burden about George. I felt it while he needed
prayer. Sometimes I could weep then. Now I shall pray with new
faith for others.

      "Oh if one soul from Anworth (Martinsburg)
      Meet me at God's right hand

My heaven will be two heavens
In Emmanuel's land."

Oh if I can have done any good I shall "Thank God and take courage."

Wednesday, May 2

A very cold day. I have had a coal fire in my school. I have had twenty-eight scholars in today. I've been hard at work drilling some little ones who were just beginning to read. I thus made out a pretty long and hard day's work. I have a little Lizzie Brown in school now who is quite cunning. She is not so white as the Martinsburg Browns and most likely no relation at all, but she is a pretty little thing. I have no special fault to find with the order of the school now. I like them far better than I thought that I ever should. I sent a long letter to Mary Brown. She needs kind words I am sure. I got no mail but the Advocate today. I must read while I do not have to write none. We had a good but very small meeting. Why don't the people come out better here? Oh for one good Martinsburg prayer meeting. I *must go* to one more.

Letter from Virginia

Harper's Ferry, May 2d, 1866 [May 23]

Dear Advocate:—When I last wrote to you I thought it possible that I might be sent to Smithfield, but now my school has come up to a list of forty, with a prospect of nearly thirty daily in fair weather. As I have thirteen in the alphabet, and all are beginners in reading, I find enough to do. I have now got the school classified and systematized, and taught to come and go by strokes of the bell. The colored children fall into systematic regulations quite well, and seem to like them too. They annoy us most of all by whispering and laughing. The little ones will forget and whisper, and all laugh easily. They improve in that however. I sometimes use their laughter as a sort of spur to dull scholars, letting them laugh at their blunders, and it works well, for they are sensitive to ridicule. We have to use all ways and means to keep up their ambition and to encourage them to study. I tried, when I first began at Martinsburg, to avoid cor-

poreal punishment. I found it impossible, but yet, by due severity
when forced to punish, I did not have it to do very often. The fact is,
the colored people are practical followers of Solomon. They show
very great attachment to their children, making great efforts to re-
claim them if they have been sold away, but they are very severe in
governing them. They expect a teacher to be so too, and the children are of the same opinion. They really like a teacher better who
compels them to perfect obedience. I followed the theory at once on
acquaintance, and it worked well. I grew to like some of my pupils
very much, and the attachment was mutual.

I spoke of the efforts of parents to recover children who had been
sold away. One woman here has exerted herself to find her four children at great expense, though dependent on her own labor altogether. She has only been able to recover two, though she has made
a journey to Richmond and back to try and obtain the others, who
were sold away in that vicinity. Not only has she found those two,
but she has bought clothing for them, and has never drawn a ration
from the Bureau, though supporting her mother also. I know two
young men who have gathered together their father and mother, a
sister and two infant children, and four nephews and nieces from
seven to fourteen years of age. By joint efforts the family dress
neatly and live entirely unaided. Where are the white men who
could voluntarily burden themselves with the children of deceased
relatives, while young, single, and dependent on their daily labor? I
think that parallel cases among us are rare, and yet we have been
asked to believe that this race are only fit for chattels, and that they
felt separation as little as the brutes. A deeper, darker falsehood was
never palmed upon the public. It contradicts itself at every stage of
our acquaintance with them. Stronger domestic affection I never
saw than some of them exhibit.

Last Sabbath we had eighty-eight in Sabbath school. I have an
adult class who can read but little or none at all. Miss Gibbs and
Miss Brackett have those who can read well and commit lessons.
Mr. Brackett has a class about where mine are. Mr. Keyes has a fine
adult class who all read I believe. The rest are taught by teachers
selected from themselves—Mr. Given being a sort of "spare hand,"
as he is not so likely to be here all the time as Mr. Brackett is. He
has been to Charlestown for a week or two. They had a good interest
there, and have had some recent conversions. At Martinsburg two

funerals were solemnized last Sabbath. George Brown—brother of
John, and a Mr. George Henderson, one of my night scholars, having died recently. George Brown has been failing all winter. He was
the first to die in a family of twelve children. His mother died about
a year ago. An old man of great piety and worth has also died since I
left my school. I should miss his prayers and exhortation were I to
go there again, for he had a kind of simple quaint originality.

Sabbath Mr. Given preached to us here afternoon and evening.
At three the colored people had their class meeting as usual. It was
good, but was marred by one woman going off into an emotional
spasm of great length and violence. The same woman has done so
here before. After the evening service we had some most excellent
singing, a young woman named Lee taking the lead. Her splendid
voice ought to be cultivated; it has a wonderful compass and rich-
ness. She is a veritable "Black Swan."

I have spoken of the variations of some familiar hymns. One oc-
curs to me now, It is this:

> "Jesus my all to heaven is gone,—
>   He's coming again by and by—
> He whom I've fixed my hopes upon—
>   He's coming again by and by.
> Christ's coming again, Christ's coming again,
>   He's coming again by and by,
> He'll come this time, and He'll come no more,
>   He's coming again by and by."

And that is about the style of their peculiar hymns. They are
nearly all chorus, but I like to hear them. They can all come in on
the chorus after one or two repetitions, and, in a full meeting, the
effect of their full melodious voices is thrilling and inspiring. As they
sing they sway back and forth in time to the music, and some even
step to it in a way that seems like dancing, only the whole body is in
a quiver of excitement. At a meeting when a number are seeking the
Savior, they will make a circle at the close around the "mourner's
bench," where the seekers kneel meeting after meeting till they find
peace. The circle then join hands, taking also the hands of their
kneeling friends, and begin to sing, swaying as I have described, or
lifting and dropping their hands in regular time. They will sing
hymn after hymn with increasing earnestness, till the more excit-

able singers, and very likely some of the mourners, are shouting.
The jumping, leaping and bodily contortions of a "shout" are beyond
all description. They must be seen to be understood. For a long time
I saw none of this at Martinsburg, and indeed the leading members
there never practiced it, but they seem to think that converts can be
brought out in no other way.

"They're going to sing over Isaac," said a colored woman to me, as
I looked a little surprised to see them grouping around the bench at
which one of my schoolboys was kneeling. I found that nearly all
thought that the way to be "brought through." Some never yielded
to it, and I am satisfied that none ever affected the emotion that con-
vulsed those who were influenced by it. Even the white Methodists
are very much the same about here; so it is not to be wondered at at
all. On Saturday night we had here the most magnificent thunder
shower that it was ever my lot to witness. The effect of the lightning,
as the vivid chains lit up the darkness and played over the Heights,
was sublime and awe-inspiring. It is quite chilly here now much of
the time. We have needed a fire all day to-day. We have had some
quite warm weather a day or two at a time, however, but we did not
realize it much except when we descended to the village below the
Hill. Here there is usually a breeze, and we can keep quite cool, I
think, as long as we shall stay.

Some collisions are constantly occurring around here between the
"chivalry" and the colored people. A sister of Mr. Keyes had an
amusing triumph recently. A poor white neighbor struck her with
no reasonable provocation, the fault being wholly her own. At first
Mrs. Poles did not resent, but when the beating was recommenced,
she retaliated in self-defense. The woman had her arrested, seeming not to know that a colored woman could have a right to defend
herself, or that she was amenable to the law for having struck first.
When the case was tried before a Justice in Bolivar, she gained a
little valuable experience, and had the privilege of paying the costs.
The justice, I learn, referred to the Civil Rights Bill, and also intimated that the Bureau had an influence upon his decision. Well it
might here, for Major Welles is an excellent and efficient officer.
Only this week a colored man was knocked down for remonstrating
a little because some white men had broken open his stable, taking
his horse to plow with, and refusing to give it back at his request.
The Justice simply made them deliver up the horse, but he designs

to bring a suit for assault, to see what will be done about it. An aggravated case of assault took place in Charlestown, the particulars of which I have not yet learned. I think that some test cases will have to be brought up to prove the extent and validity of the Civil Rights Bill. The Bureau officers will probably look out for that, and may thus benefit the Freedmen a great deal.

How Harper's Ferry is going to live this summer is more than I can see. The Government works are all idle here.[84] Times are hard for white people as well as colored around here now. Very many garments have been distributed among the white people here, and many apply for rations. The aristocracy above them has had nearly the same effect of degradation that it has upon the colored people, and the two classes are at swords points.[85]

I have the shifting part of the school—many of them being kept from the other school only by the effect of their irregular attendance. But a few are regular and doing well. My school really is about thirty. The others are not to be counted upon though I have their names. Of those who are constant, some are making remarkable progress. But we are to have a prayer-meeting here, and I must close this now. The meetings here are not full at all Wednesday nights. I miss the warm-hearted crowd that packed my school-room to overflowing each week.

More anon,
Sarah J. Foster

Diary, 1866

Thursday, May 3

Still rather cold, but not quite so cold as it has been. I've had thirty-five in school today. I have had some dull acting boys to train, but hope that they will soon do better. I got a call from the mother of one of my scholars. He has been playing the runaway. I gave him a severe whipping. I had another to whip a little too.

I took a walk down to the Ferry after school. Afterward Fannie Clemmer came up and stopped to tea. She reminds me of Ellen Caswell but is much prettier, and not near so old. I wish that I had some letters to write. I have written to the Advocate and can do no more now till some of my correspondents pay their debts. I must

read now, for next week I have a dress to make. Major Welles and
Mr. Brackett have been to a trial in Bolivar. A colored man brought
a suit for assault and battery. He gained it. Thank God.

Friday, May 4

Yet cold and windy, but tonight it is not so cold as it has been today.
In fact they do not call it cold down at the Ferry. I had twenty-eight
in school today. They really behave well. I have got them to learning
fast some of them. A few are slow and I find that I have no patience
unless I struggle for it. Mr. Brackett has been to Charlestown today.
Tonight Mrs. Smith and Miss Libby came back with him. We are
going fishing with Major Welles tomorrow if it is fair weather. How
time has flown since this term began. I wish that I could go to Martinsburg Saturdays. If I only could I should feel paid each week. No
letter yet this week. What can it mean? We have had a lively social
evening all hands down in our room. I have a bad cold, but feel
pretty well.

Saturday, May 5

It has been quite a warm day. We went on our excursion. We only
caught five fish in all and *entre nous* the Major caught all of them.
But we had a pleasant ramble. We got some wild flowers and lunched
on the grass under some evergreens near John Brown's cave. The
Major is quite good company. We have enjoyed the day pretty well.
I got a letter on my return from George Cobb. Sister Lizzie wrote a
note in it being in at their house. George, Mary, Lizzie and John
Munroe went to South Paris Maying. It must have been a better day
than we had here. I have yet a bad cold, but I am well as I can expect. How fortunate we are—not one of us has lost an hour of school
by sickness since we came out here.

Sunday, May 6

Colder again. But we had seventy-seven in Sunday School. The
Major, Mrs. Smith and Miss Libby helped us. We have heard that
the Stuart girls are not coming so I suppose that Mr. Given will stay
at Front Royal. I went in to class meeting with Binnie. Tonight Mr.
Ames preached. Mr., Mrs. and Fannie Clemmer were up. Between

whiles the Major, Mrs. Smith and I have been arguing about faith
and prayer. The Major has or professes to have just no faith at all. I
am not at all partial to him since his skeptical avowals. He is an opin-
ionated narrowminded man, but as good a Christian as the small
pattern of his mind will cut out. He borrowed my "Lectures on the
Parables" tonight, and took a Bible from the bookcase.

Monday, May 7

Oh we have had such a splendid tramp. We have been along the
Shenandoah as far as a curve beyond Bulls Falls. We fairly loaded
ourselves with flowers. We got some bees fairly drunk with fragrance
on some hair. We brought them home and they never stirred.

Our walk has been splendid. We think that it is about four miles.
Oh we have enjoyed it so much. Binnie and I are much alike about
rambling. We have a passion for it. I've written to George Cobb
tonight. He'll be glad to read about our tramp. I wish that he could
come out here. I must now to bed. I am sleepy and ought to go
to rest.

Tuesday, May 8

I had thirty-four in school today—forty yesterday. They do well.
Even David Artemous is good now, and learns quite well. I am glad
to see it so. I've begun to have the maps chanted by my first class.
They do well for a beginning. Tonight Binnie and I went down and
got the mail. Then we went with Major Welles to walk—round the
pike—over Bolivar Heights and then along home near the Potomac.
We had some hard scrambles through the gullies but found some
fine flowers to pay us. We felt well repaid. We have our table loaded
now with fragrant floating bouquets. Mr. Brackett has been to
Smithfield and back. Miss Dudley writes that there is renewed interest at Martinsburg. God help them. She says they still love me. I
love them too and pray for them.

Wednesday, May 9

A good day, not too cool nor yet too warm. There was a shower this
afternoon. On account of a tournament in Bolivar to which we did
not go our school duties were early over. After reading a while Mrs.

Brackett, Binnie and I went down to the Ferry. I got a letter from
Mrs. Cole. At noon Mr. Brackett went to Martinsburg. I sent a letter to Mrs. Vosburgh by him. Sent my letter to Lizzie off too today.
Have had thirty in school today. Some study quite well. Some white
boys have requested our school room for a party. We are going to
favor them. The petitioners appeared well. It will do good to favor
them. I must not get lazy. I do not feel like reading or writing tonight. I am sleepy. Oh if I were at meeting in Martinsburg tonight.

Thursday, May 10

We closed school today at three. I had thirty in. I had a spelling
school after dinner. They enjoyed it well. I got letters when Mr.
Brackett came at noon from Mrs. Vosburgh, Miss Dudley, Mary
Brown and also one from Mrs. John Haskell of N. G.[86] The Major
and Binnie hurried me off to Loudon Heights before I had time to
half read them. I read Mrs. Haskell's half way up. We scrambled up
where I am sure no one ever went or tried to before. Then we went
down behind into the Loudon Valley which is a perfect gem of a picture from above and the walk was splendid coming around. I have
written to Mrs. Cole and Mrs. Haskell tonight. We have no school
till Monday. So I'm going to Charlestown tomorrow.

Friday, May 11

At Charlestown tonight. I've had a very pleasant day. I've been out
walking with Mrs. Smith and Miss Libby. We passed the old court
house where John Brown was tried and the horrid Jail where he was
confined. I sent off tonight from here letters to Mary, John, and
Elisha Brown. (John sent respects and a request for a letter) also to
Miss Dudley, Mrs. Vosburgh, Mrs. Haskell and Mrs. Cole. I wrote
all the forenoon. The colored Quarterly Meeting is here tomorrow. I
was in Miss Libby's school a while this afternoon. She has a fine
school but her crooked classes would have made me too nervous
to live.

   I've been reading some little S. S. books by way of rest and talking
between whiles. I wish Lizzie could live as these sisters do. We
called while out on a sick Mrs. Welcome—colored.

Saturday, May 12

This morning before Miss Libby and I were up Jemima Dixon, the most original little yellow girl, came in as she often does to see the girls. We got her to sing and "shout" and her talk was so quaintly original for a child of five that I was very much interested. At eleven Miss Libby and I went to meeting at a house used for worship. Mr. Bowman was there and preached. He said Geo. Brown left a good evidence of his change. Mrs. Welcome died last night. A John Thornton whom we met there will not live long. Since dinner we have been to walk and have called on Mrs. Lettie Brown—Mary's aunt. She has a splendid garden. She gave me some flowers, among them some yellow roses. Her hair is straight—her features regular—color not perceptible and manners excellent. I was glad also to call on Mrs. Dixon, mother worthy of Jemima.

Sunday, May 13

Miss Libby and I rose and went to Love Feast this morning at eight. Several from Harper's Ferry were there—among them Mr. Keyes, Mr. Turner and Helen Gilbert. At eleven went to a grove in the outskirts of town where Mr. Bowzer, the Presiding Elder, preached an excellent discourse, after which was communion. A heavy shower kept us from Mrs. Welcome's funeral. Mr. Keyes took tea with us tonight and walked to and from meeting with us. Just what I've done only more so. But there were three ladies of us tonight. Mr. Bowzer's text was "And the throne had six staffs." He made them out to be Consideration. Repentance. Justification. Regeneration, Sanctification and a Triumphant Death. He sustained himself well. He is trying hard to get them to build a church here. They mean I think to do it soon.

Monday, May 14

Back again much refreshed by my rest and trip. I've borrowed the "Throne of David" and "Prince of the House of David" to read.[87] I am charmed with them. Mr. Keyes called again this morning—went into school a short while as I did too—Mrs. Smith in the morning of

course. A Mr. Arnott called who looks very much like John Brown of
Martinsburg, only he is less noble and intelligent looking. As might
be supposed he is a fine man. What with the meeting and the irre-
pressible Jemima Dixon, I have had a grand visit. Miss Gibbs took
charge of my school letting Phil Russ and Eliza Jones hear them recite. At noon I came. Got a letter from Louise Small. Tonight made
two calls with Binnie. Got Fannie Clemmer to go with us, and I
went and had my new dress cut. Our calls were on Mrs. Gilbert and
a Mrs. Morton. David Artemous stays there. She says he loves me
now. He certainly behaves well. He knows French better than English they say. I wonder he learns so well.

Tuesday, May 15

A nice cool day. I've had thirty in school today. I got on well with
them. I got a letter from William Preston one of my old night scholars tonight. He is at Cherry Rim. Binnie had a sort of social meeting
with some of her older scholars tonight. I have none but David that
come now who are old enough save one girl included in Miss Gibbs'
invitation period. Not to intrude I went upstairs and wrote to
William Preston.

A Mr. Dorcas, just in to see the girls home, knows him and Andy
Bird. Mr. Dorcas confirms the report that David is brought over and
likes me—he says best of any teacher. He says David is a pet down
town and a little spoiled but very good hearted. I believe it. I'm glad
I found the good side. Hope I shall keep it now.

Wednesday, May 16

I've had thirty-eight in school today. They do well—some very well.
This afternoon was hotter than for some time past. The air got quite
close and oppressive.

Mr. Vosburgh called a few minutes. Brought me a Magazine and a
paper. Says Miss D—— is not quite well. Mrs. Vosburgh is smart.
Mr. Cowan was here at noon. Tonight got letters from Emma,
Lizzie, Phi Haskell and John Brown. Lizzie felt hurt because I did
not name her in George Cobb's letter. I wrote to her at Gray. John
Brown wrote a noble letter. Miss Donnell has written to him about
those books. He has replied. He thanks me warmly for them and for
papers as well as all else. Oh how much good it has done me. I am

glad that I even paid away that five dollars. God will some time give
it back.

Thursday, May 17

I had thirty six today. It has been a little dull, but warm. Miss
Wright is here tonight. Her charge have a fair, and as they use the
church that she occupies, she is out till Tuesday and came here. We
went to walk with her out to Bulls Falls. I've written replies to all
my letters—to John Brown and Phi Haskell tonight. I wrote one
letter to him and destroyed it, but yet I do not fear to trust him. I
only dread to seem obtrusive. Laura has been out home and has
brought a sweet bouquet—very fragrant. The girls keep us stocked
with nosegays too. I let David have a nap this afternoon. He seems
grateful for small favors in a silent way. He never says "Thank you."
We met a poor old colored man at the railroad tonight. God send
him shelter. We saw some interesting poor white trash in a droll
coop too.

Friday, May 18

This has been a dull, almost a rainy day. As a consequence my school
only numbered twenty-one or two. Miss Wright was in. My pupils
behaved well. After dinner I had a little spelling school for a review.
They already spell better for it. Shall try it each week. Tonight
Mrs. Smith and Miss Libby came. The Major has been airing some
of his prejudices. He has a prejudice of color that I wonder at yet
seems just in theory. I'm too radical even to suit the blacks I think.
So I keep still and listen. Sent my letters off today. Have been sewing tonight. I wish I could afford not to sew but benevolence has
cleaned me out thoroughly.

Saturday, May 19

A hot day. Got off my flannels at last. Have not felt them oppressive
before. I have been sewing nearly all day resisting two invitations to
walk. So has Binnie. As Mr. Brackett has gone to Martinsburg I am
led to think of my friends there. God bless them each and all, and
keep them loving me. I wrote notes to Mrs. Vosburgh and Mary
Brown. Enclosed Mary's with an inkling that even Mr. Brackett

might not understand my love for her, for indeed I do love the noble girl. This afternoon Mr. Given came. So we are all here again save Miss Dudley. She is well enough off if she only knows it, and I'm sure she does.

We have had a fine social time. Mr. Given has a fine school, but has strong local prejudices to encounter.

Sunday, May 20

A very warm day. Fifty or sixty were in Sabbath School. I spent most of my time in teaching Mr. Robinson. He hungers for knowledge and will use it well. It seems strange to serve God on the Sabbath by teaching grown men to read about cats, bats and rats.

After S. School they had a General Class. Binnie, Miss Libby and I went in. It was very good. I have read most of the "Prince of the House of David," and have written a letter to the Advocate. We have had a good social time all together too. Tonight Mr. Given preached. Mr. Ames, Mr. and Mrs. Clemmer, Fannie and her brother were up. It is about eleven and I must to bed soon for we have to get up early in the morning.

Letter from Virginia

Harper's Ferry, May 20th, 1866 [May 30]

Dear Advocate:—It is a very warm day. I am writing this seated in the shade of our back verandah—the only comfortable places that I have found to-day being in a full draft of air. Since I last wrote you I've had the pleasure of a visit to Charlestown. We had no school from three o'clock Thursday of week before last till the following Monday. We had given up our school-room to some white boys, who were to have a tournament on the hill, and who wished to close it up with a party. They politely asked for our rooms, and of course we gladly gave them up. I at once resolved to spend the interval in visiting Mrs. Smith and Miss Libby at Charlestown. But Thursday afternoon, with Major Welles and Miss Gibbs, I ascended Loudon Heights. We scrambled up the steep side of the mountain, where I am sure no lady ever *tried* to go before. We were twice helped a little by the Major, but prided ourselves much on the feat. We found wild honeysuckle, and blue and yellow violets in profusion at the top. We also saw an abundance of strawberry blossoms. We found likewise some bullets flattened on the rocks. After duly admiring the lovely view from the Heights—Loudon valley being a perfect picture, we descended into the valley and walked home by a beautiful road that wound around the eastern extremity of the Heights. Friday I left for Charlestown. The "chivalry" all declined to board the "Yankee teachers," and so they keep house in a rough looking log building, which affords one school-room below and two small rooms for housekeeping above. Mrs. Smith teaches from eight till twelve, and Miss Libby convenes her school in the afternoon. They do not seem at all troubled by the silent contempt of their aristocratic neighbors, but go on quietly in the conscientious performance of their duties, and their schools show well how faithfully they have wrought.

Saturday and Sunday the colored quarterly meeting was held in the place. On Saturday Mr. Bowman preached an excellent discourse in a large room of a private house, which, besides the schoolroom, is their only place of worship. Sabbath morning I went with Miss Libby to Love Feast. It was my first experience of the sort, but I cheerfully partook of the bread and water, supposed to be typical of Christian love and union. After this symbolical exercise came an excellent social meeting. The testimonies were short and expressive, two or three often rising at once till the time was fully expired, and yet not half of the people found a chance to speak at all. At eleven o'clock we went to hear Mr. Bowzer, the Presiding Elder preach in a grove on the outskirts of the town. We liked him much. In the afternoon a violent shower kept us from a funeral which we designed to attend, but in the evening we went to hear Mr. Bowzer again. His text was, "And the throne had six steps." He defined those steps to be Consideration, Repentance, Justification, Regeneration, Sanctification, and a Christian's death. He sustained himself well throughout, and, though one might view a part of his steps as imaginary, it was impossible not to admire his discourse, which would not have done discredit to an educated white man. And here I must confess that the teachers at Charlestown and Shepherdstown vehemently assert that the colored people of their charges will compare favorably with any. Appearances at Charlestown indicate as much, and perhaps I judged the whole country too much by this one town. I wish that the readers of the *Advocate* could have seen the large well dressed congregations that were at Charlestown those two days. The meetings were not marred by any emotional extravagance, and would have been creditable to any society. The colored people are making strenuous efforts to secure churches for themselves now. At Shepherdstown to-morrow they hold a fair for that purpose. The church, now used by them as a school-room can be bought for a reasonable sum, being in the hands of Rev. Dr. Andrews,[88] a true friend, and they design to raise at once the purchase money. At Charlestown they must build, but seem anxious to go on. Here our school-rooms do very well for meetings, and I hardly think that they will get started to procure another place this year.

My school now numbers over forty-five, and has a daily average of over thirty. Miss Gibbs has not quite so many. As I have twelve or thirteen in the alphabet, and a number more just out, I have a plenty to do. I begin to like the school very much indeed. It is quite orderly now, and nearly all are learning well. Our Sabbath school is quite interesting. It is delightful to hear them sing together, and those who can read get Scripture lessons readily. All show a due sense of the importance of a Sabbath school.

At Martinsburg the religious interest is renewed, and they are, I learned, holding some extra meetings. Here just now the prayer-meetings are poorly attended. The evenings are short, and to come proves great interest. Want of attendance has closed all the night schools save that at Charleston, which had but thirteen pupils the night that I was present. So for hard working people, at this season of the year, to crowd a prayer-meeting as they do at Martinsburg, is a very favorable indication.

Our home friends need not fear the cholera for us here. A healthier location than this could not be found. Not one of all our party has lost an hour on account of illness since being here, and all are in excellent health now as far as I know, and to-day all are here save Miss Dudley.

It having been decided that the Misses Stuart cannot be spared from their post in Eastern Virginia, Mr. Given has opened a school at Front Royal. He likes the colored people much. He has a school of about fifty smart scholars. There is a very strong prejudice among the white people, and Mr. Given thinks that lady teachers would now have a hard chance there. We expect to leave here in about six weeks, and I have no fear of serious inconvenience from heat. We can usually find a breeze somewhere about the premises owing to our elevated situation.

But it is time that I drew this to a close. I will, to conclude this, give two choruses that were used in our last social meeting here. I like the first one much. It is:

> "We'll all unite in a heavenly union,
>   We'll all unite in a silent prayer;
>   We come here to watch; we come here to pray,
>   And we hope old Satin 'ill go away."

The other is only noticeable for its peculiarity, characteristic of the colored style of composition, for it must be original.

> "Oh hail! oh hail! I'm sorry for to leave you,
>   But you know, you know, I can't stay here."

The hymn sung with it has innumerable verses of one line each, and is a favorite near the close of a good meeting. You ought to see them sway back and forth, and shout out the chorus with indescribable energy. The effect is solemn, but, were it possible to give a verbal description it would bear a ludicrous aspect. But I seldom feel inclined even to smile at aught that I have seen or heard. So truly does the religion of Christ vindicate itself, though surrounded by extravagances born of ignorance and superstition.

Yours,
Sarah J. Foster

Diary, 1866

Monday, May 21

A windy day, but not cold. It being Whitsuntide the children took a holy day so effectually that we did not try to teach since dinner. Mr. Given, Mrs. Smith and Miss Libby left at seven this morning. Miss Wright went to Charlestown with them and came back at noon and went to Shepherdstown. Mr. Brackett came home bringing me no letters but a splendid bouquet from Mrs. Webster and Mrs. Vosburgh, and some wedding cake from John Campbell's sister-in-law whose wedding he attended. He said Mary Brown sent much love and said Elisha had been trying to get someone to write me for him. God bless the dear boy. I want to see them all. What an odd piece of conceit Major Welles is, yet I like him some. He seems to like Yankees.

Tuesday, May 22

Cold and windy. I had twenty-nine in school today. I have reduced my alphabet class by five or six. If they all had books now they'd get on finely. Have felt encouraged at the very rapid progress of some little ones. Have adopted a new way of making them read and learn the Roman numerals on which I have been drilling them some days. Tonight Binnie had her social gathering. David and another boy were in. Mr. Dorcas and three others also came up to go home with the girls. I spent the evening alone in the kitchen. I had a pleasant time. Now for bed. I have my dress almost done. I might have finished it tonight by a good light. Well rest won't hurt me any.

Wednesday, May 23

Not quite so cold but far from warm. I had thirty-five in school. I had a new scholar whiter than myself but who indignantly denied being white when the children called her so at recess. She is a lady in manners though only twelve.

I'm tired some. I kept two after school and worked hard to make them get their lessons till six o'clock.

The Major has gone to Washington. My only mail was a dead letter that somehow missed Miss Dudley at Charlestown and got sent back to me.

Thursday, May 24

Quite warm but not at all unpleasant. I had thirty-eight in school today. They were a trifle noisier than common, but did very well.

Binnie and I started to go on Maryland Heights after flowers but halfway down the hill we met Fannie Clemmer and came back. We had a grand game of ball, and a romp generally and walked down with her after tea. I got a letter from Lizzie tonight, and a good one too from John Brown again. He is in hopes soon to go to Charlestown and may come here to see me. I have determined to invite him to do so. I want him to visit my school. He says too that he has something to tell me. I want to see him and to hear that.

Friday, May 25

Well I ought to be tired and rather think I am. At half past four Binnie, Fannie Clemmer and I started to ascend Maryland Heights. We

did it too, loading ourselves with wild flowers. I had a pleasant
school and that did not tire me at all. Mrs. Smith and Miss Libby are
here tonight. We have talked till eleven or so. I have begun a letter
to John Brown—began it this morning. Shall have it to finish tomorrow. I would not like Mr. Brackett to know that I have written three
times to him. I fear he might half blame me though he thinks the
world of John. I believe that I am right though. I mean to be.

Saturday, May 26

This has been a warm day but we have not had a very uncomfortable
day for all that. I finished my letter to John Brown and carried it
down town. I got some tumblers for Binnie and I to use for roses,
and some braid to complete my dress. Then I dressed up in it and
took a nap. A bird flew into my hair through the window and waked
me up. I have had a very pleasant evening talking with and listening
to the girls. I wish that Miss Wright was here with us. I hope that I
shall ere long spend one happy Saturday and Sunday at Martinsburg. That is my home of homes out here and always will be.

Sunday, May 27

A very fine day. Seventy-eight were in Sabbath School. We had a
good Sabbath School too. I had more than I could attend to as usual
but enjoyed it. Mr. Bowman preached at eleven. Afterward they
had a Love Feast in Bolivar. So our afternoon was unoccupied. We
read and talked it away, I combing Mrs. Smith's hair for a change.
Just before night we had a splendid shower. We have had a prayer
meeting. Mr. Bowman reproved a girl sharply for laughing—telling
her how ugly she looked—"Right black and her teeth would shine."
As he is nearly jet black I could but laugh then. I wish that I had
been at Martinsburg tonight but we had a good meeting here. I
hope to hear from Mary Brown this week.

Monday, May 28

Cold again on account of the wind. I have had thirty-five in school.
A few seem slow to learn but the most are very good. I have been a
little too impatient with a dull boy. I must not do wrong. I have
finished the "Throne of David" which I began to read yesterday and
have taken up Macaulay again. No mail today. I wonder why Susan

Jordan does not write. I have some cold. My Throat feels badly and I
am sleepy. Laura as usual is here to study, but I must to bed. I wish
I had some letters to write. I could keep awake then.

Mrs. Smith and Miss Libby of course went back to Charlestown
today. How time flies. I cannot feel homesick at all and can hardly
wish time away because I have enough to do.

Thursday, May 29

Cold and rainy till most night. Had but twenty-five on that account
in school. I had therefore more time to drill those that I had. Johnny
Parker is my best speller, and doing well. Others improve. Two or
three yet vex me by slowness but those who were dull three weeks
ago now go on fast. So I must be patient. I did have more grace today. Tonight Binnie had her little meeting. Several men came up to
see the girls home. David was up again. I think that Binnie will soon
have to open her meeting and then I shall come in. She has begun to
teach some of her boys pieces for our exhibition. It is now splendid
moonlight. I have been reading Macaulay and talking to the escort
for my evening work. I'd like to teach mine some.

Wednesday, May 30

Yet cool. But I am sure that it is a great blessing to us. My cold is
nearly gone. I had thirty-eight in school. I have to make long days
work and fear that I get no thanks from Mr. Brackett for it. I do not
believe that he realizes the difference between Binnie's school and
mine. Hers is easy. Mine hard. We had a good prayer meeting tonight. But somehow I felt under a cloud. I know that I have labored
and sacrificed as no other teacher has, and I tremble lest I shall not
be appreciated by Mr. Brackett. Got letters from Mrs. Vosburgh
and Miss Dudley—love from all, but colored appreciation is not
what I need. I *know* I have had great success—Who else does!

Thursday, May 31

A fine day. Had thirty-six in school. Josh Teats is a plague. I can't like
him as I can and do Dave. Dave wants to go up North. I would
gladly befriend him. He has a cough and does not see so well. I gave
him my box of Bronchial Troches. He seemed touched. I have be-

gun to pray for him. Oh may God save him. He came to S. School since I asked him to do so. One month more. Only a little gloomy this morning but this has worn off. The root cause I know and only time can remove it—and even that may not. I know of matters why I should have [   ] of Mr. Brackett. I do not feel so now. Have been selecting pieces for my scholars to speak tonight. I want [   ] something of that kind.

Friday, June 1

A fine day. Forty in school. Josh Teats is a nuisance but I do not think that he means to be. I got a letter from Lizzie and Emma— Lizzie having gone to Lisbon Falls to help Emma a while.[89]
Mr. Brackett got me thirty dollars of my salary tonight. I owe seven dollars of it to him and Binnie. I have already written most of a reply to my letter. I feel rather tired tonight. My spelling review always tires me out more than a common school. I plan to go to Martinsburg before long—in two weeks I think. I've great hopes of a good time. Oh if I could only be there to teach again. But they will love me I hope.

Saturday, June 2

Rainy tonight. I mended all the time I got in this forenoon after completing my letter. Since dinner we have been down town and called on Mr. Ames's folks and then on Maria taking her some oranges. I bought me some gloves and a shawl. Now some books and I hope to get along. Tonight we have been up in the sitting room and I have neither read nor wrote. Mrs. Smith and Miss Libby being here spoil our work hours a little, but we like to have them here.
I feel glad to think that I shall not have to sew much more. I hope to conclude Macaulay and Shakespeare before we go home now. I must hurry in order to do it. It will be a good use of my time.

Sunday, June 3

A dull day. We had a good S. School though. Miss Libby trained the scholars awhile afterward in singing. At half-past two Mr. Richardson preached here. He is a Methodist preacher in Bolivar. He is Union and quite radical too. He staid to tea which must take some

moral courage here. Tonight Mr. Brackett preached. We had a number in though there had been a violent shower and it was yet raining
some. I wanted to read a great deal today but somehow have not. I
could not feel that it was right to read Macaulay on the Sabbath. I
wish I could finish it before I go home.

Monday, June 4

Dull in the morning but a fine day after all. I had thirty-five in
school. Josh Teats is an awful plague. Rosa, who had just come in, is
a nice girl. Josh makes Dave laugh but he tries to do well and I give
him credit therefore. I have begun to teach pieces to Laura Moulton,
Tom Smith and Martha Osborne. I cannot yet decide who shall take
one piece. Nor have I found pieces for all who ought to have them.
Tonight I have been reading the papers and Macaulay. Went down
to the Ferry on an errand. The Fenians have really begun to fight,
but some have come to grief—being taken prisoners.[90] I am not
tired at all. I hope to come out well on this exhibition with my pupils.

Tuesday, June 5

A beautiful day. Had thirty-seven in school. I've got along very
quietly indeed. Even Josh Teats is not invulnerable to kindness. I
begin to think that possibly David is serious. I've written letters
tonight to Susan Jordan and Mary Brown besides replying to one
just received from William Preston. I staid down to Binnie's meeting. It was good. Dave and several other large boys were in, and
they were very still indeed. I wish that Dave would go home with
us. He would be a good work man for someone. William Preston
says that he has a brother in Portland. Edward Madison and Peter
Winston sent their love. I was glad to hear from them.

Wednesday, June 6

Mr. Brackett has started up the valley—went this morning to see
about locating new schools in the fall. Will not be back till Saturday.
    I've had thirty-five or six in school, and got on very well. I sent
Josh Teats home for ill conduct. We had a very good meeting tonight. More than usual were in and the prayers were excellent.
    Binnie and I made three calls on colored people since tea. We
called on a Mrs. Gore and a Mrs. Jackson. I don't know who the

other one was. We had a pleasant time. I got no mail tonight. Shall
sleep alone if I sleep—have got the ear ache some and my head feels
badly on account of it.

Thursday, June 7

Had thirty-three in today. There were very good indeed. I have got
the most of them to learning fast now. They do extremely well. I am
teaching the white girl "My Angel Name." She learns it slowly but
speaks it well. I shall not try to teach any other but Tommy Smith
and he may not speak his piece well. Binnie is vexed at her's now
about the pieces. She and Mrs. Brackett are not so ready to make
allowance for them as I am. I got letters from Susan Jordan and
Addie Lawrence tonight—the latter of three sheets with a scribble
from Linnie enclosed. I was glad to hear from her. Have replied at
greater length. Shall write to Susan next week. My ear not quite
well yet.

Friday, June 8

A pleasant rather warm day. I had thirty-one in school today. They
were very good and quiet. This afternoon I got letters from Mary
Brown, Abbie Coombs and Geo. Cobb. I've been down three days
now for the mail myself. Felt well paid last night and tonight. We
went down to meet Mrs. Smith and Miss Libby tonight back of the
Hill. They are upstairs now. I've replied to all my letters, I ought to
write home. Must soon if I do not hear. Mary writes that Elisha is to
be at home the 11th and so not when I am there. Oh I am sorry. I
did want to see the dear boy. I feel grateful to all my friends at M.
for kind interest. Mrs. Howard and Anna send much love. Mrs.
Vosburgh is not well. Mary has been ill. I do hope she will spare
herself more.

Saturday, June 9

A cooler windy day. Mr. Brackett came home this forenoon. I sent
off my letters, and all that I have done since has been to read. I have
completed the third volume of Macauley. Mrs. Smith, Miss Libby,
Binnie and Mrs. Brackett have been busy all day with their needles.
Mrs. Smith and Miss Libby have arranged to take home a little girl.
They are now at work in getting her clothing ready. The others, with

advice and help from Mrs. Smith, are making over bonnets. I do not
need to do so and I am duly thankful. I am glad to have been able to
read up History a little. I am not so sanguine of getting through with
Shakespeare but mean to try. Reading is now my duty and must be
done too.

Sunday, June 10

A fine day. A little misty in the morning but beautiful since. Others
have said that it has been warm. I have been cool all day. Mr.
Bowman preached this forenoon after S. School at which we had a
large attendance. Mr. and Mrs. Brackett have been to Shepherdstown. They have just got here. It is almost eleven. We had begun to
worry about them. Mr. Keyes and Mrs. Poles stopped till this evening's prayer meeting. Mrs. Poles is handsome I think. There was a
great deal of peculiarly African singing in the meeting tonight but I
liked it. I ought and meant to have written home this day but I have
not. Rev. Mr. Green of Shepherdstown called here this afternoon.[91]
He seems loyal and radical too. He has not many friends at S.
therefore.

Monday, June 11

A beautiful day. Had forty-five in school—my largest number yet.
Was annoyed by a little more noise than common. But most were
good though. Miss Gibbs talked with David Artemous today and has
written home to an uncle to see if he will want him. He says he came
up here with the 19th Corp. He remembers the 30th Regt. but no
particular members of it.[92]
    Tonight Elisha Brown is home at a party. I do wish that I was
there to see him and all the rest of them. Mr. Brackett has gone off
again—this time for over a week. I got no mail today. I've written to
mother tonight. I hope to have a letter soon from home. I miss
Lizzie being there. Avery ought to write. I am sleepy and must now
to bed. We were up late last night and early this morning.

Tuesday, June 12

Another fine day. I had thirty-four or five in school. They were
given to quiet. A quarrel at noon annoyed me, almost decided to

whip the parties, but finally excused them. Talked with Mr. Hall tonight about Dave when I was down town. He says he is smart. We had a good meeting here tonight. They had some sweet singing. Mr. Morton was in and several young men. All were orderly. Sent off my letter to mother. Got no mail.

I've begun the fourth volume of Macaulay. I must read all I can. I have got to hurry it up. Mrs. Poles called into my school this afternoon. I wish that John Brown would call soon. I criticized his last letter and fear I wounded his feelings. I want to see him too. Hope he'll be at home Sunday at least.

Wednesday, June 13

Our warmest day yet. I had thirty-seven in school. This heat gave me a headache and I could not read much after school. I got no mail today. We had a good meeting here tonight—marred a little by the audible groans and ejaculations of a man who afterward made a good prayer. His comical singsong in lining a hymn made me laugh.[93] Mr. Morton took the lead. No one responding to one of his calls for prayer, he slowly and impressively repeated the Lord's prayer before he rose. He is a noble man. He answers my idea of Uncle Tom. A Miss Parrish was here tonight. She is a splendid character too. God grant she may find her two missing children. She has found two. Binnie is going to write to Richmond.

Thursday, June 14

Another very warm day, but fortunately today and yesterday we had showers to cool the air somewhat. Already the flies seem to act as they do at home in August. I had thirty in school. Got through quite early tonight. I have been sewing some, getting ready to go away tomorrow. Got a letter from Wm. Preston again. It was much more correct than his last one was, and that improved on the first. Mr. Given got here tonight having closed up his school. I do not think he is as earnest as we are in this work. There is a Levee at Charlestown to raise money for the Colored Church. Mrs. Poles and Laura have gone to it. I praised David tonight. He says he wants to learn to write. I would gladly teach him. He is really trying to be a noble man now. Heaven clear his way. I do wish he could go home with us. I hope he may.

Friday, June 15

I find myself at Martinsburg. I taught this forenoon hurrying up matters and having my usual spelling review so I got rather tired But I feel *so* quietly happy tonight. I am glad to be here. I have been in to see Mrs. Howard and her dear children. I found the precious babe well and handsomer than ever, and Lizzie too. Mary and Cimmie Carrie and Charlie Brown came over to see me, also Annie Leavers and her cousin. I've had a pleasant time. I went in to see Anna. They all love Miss Dudley, but they yet love me very much— just the same as ever. Everything is sweet and fresh here now. Mr. Given is coming up tomorrow.

Saturday, June 16

This has been a very pleasant day to me. With Miss Dudley I have made nine calls. I got great encouragement at Mr. Wilson's and Mr. Phinn's and Mr. Wood's. I have felt so much gratified at the love shown for me by all. Mr. Given was with us at the last three places. We all joined in prayer at each place and I was glad to do so. I have not yet seen the Brown boys. I shall not see Elisha, I knew it, but I feel sad about it. I gave Geo. Phenix an encouraging word. I wish I had a chance to see all whom I want to talk with and so have the privilege and pleasure of doing my duty by them. I am not feeling so well as I would like to for I have some slight derangement of the stomach. But I shall well enough by not eating. I am happy tonight.

Sunday, June 17

My pleasure has been a little marred by its raining, but I am too happy to think of that now. I went to meeting at the schoolhouse in the morning. Then after dinner I went to Sunday School. It was raining enough to make the attendance thin but I enjoyed it. It rained so that I could not go down street to meeting in the afternoon but I had a pleasant time with Frank while the rest went. Tonight I've been to a most excellent meeting. *Adam Howard* rose for prayers. Thank God. Another of my prayers answered. He talked of going to Bath Friday night but has held off. Mrs. Vosburgh rose too and that is another rich blessing to me. God bless them both. I shall see John Brown again in the morning, he says. He showed me a let-

ter from Miss Donnell. It was so good. Those books will be here
very soon. Have talked to my friends and have just written a note to
Elisha.

Monday, June 18

Back again to my work here. Mrs. Webster and Annie Leavers
loaded me with flowers. I went in to see Margaret and Mary this
morning. Mr. Howard gave me his picture. John Brown gave me his
and, when I came back, Mrs. Vosburgh gave me hers. I then went
into Miss Dudley's school, heard them sing and bade them all goodbye. Mr. Howard was in also to say goodbye to Miss Dudley as he
has to go to Bath. May God go with him and stay with Mrs. Vosburgh.
Bell Hopewell came in to see me this morning. Mary came to meeting for that last night. Mary Brown cannot bear to talk of our going
away. She and Anne feel so near to us because of our interest in poor
George. He talked so freely to Miss Dudley that they will feel his
loss over again in losing her. Miss Dudley loves those girls as well as
I do I think and values John too at about his true worth.

Letter from Virginia

Harper's Ferry, June 18th, 1866 [July 4]

Dear Advocate:—I have but a few hours since returned from a short
but pleasant visit at Martinsburg. I went up Friday and returned today (Monday.) I had a very pleasant time while there, though a rainy
Sabbath marred my pleasure somewhat. I had also made a slight
mistake in the time of my visit. Last week a picnic convened all my
old scholars, of whom many are at farm work in the country, and I
missed seeing many whom I might have seen had I known of the
picnic in season to go. But I enjoyed my visit much. Miss Dudley is
pleasantly situated with the family of Mr. Vosburgh—a genuine
home, not a boarding place. Her schoolroom is only across a narrow
lane, and is a much larger and more convenient room than I had
when there. It is a rude log structure, and has been used as a farm or
a slaughter house alway before this. But we do not mind that of
course.[94]

Saturday Mr. Given came up, having closed his school at Front
Royal for the present, to attend to the mission work for which he

was especially sent. The only object was to lay the foundation of a good autumn school, securing the field and awakening an interest in the matter by a session of a few weeks. He considers the people there very superior—the colored ones I mean—and was much attached to his school.

In company with Mr. Given, Miss Dudley and I made some pleasant calls. We called on two families who live on the grounds of Hon. Chas. Jas. Faulkner.[95] Summer had clothed in new beauty the grounds, which were beautiful even last summer when I visited them. The affectionate greetings, the warm-hearted pressures of the hand that met me at each place, touched a tender spot in my soul's inmost recesses. Very pleasantly and all too rapidly passed the afternoon, and yet I made not half the calls that I would have made could I have found time. Sabbath morn at half past ten, Mr. Given preached in the school-room. Though rainy, many were out. Death has claimed some since I was there, but the faces that I missed were those of faithful Christians, and so it seemed wrong to mourn them. The Sabbath school was convened at half past ten, and I was glad to take a part once more in its exercises. John Brown and Mrs. Vosburgh are Miss Dudley's chief assistants, and a sister of John has also a class. I do wish that I could introduce the readers of the *Advocate* to that noble Brown family which, till a recent invasion of death, numbered seven sons and five daughters. Notwithstanding the rain, there were about thirty in Sabbath school. A number stayed in the school-room through the intermission, and from the house we heard the quaint, sweet melody of several plantation hymns, with which they whiled away the time. We could hardly distinguish the words, and the audible stepping by which they timed themselves sounded strangely. Words are powerless in description, however. Though not at all slow in movement, the hymns seemed an embodied wail, and the memory of them will haunt me long. It blurs my eyes with tears even now to think of them. I had never before so thoroughly appreciated the beauty of Whittier's thought regarding the

> "Quaint relief of mirth that plays
> With sorrow's minor keys."

Hearts and ears steeled and dulled by years of oppression might fail to hear aught but the strange words, the quick movement of such songs: though indescribable, much more may be *felt* by a sympathetic spirit.

At three o'clock the people again met in goodly numbers at the

Methodist church, and, undismayed by the violent rain in which they were compelled to return home, quite a number came to the school-room at night. A short discourse was then followed by a social meeting which will long be remembered, by me at least, as a precious season. At its close several complied with an invitation to rise for prayers, one being a man of intelligence and excellent character, whose conversion will be an untold benefit to his people. A deep, calm, wide-spread interest still pervades the hearts of the young there, and has hardly flagged at all since its first awakening nearly six months ago. The Sabbath school is flourishing. I was happy to learn that the readers of the *Advocate* had kept up all along an ample supply of papers. Last week they failed, but a timely supply from another source was fortunately received. None would fail to save and send all that they could if they could see the eagerness with which they are taken by the little outstretched hands. It is a sad disappointment to be compelled to deny even the little ones who only value papers for the "heaps of pictures."

John Brown showed me an excellent letter from Miss Emma G. Donnell of Newcastle, Maine, regarding a box of books which she has sent to his address. They have not yet come to hand, but a letter from a shipping agent has just announced their safe arrival—at Baltimore, I think, and they are now daily expected. Already they are much needed, and they are accepted with the deepest thankfulness. But they will doubtless be acknowledged by a letter to the kind donor. I do not think that I have ever mentioned that John Brown learned the art of penmanship while in the army, without any instructor; yet such is the fact. By copying the letters and practicing, all unaided, he became able to write a letter in three months. Perhaps Miss Donnell will not need to be reminded that the past winter has been his only school privilege. But I thought I would name it to enhance the pleasure or reading the letter that I am sure she will soon receive.

But, after this long ramble, I will hasten back to my present location. My school this month approaches fifty. Surely no children could learn faster than many of them do, and they are not troublesome at all when all things are duly considered. The school of Miss Gibbs is smaller than mine now, and has been so for some time. She now has classes in the Third Reader, and in Arithmetic and Geography. To be sure such pupils had made a good start before we came, but it seems to me that they have crowded the work of a full year into a little over six months, even when their starting point is taken into the account. They learn all oral exercises with incredible rapidity. Study comes a little hard at first to the most of them, but they are well in the habit now. We hope to arrive at our homes before the Fourth of July, when we anticipate a vacation of ten weeks. Mr. Brackett has just returned from a vacation of nearly two weeks up the Valley, looking out locations for new schools another season. For the good work must go on here, and must be as widespread as Northern benevolence will permit. The society which sustains us now has at its disposal the Shenandoah Valley, excepting Winchester, and must bring many more teachers into the field.

Next Saturday we plan to have a Sabbath school picnic on the hill. Already we have done much to prepare for it. The children will be able to sing and recite some pieces. We anticipate a pleasant time. How we are to travel home is not yet decided, but home begins to be in all our thoughts. Still I should feel sorry indeed if I could not hope some time to visit these scenes again. Strong cords of affection bind my heart to each of my schools, and some photographs given me this morning will ever hold a place among my choice treasures.

Sarah J. Foster

Diary, 1866

Tuesday, June 19

A nice cool day, I only had twenty-seven in school. I have been out to Bolivar Heights and beyond to make some calls with Binnie. We made three and had a very pleasant walk. We had but few into our little social meeting tonight but it was good. I got my Photographs today and I have written to Mrs. Vosburgh and Mary Brown sending enclosed the pictures for Mrs. Vosburgh and Mrs. Webster, Mary and Mrs. Howard. I feasted my eyes on the others several times today. I showed them to Mr. Brackett. I shall always love to look at them. But I'm too sleepy to think and I must retire for I want to rest. I yet feel to pray for special grace and want new strength. Thank God.

Wednesday, June 20

Another nice cool day but only twenty-seven were in. Mary now will have to go to work. I have been teaching the "Angel Names" to Levenia Comb, Martha Asbury having gone away to work.

Got nice letters tonight from Mary Bradbury and Addie Lawrence. Have written replies since school. Tonight Mr. and Mrs. Clemmer and Fannie were up. They kept us females out of meeting.

It is late. I am sleepy. I sent off letters to Mrs. Vosburgh and Mary Brown as I had got them ready, pictures and all. I find that I am true as a magnet to my attachments. I shall ever love the colored people of Martinsburg, especially the noble Brown family.

Thursday, June 21

A delightful day. A little warm but not uncomfortable up here. Our school was a little broken by rehearsals for our picnic. Mr. Brackett was in my school in the morning. He seemed to think that my scholars done well. They do better sometimes when none are to hear them. Tonight I got a letter from Avery—good but short, and a note in from Nellie. Lizzie is on her second week of teaching. Hope she will like it much.

Sent off my letters today. Lizzie or Emma sent me in a paper a fancy necktie to give as a present. I mean to give it to Dave. We have no school tomorrow, only three days more anyway.

Friday, June 22

Oh my soul give thanks to the Lord. My dear friend Anna Brown has started to be a Christian and Mrs. Vosburgh has found peace fully. Mr. Given came at noon and brought me a good letter from Mrs. Vosburgh. A strong renewal of interest made it hard for him to leave. Oh may God lead and guide them all.

I've written to Anna and sent that enclosed in one to Mrs. Vosburgh, and sent both with one to Avery down by Dave, who, with others, has been here helping to prepare for the picnic tomorrow. I hope it will go off well and be a pleasant affair. I fear a rain now.

Saturday, June 23

Over and done. All was harmonious, and the children done themselves much honor. Levenia Comb did wonders in her piece. But all went well. The singing was splendid.

Several hundred must have been here. They were not noisy. They had the speaking before dinner, all but the men's parts and one recitation by our Black Swan. After dinner speeches and music—

enough of it and plays at which Mr. Brackett slightly helped. We
had a grand dinner—a great profusion of excellent viands. The
young people marched around the front of the Hill with a drum and
fife and two flags. All good but I'm tired and must to bed now.

Sunday, June 24

Our warmest day yet. We had a very large Sabbath School. We lent
books to those who can read to exchange among themselves till we
get back. There was a class meeting here at three. The rest did not
go in and so I did not. I wanted to and *would* had I been at Martinsburg. Here I do not know why I did not.

Tonight we had a good meeting—Mr. Brackett preached on the
Parable of the Good Samaritan, and a man from Charleston prayed
and talked. I do not feel as homesick as the rest. I love my work
better I think. Had half a mind to write to John Brown but thought I
would not today. Have felt to pray for Mary tonight with new zeal.

Monday, June 25

Quite as warm today. I had but twenty-five in school. They were
very good and quiet, but at noon I had to punish two boys for a fight.
Mrs. Smith and Miss Libby as usual went away. Next time they'll
come to stay till we go. Mr. Brackett has gone to Martinsburg. I expect to hear that Mary Brown has started. I do think that she will be
thus affected by Miss Dudley's coming away.

I got a good letter from Lizzie. She is in a good training place for a
colored school. Caleb has a meeting appointed in Webster. Has
been asked to preach in Lisbon.[96] Oh if he only would. I believe he
soon will. I am thankful and very hopeful now.

Tuesday, June 26

Yet very warm. I had but about my yesterday's number. All were
very good and still. Miss Dudley and Mr. Brackett came at noon. I
met a great trial first. Mrs. Bales denied all knowledge of the bed-
ding that Mr. Brackett had there. I fear he will blame me. But I can't
help it. Then I had a great pleasure. Mary Brown sent me her picture. She has not really started, but Anna has become a Christian
and wrote to tell me so. I thought that I'd wait till I got home at first

before answering. Then I could not wait and wrote at once as good a letter as I could. I never felt to love the dear Brown girls so well before as I do now. Anna writes that they'll send me their pictures. I shall be glad of them. Miss Dudley has Mary Hopewell's and John Brown's. Fannie Clemmer was up. I showed her my pictures.

Wednesday, June 27

Quite comfortable today, and tonight we've had a fine shower. Our schools closed at noon. I gave small prizes to a number selected from our books here. A lady from Northern Ohio came early in the afternoon. She came to visit these schools. She did not know that they were done. She staid on account of fatigue and the shower till just now. While she was here Helen Gibberd, Eliza Morton and Lizzie Harris came up with Geo. Harris and Geo. Christie from Martinsburg. I was very glad to see them. I gave Geo. Christie my address. He will write he says. I hope he will. Mr. Brackett has been over and he has brought home Miss Wright. They came in the rain. No meeting for the rain. Mr. Keyes and four young men were in and made a long call. An old man called today too.

Thursday, June 28

Quite cool, especially since dinner. Mrs. Smith and Miss Libby came at noon bringing their little Virginia. Very many were in the cars returning from yesterday's decoration of the graves of the rebel dead. They showed their usual spirit about the beautiful child. I got nice letters from Mary and John Brown and Miss Dudley got one from Fannie Ransom—very good. Mary says all send love. Elisha was very proud of his letter. Miss Dudley says he fairly leaped for joy. Dear boy may God bless it to him. I love to hear from my dear Martinsburg friends. I must write to them just as soon as I get home. We've had lots of goodbyes today. Mr., Mrs. Clemmer and Fannie were up.

Friday, June 29

On our way? We are now waiting for the Light Express at Baltimore. Thus far the girls Amanda Biner and Laura Keyes had had to ride in the colored car. At first they were homesick and cried a little and

even Dave looked sober. But Mr. Keyes looked jubilant, and little
Virginia seems perfectly happy. Twice some depot official has tried
to order out the girls but, by claiming them as our servants, we have
kept them with us. People stare a little and the express agents did
not like our getting a Colored carter to take our baggage across
the city.

Saturday, June 30

At New York. We got here at five. On the Jersey Ferry we saw a
party of colored people in charge of a lady. They had come from
some Employment Agency.

Here at Mr. Newton's we have met a Mrs. Mains, Mrs. Shaw and
Mrs. Russell, and a colored man named Sanders going on with us
all. There was till noon also a Mr. Payner and a colored girl going up
the Hudson. We are to take the boat for Portland tonight.

On the boat. It is a splendid night. I have a state room with Mrs.
Shaw. She looks like Marion Higgins. Amanda is going to sleep in
our room on the floor. She was very kind letting me sleep in her lap
on the cars last night. Our party is all happy.

Notes

1. SJF was one of the original four teachers and a minister employed by
the Freewill Baptist Home Mission Society, in conjunction with the American Missionary Association and the Freedmen's Bureau, to establish the
Shenandoah Mission in 1865 with schools in Harpers Ferry, Charles Town,
Shepherdstown, and Martinsburg, West Virginia (Freewill Baptist Home
Mission Society, *Thirty-Second Annual Report* [Dover, N.H., 1866], 82–
89; "Home and Foreign Missions," *MS*, Dec. 6, 1865).

2. Rev. Nathan Cook Brackett was superintendent of the Shenandoah
Mission. Later he became a founder and principal of Storer College, a normal school for black students established in 1867 at Harpers Ferry as an
outgrowth of the mission effort. Born in Phillips, Maine, in 1836, he attended Maine State Seminary in Lewiston and was graduated from Dart-
mouth College in 1864. During the Civil War he served in the U.S. Christian Commission as a field agent in Sheridan's army, headquartered in
Winchester, Va. He received an honorary Ph.D. from Bates College in
1883 (Rev. G. A. Burgess, A.M., and Rev. J. T. Ward, A.M., *Free Baptist
Cyclopaedia* [Chicago, 1889], 67; *Rev. N. C. Brackett, PH.D.*, undated
pamphlet at the American Baptist Historical Society, Valley Forge, Pa.

3. Rev. Daniel McBride Graham (Burgess and Ward, 236–37).

4. Anne S. Dudley was born in Kingfield, Maine, in 1833. A graduate of the Maine State Seminary at Bates College in 1864, she succeeded SJF in Martinsburg and later played a role in the founding of Storer College. She married Rev. L. E. Bates in 1874 (ibid., 43–44).

5. Rev. George Barrell Cheever, a fearless abolitionist, was pastor of the Church of the Puritans, Union Square, New York City, between 1846 and 1867 (*DAB*, s.v. "Cheever, George Barrell").

6. The story of Naboth's vineyard is told in the Bible in 1 Kings 21.

7. The abandoned government buildings on Camp Hill, overlooking Harpers Ferry, including the original building used by the Shenandoah Mission, in 1867 became the site of Storer College (Kate J. Anthony, *Storer College* [Boston, 1891], 5–6).

8. Located across the Potomac and Shenandoah rivers, respectively, from Harpers Ferry, Maryland and Loudoun Heights were the scenes of military engagements during the Civil War (Harpers Ferry National Historical Park, informational pamphlets).

9. Lt. Henry E. Smith of the 193d New York Volunteers was one of the officers who represented the Freedmen's Bureau in Harpers Ferry in the last quarter of 1865 (Stealey, "Freedmen's Bureau," 102).

10. At Martinsburg and Charles Town "we hired buildings of colored men for our schools," said Brackett; conditions were primitive (Freewill Baptist Home Mission Society, *Thirty-Second Annual Report*, 83). The location of the Knowlton School, as Foster's school was called, is unknown.

11. Attendance at SJF's day school averaged twenty-eight students in December and then rose to nearly fifty for the remainder of the time she was there. In the night school attendance began at an average of forty-five and dropped off to about thirty. Males outnumbered females by a substantial margin, nearly double in the months of January and February. Most of the day students were under the age of sixteen, and most of the night students over that age. "We open our [night] school by reading and prayer alternating with each other in this duty. Such as can read intelligently in the Bible use that for a reader," she wrote to the AMA in December. Teaching materials consisted mainly of tracts and papers, with few books. In the month of February, for example, SJF indicated she distributed 150 papers but no books. Writing was taught separately one evening a week to about fifteen students. Only four or five students could write in the day school. The only singing taught was "the multiplication table as introduced by Mr. Brackett" (Teacher's Monthly Reports, SJF to the AMA, Nov.–March 1865—66, SJF to the AMA, Dec. 4, 1865, SJF to Samuel Hunt, Jan. 1, 1866, AMAA).

12. James Matthews (Willis F. Evans, *History of Berkeley County, West Virginia* [Martinsburg, 1928], 275).

13. William Hoke was a tailor, and lived with John Hoke and his family. They were fifty-eight and fifty, respectively, in 1870 (National Archives, *Population Schedules of the Ninth Census of the United States, 1870*, West Virginia, Berkeley County, Martinsburg District).

14. "Although no major battles were fought in the county [Berkeley], its seat of government [Martinsburg] changed hands in a major sense no less than ten times during the war. . . . A rough time estimate of occupation would place Martinsburg under supervision of Union forces for about thirty-two months and under control of Confederate forces for about sixteen months" (William Thomas Doherty, *Berkeley County, USA: A Bicentennial History of a Virginia and West Virginia County, 1772–1972* [Parsons, W.Va., 1972], 136–37).

15. Of her impending change, Dudley wrote, "I am going to Charlestown to open a school there next week. The spirit that hung John Brown still lives, and the people are strongly opposed to schools for the Freedmen there, as well as here. I go alone, but I trust the law and the Lord will shield me." The trip to Charles Town was made with "a company of soldiers" for protection against "the promise of 'bloody heads' and 'broken windows.'" In February, Dudley wrote, "No one can ever know the anxiety I have felt, and the effort I have had to make these two long months since I came here, occupying a rough log house, cold as a barn; teaching and boarding in the same rooms because I could not get board elsewhere; sleeping there with no man or boy in the house for a single night, while the enemies of the school were threatening without, and not knowing what the next hour might bring; hearing a hundred different scholars recite lessons in a single day, doing my own work, receiving company, writing letters, etc., etc. All this and much more I have had to do in getting this school fairly started; and I can rejoice now in the belief that *it will go on!*" (Anne S. Dudley to Rev. George W. Whipple, Dec. 9, 1865, AMAA; Dudley to Rev. S. Curtis, Dec. 23, 1865, "Freedmen's Mission," *MS*, Jan. 24, 1866; Dudley to *MS*, ibid., Feb. 28, 1866).

16. John H. Brown's family was listed among the free inhabitants of Martinsburg in the 1860 U.S. Census. The son of Perry and Elizabeth Brown, John, who was twenty-one in 1860, was one of twelve children. His father was listed as a sixty-year-old carpenter. John's siblings and their ages in 1860 were Margaret Howard, twenty-eight, wife of Adam Howard, a thirty-year-old barber; Mary, twenty-five; George, twenty-four; James, nineteen; Jacob, fifteen; Ann, fourteen; Isaac, eleven; Lucy, nine; Elisha, six; Caroline, four; and Charles, two. John, George, James, and Jacob were listed as laborers, and Mary was a washerwoman. John served in the Union army

during the war. N. C. Brackett was impressed enough with his abilities to encourage him to go to Lewiston, Maine, to study at Bates College, the chief educational institution of the Free Will Baptists. Brown married Hannah F. Robinson in 1867. He died in Berkeley County on Oct. 27, 1874. At that time, he was employed as a carpenter (National Archives, *Population Schedules of the Eighth Census of the United States, 1860*, Virginia, vol. 3, Bedford and Berkeley counties; SJF, "Letter from Virginia," May 2, June 18, 1866, ZA, May 23, July 4, 1866; SJF, Diary, Jan. 6, 1866; Guy L. Keesecker, *Marriage Records of Berkeley County, Va. and W. Va.* [Martinsburg, 197–], 32; Keith E. Hammersla, Staff Historian and Genealogist, Martinsburg–Berkeley County Public Library, Martinsburg, W.Va., personal communication, May 15, 1989).

17. Students' intelligence relative to their blackness was a common subject of discussion; N. C. Brackett wrote in his annual report in 1866: "The capacity for the colored people for education is rather a stale subject, and I will simply say that my experience tends to prove that they are every way human, subject to the same passions and incited by the same motives as other men. Some of them are very sharp, some very stupid. It must necessarily be a long time before they become a race of scholars" (Freewill Baptist Home Mission Society, *Thirty-Second Annual Report*, 83).

18. On Nov. 30, 1865, the *Martinsburg New Era* noted sarcastically: "We are much pleased to learn that a large school is soon to be opened for the benefit of the negroes in our midst. We believe the teachers are to be ladies from Massachusetts. These ladies will, of course, receive a cordial welcome by the elite of our place, and be at once admitted into our heartfelt sympathies. We have not yet heard where they are to board, but suppose they will bring their board with them."

19. Sunday school newspapers.

20. Of the four communities visited by the members of the Shenandoah Mission, opposition was least expected in Martinsburg. N. C. Brackett wrote that in the other three communities the "people are exceedingly hostile to any measure that benefits the colored people, especially a school." In Charles Town and Shepherdstown "threats of violence have been made against any one who attempts to establish a 'nigger school.'" Then he wrote: "Thank God for Martinsburg. I was cordially received by prominent citizens of that brisk little city. At a meeting of colored people for the purpose of organizing a sort of 'Education Society,' the mayor cheered us with his presence and his voice." J. H. McKenzie, a Freedmen's Bureau agent, gave a different account of the climate in Martinsburg. "The late rebels here manifest a purpose to oppress the colored people all they can. The majority of the people being loyal and the rullers loyal, the disloyal element vent all their spite upon the heads of the poor Blacks, and I am sorry to say that I

have Observed many loyal persons as strongly prejudiced against the freedmen as the disloyal" (N. C. Brackett to the Editor, Nov. 18, 1865, *MS*, Dec.
6, 1865; J. H. McKenzie to Capt. W. Stover How, Jan. 31, 1866, Letters
Received, No. 1102 [1000], Assistant Commissioner, Va., BRFAL, quoted
in Stealey, "Reports," 99).

21. SJF recorded in her school reports that she visited no families in December, fifteen in January, but only three in February at the height of her
troubles. On Jan. 1 she wrote: "As to visits I have waited till the excitement
against the school subsided. Now I shall visit some each fair day. A gentleman who walked out with me a few weeks since received an anonymous and
insulting note the next day. But that has passed by now, and I meet with no
trouble at all. I have never been *personally* insulted" (Teacher's Monthly
Reports, SJF, Dec.–March 1865–66, SJF to Samuel Hunt, Jan. 1, 1866,
AMAA).

22. Louise N. Wood married N. C. Brackett on Oct. 16, 1865 (Burgess
and Ward, 67).

23. SJF apparently was referring to St. Joseph's Catholic Church in Martinsburg (Keith E. Hammersla, staff historian and genealogist, Martinsburg–Berkeley County Public Library).

24. The Lockwood House, the former office and home of the armory
paymaster on Camp Hill, became the first residence and classroom building
for the Shenandoah Mission teachers in 1865. The cemetery is presumably
Harper Cemetery. Anne Dudley described the house as "shattered by
shells and defaced by soldiers but with some repairing it is quite comfortable. The large rooms are convenient for schools and meetings and we consider it an excellent location for our school." The kitchen and a classroom
have been restored, as has been the building's exterior (ibid.; Anne Dudley
to Rev. George Whipple, Dec. 9, 1865, AMAA).

25. Thomas Jefferson stood on the rocks in 1783 and thought the view
"stupendous" and "worth a voyage across the Atlantic" (Harpers Ferry National Historical Park map).

26. Brown stored the pikes, with which he planned to arm the blacks he
expected to join his insurrection, under the beds in his rented farmhouse
and in a small cabin across the road from where he was staying with his band
six miles from Harpers Ferry (Allan Keller, *Thunder at Harpers Ferry*
[Englewood Cliffs, N.J., 1958], 14–15).

27. "We were bent upon looking up the church which gave rise to his
[Thomas Gray's] Elegy in a Country Churchyard, intending when we got
there, to have a little scene over it; Mr. S., in all the conscious importance
of having been there before, assuring us that he knew exactly where it
was. . . . After all, imagine our chagrin on being informed that we had not

been to the genuine churchyard. The gentleman who wept over the scenes of his early days on the wrong doorstep was not more grievously disappointed" (Mrs. Harriet Beecher Stowe, *Sunny Memories of Foreign Lands* [Boston, 1854], 48).

28. SJF was listed in the U.S. Census of 1860 as a domestic in the family of Frederick M., thirty seven, and Mary A. Cobb, thirty-four, of Portland, Maine. Their children were Frederick M., age thirteen; George C., ten; Mary A., seven; Lizzie L., five, and Ella F., two. Cobb was a railroad engineer. In 1864, SJF was still working for the Cobbs between January and the end of March. When the family moved to another address in the city, Foster returned to her home in Gray (National Archives, *Population Schedules of the Eighth Census of the United States, 1860*, Maine, vol. 3, Cumberland County; SJF, Diary, 1864).

29. Lizzie was the nickname of Hannah Elizabeth Foster, SJF's seventeen-year-old sister (Family genealogical record).

30. Rev. Silas Curtis was corresponding secretary of the Freewill Baptist Home Mission Society from 1839 to 1869 (Burgess and Ward, 145).

31. Samuel Howard Foster, SJF's twenty-three-year-old brother, had recently had charges of desertion from the Union army lifted against him. He was "rather headstrong," reported his niece Edith Thompson Libby many years later. Military records show that between 1861 and 1865 he served as a volunteer for a total of three-and-a-half years in three Union regiments. He suffered sporadically from chronic diarrhea, chills, and fever, a combination that killed many soldiers. He was hospitalized in four army hospitals between 1861 and 1863. In 1864 he complained in letters to his family of a recurrence of his medical problems that made it difficult for him to keep up with his regiment. On July 1, 1865, several weeks after the last Confederate army had surrendered, he was listed as having deserted from his regiment at Savannah, Ga. He was arrested July 24 at Gray. His niece described the circumstances surrounding his desertion: "While waiting to be mustered out he contracted a southern fever. His temperature ran high. In his dreams he seemed to hear his mother calling him. She seemed so far away and in his delirium he called, 'Mother, oh Mother, where are you?' When morning dawned, ill as he was, and burning with fever, he started out. His one idea was to get home before he died." He set out for Maine, hitching rides, living off the land and handouts, and sleeping in barns. "One nice old lady fed him, and gave him some medicine, then let him sleep in her son's bed." He hitched a ride on a charcoal wagon for the last leg of the trip from Portland, arriving home at 2 A.M. He was mustered out on Aug. 29, and the charges against him were dropped on Sept. 11 with the forfeiture of pay and allowances due to him. In 1888 his schoolmate and former comrade in arms Edwin A. Rich testified that Howard returned home "very

much broken down in health" and that he lived at home for two or three
years afterwards doing little work (Edith Thompson Libby, undated manuscript, Gray Historical Society; Regimental and pension records, Samuel
Howard Foster, National Archives and Maine State Archives).

32. Emma Ann Foster was SJF's nineteen-year-old sister (ibid.).

33. Rev. Charles H. Pearson, "a gentleman who is well known in literary
circles," purchased the *Home Monthly and Mother's Assistant* in 1864.
Proving less than successful, the Boston-based monthly was merged with a
new publication, *Sabbath at Home*, published by the American Tract Society, in 1867. Emily C. Pearson, the publisher's wife, was the author of
Ruth's Sacrifice; or Life on the Rappahannock and *The Poor White; or the
Rebel Conscript* (*HM*, 1864, 217–18, 276; *HM*, 1865, 531).

34. Samuel W. Hopewell, listed as age forty-five in the 1870 census, was
described by one historian as representing "one of the energetic, clever and
industrious colored citizens of Martinsburg." During the war he was con-
scripted into the Eastern Maryland Regiment, but he served only a short
time because of ill health. During his life he worked as a farmhand, caterer,
and barber. "As a tonsorial artist he cannot be surpassed in hair cutting,
shampooing, dying and shaving. He employs two skilled workmen regu-
larly, and has his shop conveniently arranged." His home was located over
his shop in a brick building on the northwest corner of Martin and Spring
streets. He trained his two sons, Henry and John, as barbers. He was steward and trustee of the Mt. Zion Methodist Episcopal Church. He and his
wife Eliza had been the slaves of Belle Boyd, the Confederate spy (F. Vernon Aler, *Aler's History of Martinsburg and Berkeley County, West Virginia* [Hagerstown, Md.: Mail Publishing Company, 1888], 365, 437; *Martinsburg News*, June 22, 1951).

35. This is presumably a reference to the Maine State Seminary at Bates
College, which Brackett, Dudley, and SJF's brother Caleb had attended.

36. Caleb was SJF's twenty-eight-year-old-brother. He attended Maine
State Seminary in 1862 and was later a minister in churches in Parsonsfield
and Otisfield, Maine (Family genealogical record; *Catalogue of the Officers
and Students of the Maine State Seminary* [Lewiston, 1862], 9; Minna J.
Thompson, personal communication).

37. This seems to be a reference to SJF's brother Howard, who had
served in the Union army in the area and was hospitalized at Harpers Ferry
during the war (Pension records of Samuel Howard Foster, Records of the
Veterans Administration, Record Group 15, National Archives).

38. J. H. McKenzie, Freedmen's Bureau agent, wrote from Martinsburg
to his superior, Capt. W. Stover How, on Jan. 31, 1866: "The condition of

the freedmen in this county is fair. they are most all employed at fair wages, most of them have entered into agreements with their employers for this year." And on Feb. 28 McKenzie wrote: "The freedmen all that are able are at work for fair wages, and many at profitable wages. A majority of the citizens are disposed to deal fairly with them and to treat them Kindly" (McKenzie to How, Jan. 31, Feb. 28, 1866, BRFAL, quoted in Stealey, "Reports," 99–100).

39. Shepherdstown had the reputation of being "the most intensely bitter rebel town in Virginia," according to a minister from the North (E. A. Stockman to Bro. Burr, "Notes from the Shenandoah," MS, Feb. 14, 1866). Anna Wright wrote an account of her activities in Shepherdstown: "My school is progressing quite well—75 scholars on the list. The most of them are under twenty years of age; but one calls his age 55. Of course, I find all sorts of scholars—some very diligent, others very delinquent. They were at first very much inclined to fight. One morning I found two boys having so hard a battle that I thought I had better have a hand in it. I gave them both a comfortable whipping, and have had no trouble in that line since. I have one large class who have learned their letters, and read and spell quite well in words of three letters.

"Dr. Andrews, pastor of the Episcopal church, looked in upon my school one morning and offered to give each of the scholars a Bible as soon as they can read it. He has always been a friend to the colored people. The night school numbers 35. No idlers there—It is very pleasant teaching those who so anxious to learn. Sabbath school is well attended—those who are able are ready to assist in teaching others.

"I have a little boy in my school who is a very good reader and is studying mental arithmetic and Geography, who learned his letters from a pocket handkerchief. He is now teaching his father. The father of one of my scholars enlisted in our own army, and his mistress was so enraged that she took his wife and sold her to go South, retaining his girl and her two little brothers. The father has recently returned, but the mother has not been heard from. She was a feeble woman and is no doubt dead. Such is the spirit of slavery, but, thank Heaven, slavery is now no more" (Wright to MS, "Freedmen's Mission," ibid., Feb. 28, 1866).

40. The Morning Star was a Freewill Baptist newspaper published in Dover, New Hampshire. It chronicled the establishment of the Shenandoah Mission with letters from N. C. Brackett and some of the teachers, but SJF's article never appeared (Burgess and Ward, 435).

41. Mr. or Capt. McKenzie was J. H. McKenzie, an assistant superintendent for the Freedmen's Bureau stationed in Martinsburg (Stealey, "Reports," 100).

42. Jacob Brown, one of the twelve Brown siblings, was listed as a barber in the 1870 U.S. Census for Berkeley County, West Virginia, Martinsburg District.

43. Other versions of the events leading up to the arrests of two teen agers on Jan. 25 cast additional light on the incident:

"There was an intention manifested by the rowdy to brake up the freedmens School at this place which is under the charge of Miss Foster, they were encouraged in their proceeding by the disloyal and prejudiced residents of the town. They inturupted (or rather attempted to interuppt the school) four or five different times, one eavening a Revd gentlemen (a white man) was preaching to the freedmen, when a large stone weighing about twenty pounds was thrown against the door it was (the door) carried clean off its hinges I instructed the freedmen (as the only way to catch them) for some of them to run out and nab them in the act, the next time they inturupt the school they done so, and caught two of them boys, boys sixteen, and seventeen, and years of age. I was sent for and I arrested the boys and took them to the Jail. I examined them the next morning at my office, which was crowded by all class of citizens, such an interest being manifested in the case. after confineing the boys twenty four hours in the county jail, I released them upon their parents vouching for their appearance when demanded. The fuss that I have made in this matter I think will prevent any future disturbance" (J. H. McKenzie to Capt. W. Stover How, Jan. 31, 1866, BRFAL, quoted in Stealey, "Reports," 99).

"Our school at Martinsburg has been several times disturbed—the doors smashed and the building clubbed, etc. But the wise management of the superintendent, and the presence of a few soldiers called in from Harper's Ferry, soon restored quiet, but not until two of the leaders were arrested and furnished with comfortable quarters in jail. So the good work goes on in the Shenandoah Valley.—'If God be for us, who shall be against us'" (E. A. Stockman to Bro. Burr, "Notes from the Shenandoah," *MS*, Feb. 14, 1866).

44. From October 1865 to May 1866, Winchester, Va., was the location of central headquarters for the Freedmen's Bureau's Sixth District of Virginia, which included Jefferson and Berkeley counties (Stealey, "Freedmen's Bureau," 102).

45 George Honnett was a "practical watchmaker and jeweler" whose office was located "two doors south of the Everett house" (advertisement *NE*, Jan. 4, 1866).

46. *Theodosia Ernest; or, the Heroine of Faith* (1856) was written by Amos Cooper Dayton.

47. Mrs. Bayles or Bales may have been the woman mentioned by J. H. McKenzie: "Some months ago, a young lady a resident of this city com-

menced a night school for colored children, at three different times, a mob of from thirty to forty men came to her house for the purpose of entimidating her, but her father who is a resolute man drove them off with a double barreled shot gun. I state this fact to show you the spirit of Mobism that exists here, and to demonstrate the necessity of haveing a small detachment of troops here, many of those who have engaged in these acts are discharged union soldiers, who are bolder than rebels dare to be from the fact that they have been in the union army they dont seem to Know that rebellion against law and order makes them rebels" (McKenzie to Capt. W. Stover How, Jan. 31, 1866, BRFAL, quoted in Stealey, "Reports," 100).

48. "Mr. Cowan" was W. L. Coan (American Missionary Association, *Twentieth Annual Report* [New York: American Missionary Association, 1866], 18).

49. Susan Jordan, a cousin, lived in Raymond, Maine, where SJF frequently visited her and helped with chores (Diary, Aug. 30, Sept. 17, 1864).

50. The Vosburghs became one of SJF's chief sources of friendship and support at Martinsburg. Charles D. Vosburgh was born in Buffalo, N.Y. He served as a first sergeant in Co. K, 1st Regiment of the New York Lincoln Cavalry and was discharged in 1864 at Halltown, W.Va., near Harpers Ferry. He was listed as a thirty-four-year-old painter in the 1870 U.S. Census. At the time of his death in 1895 at Big Rapids, Mich., he was a veterinary surgeon. He married Sarah K. Luce in 1857 at Wright, Mich. She was born in 1841 at Bristol, R.I. Their son Franklin, who was age eight in 1870, was born in Michigan. Living in the household with them at Martinsburg was Henry Webster, a twenty-one-year-old painter (Pension file of Charles D. Vosburgh, Records of the Veterans Administration, Record Group 15, National Archives; National Archives, *Population Schedules of the Ninth Census of the United States, 1870*, West Virginia, Berkeley County, Opequon District).

51. J. H. McKenzie blamed "discharged union soldiers," rather than former rebel soldiers (Stealey, "Reports," 100).

52. The *Freedman* was an instructional newspaper published by the American Tract Society (Butchart, 139).

53. Avery, age fourteen, was SJF's youngest brother (Family genealogical record).

54. A Freewill Baptist church was organized under SJF's successor, Anne S. Dudley, in 1868 in a log cabin on Connors Street in Martinsburg. A brick building was built soon after on North Raleigh Street with donations from the children of the Northern Baptist churches of New England. It was described as "the largest and strongest colored church in the Shenandoah

Valley" (Frances Staubly Pine, *History of the First Baptist Church*
[(Martinsburg, W.Va., ca. 1958)], 59; Aler, 364).

55. SJF describes a "shout" in her May 2 letter ("Letter from Virginia,"
ZA, May 23, 1866).

56. These towns are all Maine communities.

57. For Phi Haskell, see Introduction, p. 4.

58. Besides a Freewill Baptist church, the black community also formed
the Mt. Zion Methodist Episcopal Church after the war and erected a
building on West Martin Street. Samuel Hopewell was a steward and
trustee (Aler, 364).

59. The Baltimore and Ohio Railroad.

60. This "better room" for the school was "a stable fixed at a little in a
remote corner of this town" (N. C. Brackett, superintendent's report, April
1866, AMAA).

61. Mr. Snyder may have been James Snyder, a county superintendent
of schools (Evans, 274).

62. *Alone* (1857) was written by Marion Harland.

63. Rev. Lincoln Given of Brunswick, Maine (Freewill Baptist Home
Mission Society, *Thirty-Second Annual Report*, 89).

64. Mrs. M. W. L. Smith of Candia, N.H. (ibid.).

65. Phebe P. Libby of Candia, N.H. (ibid.).

66. Almost 23,000 casualties were reported at the battle of Antietam on
Sept. 17, 1862, near Antietam Creek at Sharpsburg, Md. The Confederate
retreat gave President Abraham Lincoln the occasion to announce the
Emancipation Proclamation (Stephen W. Sears, *Landscape Turned Red:
The Battle of Antietam* [New Haven, 1983], xi, 44–45, 317–18).

67. Hamilton E. Keyes of Front Royal, Va., accompanied SJF and other
teachers back to Maine in June. He attended Maine State Seminary at
Bates College as a student in the "academical" course during the 1866–67
and 1867–68 terms (*Catalogue of the Officers and Students of Maine State
Seminary and Nichols Latin School, Lewiston, Maine, 1866–67* [Lewiston,
1866], 12; ibid. [1867], 13).

68. Rohrbach Bridge, a triple-arched, 125-foot-long bridge crossing
Antietam Creek southeast of Sharpsburg, was nicknamed Burnside Bridge
because of the effort by the Ninth Corps, led by Gen. Ambrose E. Burnside, to capture it (Sears, 183, 260, 267).

69. Bloody Lane was the Sunken Road, which ran from Hagerstown

Turnpike to Boonsboro Turnpike northeast of Sharpsburg. Over the years heavy travel combined with erosion had worn down the road surface until it was several feet below ground level, making it a naturally defensible spot for its rebel defenders. The Yankees prevailed, however, after hours of particularly brutal fighting that produced thousands of casualties (ibid., 183, 236, 246).

70. Lincoln Given had a brother, Rev. Arthur Given, who graduated from Bates College in 1867. Burgess and Ward make no reference to service in the Shenandoah Valley in either of their biographies in the *Free Baptist Cyclopaedia*. However, Lincoln is identified as the Given who came to Virginia by the *Thirty-second Annual Report* of the Freewill Baptist Home Mission Society.

71. Mary Clemmer Ames, novelist and journalist, had just launched her career as Washington correspondent on March 4 with the first installment of a regular column in the New York *Independent*. She had separated the year before from her husband, Daniel Ames, a Methodist minister and federal officeholder at Harpers Ferry, but they were not divorced until 1874 (Maureen Hoffman Beasley, *The First Women Washington Correspondents*, GW Washington Studies, no. 4 [Washington, D.C., 1976], 10–12).

72. Commanded by Brig. Gen. Thomas F. Meagher, the Second Brigade in the Second Corps of the Union army was known as the Irish Brigade. Recruited primarily from New York City's Irish population, three of its regiments went into battle under emerald flags bearing gold shamrocks and harps (Sears, 242).

73. Bvt. Maj. George W. Wells was local superintendent of the Freedmen's Bureau at Harpers Ferry from Jan. 15 to June 1866 (Stealey, "Freedmen's Bureau," 103).

74. Kitty was Miss Anna A. Wright.

75. President Andrew Johnson delivered his veto of the civil rights bill on March 27. The bill was a response to the "black codes" passed in southern states. It forbade discrimination between citizens on grounds of race or color and represented an effort to assert federal jurisdiction over matters that, owing to the looseness of presidential policy, had been allowed to pass to the recently rebellious states. By vetoing it and the Freedmen's Bureau bill, Johnson removed any possibility of compromise with Congress. His veto of the civil rights bill was overcome, and a new version of the Freedmen's Bureau bill was passed over another veto. The Fourteenth Amendment was approved by Congress and sent to the states for ratification in June (Eric L. McKitrick, *Andrew Johnson and Reconstruction* [Chicago, 1964], 11, 12).

76. Binnie was Sabrina L. Gibbs.

77. Tennyson wrote both poems.

78. The National Freedmen's Association was one of the leading organizations sponsoring schools for the freed slaves (Swint, 173).

79. Jennie M. and Emily Stuart of South Hill, N.Y. (Freewill Baptist Home Mission Society, *Thirty-second Annual Report*, 89).

80. Rev. George Barrell Cheever compiled *The American Common-Place Book of Poetry.*

81. The United States Christian Commission was a church-supported organization formed in New York in 1861 to provide comforts and supplies to Union troops not provided by the federal government (*Dictionary of American History* [New York, 1976], s.v. "Christian Commission").

82. The Black Swan was Elizabeth Taylor Greenfield (c. 1824–1876). A former slave, she was the first Afro-American concert singer acclaimed on both sides of the Atlantic. In the 1860s she directed an opera troupe (Eileen Southern, ed., *Biographical Dictionary of Afro-American and African Musicians* [Westport, Conn., 1982], s.v. "Greenfield, Elizabeth Taylor").

83. Nellie, SJF's sister Eliza, was thirteen. Like Eliza and Hannah Elizabeth (Lizzie), Sarah Jane also went by shortened names. She was called Jenny or Jane and is recalled as Aunt Jane by grandnieces who never knew her.

84. U.S. armory buildings.

85. SJF's assessment of hard times in Harpers Ferry was echoed by other observers. For example, on March 31 J. H. McKenzie wrote: "In Jefferson County there are many helpless destitute persons both Freedmen and Refugees. The refugees are principly women and children some of whom are perhaps able to work, but their is no work here for them, nor is their likely to be any. There is but little prospect of their ever being able to provide for themselves so long as they remain in this place. The destitute freed people to whom rations are issued are old and helpless ones, and women who have large families and no husbands. There is a great deal of suffering here among the freedmen for lack of Medical attendence and medicines. There has been considerable suffuring for the want of sufficient clothing, but they have been relieved in a measure by the Rev. Mr. Brackett" (McKenzie to Bvt. Maj. W. S. How, BRFAL, quoted in Stealey, "Reports," 101).

86. New Gloucester, Maine.

87. Both novels are by Rev. Joseph Holt Ingraham (1809–1860), a Portland, Maine, native and Episcopal clergyman.

88. "At Shepherdstown, the colored people have a worthy and influential friend in Rev. Dr. [Charles] Andrews, an episcopal clergyman. The Dr. was formerly a colonizationist, but after Virginia seceded, a rebel. He has preached to the colored people occasionally during the war, and has lately done much to stimulate them to industry and sobriety. He advises them to send their children to school, and if possible to pay their own bills" (N. C. Brackett to the Editor, Jan. 11, 1866, *MS*, Jan. 31, 1866).

89. Emma worked for a milliner in Lisbon Falls (Minna J. Thompson, personal communication).

90. The Fenian movement originated in 1858 among Irish-Americans to aid the Irish Republican Brotherhood in an uprising against Great Britain. In the 1860s Fenians launched unsuccessful invasions of Canada. Four days before SJF's diary entry, an army of 800 Fenians crossed the Niagara River near Buffalo, N.Y., into Ontario. On June 2 they routed Canadian volunteer forces at the battle of Limestone Ridge near Ridgeway and at Fort Erie before surrendering to American authorities as they retreated back into the United States the next day (W. S. Neidhardt, *Fenianism in North America* [University Park, Pa., 1975], 59–75).

91. "We clip the following items from the Shepherdstown *Register*, of the 24th inst.: . . . The Rev. J. M. Green, the minister sent by the Baltimore Conference to take possession of the church and other property here, has arrived, but the minister in charge, Rev. Mr. Kreglo, and members, refuse to give it up, and we presume the matter will finally be settled by the Courts. Rev. Mr. Green preached on this circuit about 18 years ago, and has latterly been connected with the Freedmen's Bureau" (*NE*, March 29, 1866).

92. SJF's brother Samuel Howard was a member of the 30th Maine Regiment, which fought in Louisiana and then in the Shenandoah Valley toward the end of the war.

93. Lining out referred to the practice of having a church official recite a line of a hymn or psalm which was then repeated by the congregation. Introduced from England to New England, it was common practice around 1750. It came into existence where many of the congregation were unable to read and where books were limited. The practice was abandoned by most religious bodies by the mid-nineteenth century, "with only isolated vestiges of it remaining" (James Robert Davidson, *A Dictionary of Protestant Church Music* [Metuchen, N.J., 1975], 193).

94. Anne Dudley described her school in a letter of June 2 to the *Morning Star:* "Our school here is prospering finely. No lack of interest. The scholars are progressing well, and do not get tired of going to school At first it seemed dark here. I came only because I thought it was my duty, for I had

expected to remain at Charlestown, but the clouds have passed away and all is bright now" ("Freedman's Mission," *MS*, July 1, 1866).

95. Charles James Faulkner (1806–1884) was a prominent lawyer who served as a congressman, diplomat, and Confederate soldier. His home, Boydville, is located on South Queen Street in Martinsburg (*DAB*, s.v. "Faulkner, Charles James").

96. Webster and Lisbon, Maine.

MAINE, 1866

Diary, 1866

Sunday, July 1

I was comfortable till nearly noon but now I am seasick. The boat rolls terribly—not laden good the captain says. I'm tired and feel wretchedly.

Monday, July 2

At home. When I got in I found myself quite weak and so wanted to get home but thought I could not. Geo. Cobb came down to get Fred's clothes. I did not know before that he was on the boat. I told Geo. that I was going up there but I am not there because at the Stage office I saw Kimball and found out that I could come right out.[1] So I left a note for Mrs. C. and came on. I feel better than I did. We had a general parting time in the boat. Miss Gibbs fairly scared Laura by kissing her. We went to each that we had to leave and shook hands with them and bade them a kind goodbye. The blacks are much pleased at the differences as they get up North. Mrs. Fogg, Mrs. Hutchinson and several others have been in. Mrs. Doughty and a lady visitor of hers were on the stage with me.

Tuesday, July 3

A warm day. Here I have felt the heat from the sandy nature of the soil as much or more than at the Lockwood House. I've done some washing and have written to Emma and Lizzie, John and Mary Brown, Mrs. Vosburgh and Mrs. Webster. I must not be selfish now that I have got home. I said a few words about what John Brown and I have been talking about. It seemed to be best. Now I have dropped the matter. I can but feel that I have done right. I've made no calls today. Meant to this afternoon but delayed too long. I feel somewhat tired and nervous. People think that the boys will act badly tonight, as they will be angry at not having a chance to ring the bell. Mary Small is near her end, and Father and Howard have unyoked the bell. They are going to watch tonight.[2]

Wednesday, July 4

A very warm day. Mother, Father, Avery and Nellie went over to the picnic. I staid at home in hopes that Lizzie would come and she did at noon. I had a good chat with her and told her all about my mental and social experiences in the South. She has full sympathy with me and I am glad that I told her. All had a good time at picnic. Tonight an awful fire has been raging for some hours in Portland. Oh how I hope that it will not burn out my friends.[3] I'm glad that I did not stay in Portland till today. I had not thought of it but Mother thought I might. I feel nervous tonight. I shall soon get rested though. Lizzie will know now how I feel about my work. She says I may apply for her. I want to have her there. Mr. Bean has been in.[4] We have called on Mr. Patrick Doughty's folks.

Thursday, July 5

The fire is subdued at last but more than half of Portland is gone. Father is down to see how it looks. It has made us nervous all day. I have been talking to Lizzie and ripping up my brown dress for work. After noon we called at Mrs. Bean's, Mrs. Hutchinson's and Mrs. Doughty's. Tonight Lizzie went back to her school. I think that she is having a good time in her school. She says that she would like to go out South. I hope she will. I do wish that Father would come and tell us how the fire is. I am very sleepy and must now to bed. I wonder if my letters were burned. I hope not.

Friday, July 6

Father came home last night at ten. This morning he could not speak of the fire without tears. I've written a report for Elder Curtis and letters to Caleb and Howard.

We had a good meeting at the Congl. church this afternoon. Mr. Bean wants me to tell the people about the schools Sunday. I've said I would do so.

Saturday, July 7

A very warm day. I have seemed to feel the heat about as much here as I have anywhere. I have been sewing all day nearly. I wrote none at all today. I've read some to Father. This afternoon Mother and I went up to the F. W. B. Conference. I felt constrained though I was cordially welcomed. The people do not feel that lively interest in my late work that they do at the other house. They do not seem to view it as a special work of the F. W. Baptists as I am sure that they ought. Still, for the good of the cause, I must go there a part of the time. I do not know as the church here will help at all at any rate. I got no mail today. Howard got a letter from Hannah Adams with whom he has corresponded some time. She is in Lowell, so the mail is all right. I must wait a while.

Sunday, July 8

Still very warm. I went to meeting at the Lower House forenoon and afternoon and also to Sabbath School. After the afternoon service I took Marion Higgins's place—she being ill—and rode with Mr. Bean to a school house a mile or so from here to assist in a Sabbath School. We had to hurry home on account of a shower, and made out to get about the whole of it. Then we went down to the five o'clock meeting and I was called on to give some account of my labors out in [   ]. I enjoyed telling only I had not time to half tell what one ought to name. I feel glad that I did as well as I did though. I think that I shall get papers at least for the Martinsburg Sunday School. At the Ferry I do not know who to address them to.

Monday, July 9

Caleb is at home tonight. I started after we had got through washing and met him before I got near up to Uncle Shadrach's.[5] So I turned and come back. He is quite tired. He has begun to do his appropriate work. He has preached several times in Lisbon and in Webster.

We have had some good talk together. I am proud of my brothers and sisters, and we all live harmoniously too.

Tuesday, July 10

At Uncle Shadrach's tonight. Lizzie and [   ] are at home. The folks are better than they were last Summer here.

I have been thinking that I have a very pleasant home. And these fine people here are all my relatives. Yet I like my own home best.

The people here have no prejudice against color. I have their full sympathy.

Wednesday, July 11

At Uncle John's tonight.[6] Uncle John and Aunt Mary are both feeble—very. They can hardly last long either of them. Abbie is but little if any lower than she was last summer. I've been reading the life of Toussaint L'Ouverture and looking over "Uncle Tom's Cabin." It seems very interesting to me now. They think that Adam Howard's picture looks like Erskine Ford. I do now that they mention it. I have been feeling better than a few days since I got over my sickness. I have nothing to *do* with me. I must plan more than I have yet to make my money last, and so I now am idle. I shall get up a lot the work to do soon of some kind.

Thursday, July 12

At Uncle Shadrach's tonight. Lizzie was over to spend the afternoon with us and I have returned with her. It has been a very warm day. I feel to rejoice that so many sympathize in my work. What good people all there are up this way. I got a letter yesterday from Lizzie sent up from home. She will be at Susan's this next Saturday and wants me to meet her there. Caleb was up this way day before yesterday. I did not meet him though. I must go home early tomorrow morning. I hope I shall get a letter or two from Martinsburg very soon. I shall fear that my pictures were lost in the fire if I do not. I want them all very soon. I have got the best ones, but I want the others also.

Friday, July 13

At Aunt Jordan's.[7] It is a warm day. Lizzie is here too. I came from Uncle Shadrach's this morning. I got a ride a part of the way with Mrs. Leonard Cummings. Then I started up here. Providence favored me and I got a ride to the foot of Sabbath Day Pond with a man named Goss, formerly the chaplain of Mt. Pleasant Hospital near Washington. He was good company. He got dinner and we rested an hour or two at a Mr. Cobb's just beyond Dry Pond. I walked from where he left me to here. Lizzie got here just before dusk. We had a pleasant evening. Susan is very glad to see us. She is not disposed to find fault with my favorite pictures as I feared she might be. I should not like that ever in her.

Saturday, July 14

Well, Lizzie has gone back to her school.[8] I walked quite a piece of the way out to where I landed yesterday with her. She was then to take the stage for her place of duty. I have enjoyed the day very much. I do feel to hope that if I go back South Lizzie may go with me. She will do me good and, though not half so good as she is, I hope I may benefit her. She is getting on well. I wish I knew if I had any mail at Gray now. I sent yesterday 50 papers to John Brown that came from Mary Stevens. It is yet very warm. I miss the pet lambs that Susan had last Winter. They are killed and two little ones now supply their places—in part, but not quite for me.

Sunday, July 15

A long, warm day. We have read, talked and thought it away though. Sidney and Mary, brother and sister of Susan's girl, Lottie Bennett, have been here and have taken her away home to make a short visit while I am here. Mrs. Wardsworth Merrill has been in. I could hardly hold my temper at her remarks about the "niggers." She seemed to have but little human sympathy for the blacks—save the modified, very light specimens. I thank God that I have a broader interest in humanity. God forgive me that I ever lacked it at all. Now I shall do all that I can henceforth to help the colored people rise. Susan is good enough to get over prejudice, I am sure.

Monday, July 16

Still very warm, but a slight shower has cooled the air so that we can sleep I hope. I've helped Susan a little today as she has washed. I feel better to do something. For the rest I have read and we have talked. I've been reading the Second volume of a book called "Herman or Young Knighthood." I only wish I had it all. It is a book of those times, good and up to the mark. I feel a hope to be able soon to write at least a Magazine story that shall do some good by unmasking brutality and selfishness in contrast to pure self devotion. I have

not the proper time or chance now. I must not let all this training go
for nothing though. I must reap its benefits in a harvest of new
capabilities.

Tuesday, July 17

Very warm. I have been reading some old school books and various
small volumes. I wrote to Emma today. I then went up to the office.
I dallied along picking flowers and raspberries and *lost* a paper and
letter. Dr. Shattuck has been here. Caleb is here now. He has been
up to Poland to see Lizzie. When she left here she did not go right
to Poland as she intended but she staid at the Pond the next day
with Miss Abbie Grant teacher there. She scraped acquaintance on
the strength of knowing a sister in Lisbon.

Caleb is very tired. He has decided to leave an appointment to
preach here Sunday forenoon. I am glad for him that he has found
and chosen his work.

Wednesday, July 18

Lizzie's birthday. It has been dull and partially rainy all day. Susan
has been over after Lottie. Caleb left with her and made an appointment at the Pond at two o'clock Sunday. Now he'll have a chance to
feel justified in resting at home.

I've done all that I could to lighten Susan's tasks when she got
home. She has had a very pleasant day. She consulted Dr. Sturgis at
New Gloucester to see if he agreed with Dr. Shattuck. He did and
now she feels sure that Dr. Anderson has been mistaken in her
case.[9] She has dropped him at last. Thus all his old friends go. Well
thus may we see the downfall of pride and arrogance. He has been a
tyrant in his sphere, and raves now at its restriction.

Thursday, July 19

Quite cool this morning. I looked over old books and talked to pass
away the forenoon. Since dinner Susan and I have been up the road
as far as the store and have made calls at Jonas Morrell's, Wardsworth
Merrill's, Sewell Brown's, Isaac Adams's, Stephen Thurlow's, and
Edward Files's. I am glad that I do not have to make it my home in
this neighborhood. Six duller calls it was never my lot to make. The

people are all mere domestic drudges. Here is the only place where
I would be willing to stay. Here there is an atmosphere of something
more than work. In this neighborhood there will be four or five hundred yards of cloth made this Fall. I wish I had one of the nice
Balmorals.

Friday, July 20

Still rather cool, and so much more comfortable than the early part
of the week.

Since dinner Susan and I have called at Bella Leathem's, Geo.
Morrell's, John Smith's and John Spiller's. We had a better spell of it
than we had yesterday. Mrs. Spiller showed me the finest homemade Balmoral that I ever saw. I would not sell it for ten dollars if I
had it. I wonder if I should be willing to be such a slave to work as
those people all are. No I feel that I shall not. I could not marry for
such a destiny. It can not be a duty. Yet all praise women who toil
every moment and never spend an hour in self cultivation. I will
never be such a drudge, however. Very likely I shall never marry at
all. Certainly not now nor very soon.

Saturday, July 21

I am at Mr. John Elwell's in South Poland.[10] I started and walked
over here this forenoon. I have spent the afternoon in Lizzie's school.
She has a small school, and rather backward, but yet good to manage.
She boards around but Mr. Elwell's is a sort of home for her. With her
and Mrs. E. I have been to the famous Poland Mineral Spring. It is a
sort of gaseous water—very sweet and pure—impregnated with
soda I should think rather than with any mineral.

Lizzie and I have been having a good social time tonight. How
strangely we all seem to get acquainted with the friends of each
other. I want to have Lizzie know some of my Martinsburg friends
and believe that some time she will.

Sunday, July 22

A dull, overcast day, but Lizzie and I walked out to the school house
on White Oak Hill at least two miles and a half each way. Eld.
Austin preached two good sermons. He could hardly tell Lizzie and

I apart and did not know that I had been away when he found out who I was.

I suppose that Caleb has preached twice today. I'd like to hear him. Tonight Lizzie and Mrs. Elwell had a little S. School here at the house. They seemed all to enjoy it. This has been a pleasant day to me. I am very glad to have made the acquaintance of Mrs. Elwell and her husband but then I have found as good friends far away when I needed them more than Lizzie did there.

Monday, July 23

As blue at heart as this ink tonight. I have just got a letter from Mr. Curtis to tell me that my commission will not be renewed this year. It is all because I had trouble in the Martinsburg school with the white outsiders. I can't blame myself. For better cheer I also heard from Emma—a good letter, and from David Artemous and dear Mrs. Vosburgh. John Brown has gone away and is at Bath working. Mrs. Webster and Mrs. Vosburgh with Mary Brown and others take charge of the school. I came down home this morning in Kimball's stage. I found a letter from Geo. Christie awaiting me. I've sent a reply to that and have written to Emma to meet us in Lewiston Wednesday. I wrote that before I got here. I mean to stop in New Gloucester, when we come back from Lewiston.

Tuesday, July 24

Howard has been fretting today about going off to work. I've paid him the money that I owed him—twenty-five dollars, for Mr. Curtis sent me some money. This forenoon I helped mother about house and wrote replies to nearly all my mail. Shall hope to see Emma so did not write to her. Since dinner I have written to Mrs. Webster to send in Mrs. Vosburgh's letter. I hope they'll not forget me. I love them certainly. I feel some calmer. I have decided to be frank and tell everyone just how I am circumstanced for I do not feel to blame, and no one can say ought that is against me save that I am a little unpolished and no toady. I do not quite like to think of not going back but hope to be able to see that it is all for the best by and by as I doubt not that it is.

Wednesday, July 25

At New Gloucester and rather tired tonight. Mother, Caleb and I have been over to Lewiston. We had a pretty good time. I saw none of our Mission party to speak to but Mr. Brackett and only had a bow at a distance then. I fancy he did not care to encounter me there for fear I should say something. The exercises were good. Emma was there. We walked about town considerable. I also met some of her Lisbon friends. We did not have time to stop for the after dinner speeches. Emma wanted to get a return ticket from President Cheney so we went up to the chapel.[11] I saw Keyes, Miss Dudley. Miss Gibbs and Miss Russell were inside but I felt fretted and did not try to see them. I was cross at Caleb too. He *is* fussy but I was fretted. Here I found them glad to see me. I am at Jos. Coombs's. I've met Abbie, her mother, Delia Haskell and Mrs. Angelia Whitman here tonight. Mrs. Abbie Coombs is soon going to the Water Cure for a month. I am sure I would not like that at Waterford.[12]

Thursday, July 26

I have been lounging all day reading and talking. Tonight with Mrs. Combs I have been up to the corner. We called on Miss Helen Crockett who is teaching here. She is going out South.[13] I had a good long talk with her.

Since I have made up my mind to talk freely about my dismission I feel better than I did. While Mrs. Coombs was calling elsewhere I called on Mrs. Mosely. Helen was not at home but I had a pleasant call.[14] I've bought me some cloth to make some drawers and now I shall have some work.

I felt more than of late to make special prayers. Oh may I be enabled to hold a correspondence that will keep me advised of the answers to these petitions. I long for the rest of the pictures that I am to have. They will keep my heart on my far off friends.

Friday, July 27

I've been sewing today and have had quite a pleasant day. We invited Miss Crockett here to tea but she could not come. She had to prepare for a picnic tomorrow and her school closed today. She is

positive enough to dare Southerners and with her Melodian and
ability to dress may pass for lady enough to do well. She'll be independent though.

Delia Haskell was here to tea. She graduated at the Edward Little
Institute at Auburn last week.[15] Ah well such privileges are not for
me and I must do as well as I can without them. I am going to begin
regular writing again directly. I must soon take up something. Oh
My Father help me and soon prove to me that all clouds are for the
best. I begin to dare to believe it. I have not lost the wonderful
friends in human nature that I gained last winter.

Saturday, July 28

This forenoon I helped Mrs. Coombs a little and at noon Mrs. Joseph
Cross called for me to go over to the school picnic on the back road.
We went over. I staid an hour or so and had a good time. I met Miss
Crockett's father. I had a good talk with him. After coming back
Mrs. Coombs and I went over to John Haskell's. We had a very
pleasant visit to Mrs. Haskell and Delia. We had a splendid shower
in the course of the time.

Gerty is a good observing child, rather backward and I fear going
to be dwarfish in size but I love the darling. Here too her aunt and
cousins all seem to love her dearly. Well I find friends to love but
shall I ever have a home? I'm further off seemingly than ever, for I
can never lightly throw myself away. I am sleepy now and may as
well rest. I begin to plan about writing now.

Sunday, July 29

Mrs. Coombs is not at all well. With Grandma Coombs I have been
up to church. Mr. Cross preached two good sermons. At noon
Jennie Haskell invited me into their Bible class. The teacher being
absent Mr. Cross officiated. He and I had some talk. He seems to be
a very fine man. This afternoon I have been reading "Livingstone's
African Explorations." I have been very much interested in it. I have
been thinking that I would like to be a Missionary in Africa or some
such place. Well perhaps I may do as much good in some other way.
God can lead me aright. I can only wait and pray. I trust that He
knows best what is good for me and will allow me to be the most
useful.

Monday, July 30

Mrs. Coombs still being far from well, I have washed and have cleaned the floors and passages for her. Tonight Delia called in at Mrs. C.'s and at her invitation I've come over with her. We dropped in a minute at Mrs. Marilla Haskell's as Mrs. Betsy being there. I had a few minutes talk about my schools with the folks and, having my pictures with me, I showed them. Mrs. H., though a professed Republican, gave a gratuitous exhibition of a little caste prejudice. Well it did not offend me as I've got used to expecting it. I will not be driven from right by ridicule. I *know* that Negroes are not disposed to be over forward. I will not then pretend to think that they are.

Tuesday, July 31

Back again at Mrs. Jos. Coombs and, for a wonder, having a headache. I have been reading and sewing. I have been reading some of Delia's exquisite manuscript poetry that she has written of late. She is a real poetess. I can but admire her, and yet she is girlish and unaffected and does not half know her worth. I needed this spur to make me start up. I *must* certainly begin writing again. I must polish up and find a publisher for my last year's work. Oh for the money to send it forth myself. But it must go somehow. It is not worthless I know. Will read it over to Lizzie next week and see how it seems. I now need to begin new work. I see that I was in part dropping that aim and it may be that that after all is my life work. I have certainly been blessed in it. Well God still will lead me on.

Wednesday, August 1

At Mrs. Thos. Coombs's tonight. I find Abbie senior in the thick of preparation to go this month to Waterford to Dr. Shattuck's Water Cure. I somehow do not just like this doctor who has been here today.

Abbie's general health is better than it used to be; but I fear that her knee is not to be cured—cannot see that it is much if any better. I've been reading, chatting, and sewing. I do not feel as if this idling around agreed with me. I need to be set at steady work. I must write and improve my time. The Advocate is not suspended and I

must write them a line soon. I shall need to keep before the public
in some way. I've begun to think of a piece that I can write soon. Oh
Father help me to do right. A very interesting deaf mute—Mrs.
Saml. Rowe and her niece have been in here just now.

Thursday, August 2

Last night it rained hard, and it has rained nearly all day. This afternoon I have finished my sewing work. Delia has been over here this
afternoon. Tonight her father and mother have been here. I still feel
not quite as energetic as I could wish. I have seen Mr. Cobb on his
train tonight by going out to the station. He looked very glad to see
me. Have not seen him before since I got home. Abbie will get too
tired to rest in a month in getting ready to spend her month away.
She is too particular for an invalid. She is not able to sew much and
does a great deal that is unnecessary or that I should think was so.
I wish that I could peep at my home mail tonight but if there is none
I should feel soberer than I do now. I've been thinking so much of
Mary Brown that I've seen her in my mind's eye. I wish *she* and
[   ] would come to Portland ere long.

Friday, August 3

Tonight finds me at Mrs. Moseley's. I left Abbie's just after dinner
and calling a short while at Inez's by the way I came right over here.
I found Mrs. Moseley, Helen, Henry and a niece who was there a
part of the time while they were sick. Mr. and Mrs. Cross have been
out to tea. I have merely seen Mrs. Cross a few minutes. With
Helen and her cousin Lizzie I have been down in an old orchard
after apples. Somehow I yet feel singularly indolent. As usual I've
had a pleasant time here. I bought me some more sewing work but
have not yet put scissors to the cloth. I've had to tell yarns all the
while I've been here. I usually do for Helen's amusement when
here. I am rejoiced to see Helen able to walk with neither crutch
nor cane. She merely limps a little. I think that she is a lovely girl
and very patient in all that tries or has tried her. I love her very
much and always shall.

Saturday, August 4

A dull day for me. I came down to Mrs. Coombs's early but have felt
ill all day. I do hope that I shall not be sick. I've been able to sew

and to write some this afternoon. I must not allow my sadness to affect my nervous system. I do believe that it has. I shall have to nerve myself up. Mrs. Peter Haskell has been in to get me to agree to come there for next month. I promised but do not feel as if I should be good for much today.

From Our West Virginia Correspondent

New Gloucester, Aug. 4th, 1866 [Aug. 22]

Dear Advocate:—I ought to apologize for not having said a word since getting home. But your sad experience in the flames deterred me for a time, and then, since getting home, I seem to have felt a great lack of my usual strength and energy. It seems as if my nervous system had been revenging itself for the discipline of the past seven or eight months. I am not ill, but not yet my indefatigable self. I have decided not to return for the next season. Yet I thank God that I was ever led to go out in that great and glorious work. Not for any earthly consideration would I have missed the experience that I have had. Whether I have done any permanent good or not, the great day of reckoning alone can reveal, but I have benefitted myself mentally and morally, if I have not others, and thankful letters from colored friends prove at least their gratitude and affection.

When we came on we brought five colored people from Harper's Ferry with us. At New York we met three teachers from Hampton, Eastern Virginia, and a young colored man with them. At New York Miss Wright left us to go by rail thence to Montpelier, but, with the additions above named we numbered when we took the boat for home, July 31st, eleven white and six colored people. Our colored delegation comprised all shades of color from perfect black to pale yellow, and seemed well selected for intelligence and agreeability. We passed our Sabbath on the water. At evening Mr. Brackett got our colored friends to sing. I was prostrate in my stateroom from sea-sickness, but daresay that the listeners enjoyed it well. One of the number from my own school came up from New Orleans with the Nineteenth Corps, and can speak both French and English, the latter acquired since his coming to West Virginia. As a scholar he was very good indeed. A letter received since his settlement on a farm in Wells proves him well satisfied with New England. He writes, "I study all I can, and go to meeting every Sunday." He is a full black of seventeen, and will prove to all that meet him that his color does not make him either stupid or lazy.[16]

I have heard from the Sabbath school at Martinsburg through Mrs. Vosburgh. At the date of her letter it was in her charge, John Brown being away at work. With the aid of a neighbor always friendly to the school, and those colored people able to help, she succeeds in keeping things in working order. She wrote an urgent request that I would forward Sabbath school papers if I could get any. One Sabbath they had been destitute of papers, though Miss Dudley had sent some, and I had forwarded fifty. They now need about three hundred a month, as so many are now able to read who have learned since our schools began. I was sorry to hear that there was an apparent diminution of interest in the meetings. They doubtless miss Miss Dudley, who has more of a missionary spirit than any other teacher I ever met. I will not encroach more at this time upon your space. Whatever of interest my letters from Southern friends may contain I will impart to your readers: as I doubt not many will be glad to hear that they are doing as well, as I hope and expect in the places where we have been striving to sow good seed.

Papers, if sent, may be addressed to Mrs. Chas. D. Vosburgh, Martinsburg, West Virginia, to which address none need fear sending too large a supply. It matters not if the dates are old if the papers are not worn out.

Sarah J. Foster

Notes

1. Instead of going to the Cobbs in Portland she went directly to her home in Gray on Kimball's stage.

2. SJF's father was sexton of the Congregational and Freewill Baptist churches. Since the latter had no bell, this is most likely a reference to the Congregational Church (Edith Gray Thompson, undated manuscript, Gray Historical Society).

3. The fire raged for fifteen hours, destroying 1,500 buildings and leaving 10,000 people homeless. The office of *Zion's Advocate* was burned. For several weeks afterwards it was printed at the office of the *Oxford Democrat* in Paris, Maine (John Neal, *Account of the Great Conflagration in Portland* [Portland, Maine: Starbird and Twitchell, 1866], 8; Burrage, 255–66).

4. Rev. Ebenezer Bean was pastor of the Congregational Church of Gray (Hill, 301).

5. Shadrach Humphrey was a sixty-eight-year-old farmer living in Gray in 1870. His family included his wife, Betsy, sixty-three, and children, Delphina, twenty-seven, and Shadrach, twenty-five (Minna Thompson, personal communication; National Archives, *Population Schedules of the Ninth Census of the United States, 1870*, Maine, vol. 3, Cumberland County).

6. John Humphrey was an eighty-year-old farmer living in Gray in 1870. Abbie Humphrey, thirty-eight, a name that appears occasionally in the Foster diaries, lived with him (National Archives, *Population Schedules of the Ninth Census of the United States, 1870*, Maine, vol. 3, Cumberland County).

7. Aunt Rachel Jordan was a ninety-three-year-old "invalid" living with Susan Jordan in 1870 in Raymond, Maine. Susan's occupation was "keeping house" (SJF, Diary, 1864; National Archives, *Population Schedules of the Ninth Census of the United States, 1870*, Maine, vol. 4, Cumberland County).

8. In Poland, Maine.

9. Dr. Abraham W. Anderson's office was located two houses away from the Fosters on Church Street. Dr. J. I. Sturgis occupied an adjoining building. Anderson's home was located across the street. Anderson "was highly regarded and his practice, which he continued until his death in 1876, extended from Yarmouth to Bridgton" (Hill, 104, 299).

10. John Elwell was listed as a fifty-three-year-old farmer in 1870. He lived with Margaret, forty-one, and Ida, thirteen (National Archives, *Population Schedules of the Ninth Census of the United States, 1870*, Maine, vol. 1, Androscoggin County).

11. July 25, 1866, was the "Ninth Anniversary at Bates College, Maine State Seminary, and Latin School" according to a schedule of events by that title published by the Lewiston *Evening Journal*. Oren B. Cheney was the president of the college.

12. The Coombs family included Thomas T., a shoemaker, and his wife, Abbie B. Their children were Abbie R. and George W. They were living in New Gloucester in 1860. Tom was thirty-two and Abbie twenty-nine in that year. SJF wrote letters to Abbie's brother, Clifton Jones, in 1864 and conducted a brief flirtation with him when he returned from the U.S. Army. Around that time, she named a book-length manuscript, now missing, "Clifton." Joseph L. Coombs, forty-seven, and Lucy H., forty-two, and their daughter Gertie, eight, lived in New Gloucester in 1870, along with seventy-nine-year-old Shuah Coombs. In 1860 Delia Haskell was the sixteen-year-old daughter of John, forty-six, and Betsy Haskell, forty-two. They were living in New Gloucester and John was a farmer. Delia had three brothers, George, John, and William (Diaries for 1864 and 1866; National

Archives, *Population Schedules . . . of the United States, 1860* and *1870*, Maine, vols. 3 and 4, Cumberland County).

13. Helen Crockett of Portland, Maine, worked in the Shenandoah Valley supported by the Freewill Baptists in 1866–67 (American Missionary Association, *Twenty-first Annual Report* [New York, 1867], 23; Swint, 181).

14. Helen A. Moseley was twenty-one and living in New Gloucester in 1870 with Sophia, fifty-two, and Frank H., eighteen (National Archives, *Population Schedules of the Ninth Census of the United States, 1870,* Maine, vol. 3, Cumberland County).

15. Edward Little Institute became Auburn's public high school in 1874 (Auburn Centennial History Committee, *Auburn, 1869–1969, 100 Years a City* [Lewiston, Maine, 1968], 243).

16. David Artemous.

SOUTH CAROLINA, 1867–68

Letter from the South

Charleston, S.C., Oct. 26th, 1867. [Nov. 6]

Dear Advocate:—I arrived here several days since. I had a pleasant trip, and only had one day of sea-sickness, which was to be expected when we rounded Cape Hatteras. I had seven traveling companions as far as here. The next day after our arrival they took the Beaufort Steamer, being destined for points farther down. My own destination is a plantation about three miles from here. It is not thought best for me to go out there just yet, and I expect to assist in one of the departments of Mr. Cardozo's school here for a few days until another teacher arrives.[1] I visited his school yesterday. It is nicely graded, and contains four hundred pupils. They occupy the upper story of what is here known as Military Hall.[2] The lower story is occupied by as large a school, under the auspices of the National Freedman's Association. When I arrived at the Hall, the eight hundred were at recess. It was interesting to watch them march in and out. Seeing them I was moved even to tears at the thought of the long years of injustice which we are trying to blot out. We have a very pleasant home here. Five teachers are here at present, and one more is to come, besides a clergyman.

The farm where I am to go is owned by Father Haynes, a colored man, who has built a chapel for the people out there.[3] I shall remain there all except Saturdays. I look forward to a period of independent enjoyment. When I get started I will write again. I like Mr. and Mrs. Cardozo very much and their little one has crept into a warm corner of my heart, as the representation of a dear child now in heaven.[4] Should any kind friend wish to address me, write to Box 175, Charleston, S.C.[5] In haste   Yours.

Sarah J. Foster

Letter from the South

Charleston Neck, Nov. 22d, 1867. [Dec. 4]

Dear Advocate:—I opened my school out here[6] on the 7th of this month, with thirty-seven pupils. The number is now upwards of

fifty and still they come.[7] I opened night school Nov. 11th, and now
have over twenty, to all of whom I give personal attention. As most
are farm hands, and can come only at a late hour of gathering, I
never get out before ten, and am sometimes even later. One young
man, nearly or quite black, named James Gadson, reads well in the
Third Reader, and is to get a Fourth. He spells excellently, writes
a good hand, studies Geography, and has commenced Grammar.
Seven of that family come to school—four in the day, and three
at night.

I lodge in the house of Father Haynes, the colored proprietor of
the farm. He and his wife are excellent people. I have no white
neighbors at all. But I am within a rod or two of the little chapel
where I preach, and I like it much. Out here nearly all the pupils
are black, or near it. I have but two or three yellow ones, but they
are as a whole good and smart.[8] We have a nice little Sabbath school,
in which I am aided by a white man from town, who often preaches
to the people here too. We need papers, but I can only get my mail
once a week, and should hardly care to bother Mr. Cardozo with the
constant receipt of such bundles of papers in his box as used to come
to me in Virginia.

A better superintendent than Mr. Cardozo need not be looked
for. He himself is of partial colored extraction, and is by birth a
Charlestonian, but he was educated in Scotland mostly. We all like
him very much.

But I will not weary you. I cannot picture by words this place,
bordered with trees, fringed with long grey atmospheric moss, but
can only assure you that it is very pretty and pleasant. Two bouquets
of roses on my table as I write attest that I am in the far South, but I
already feel somewhat at home.

                                        Yours in haste,
                                        Sarah J. Foster

Letter from South Carolina

Charleston Neck, Dec. 14th, 1867. [Jan. 1, 1868]

Dear Advocate:—Although I am in the South, I was of the opinion
that winter came on the day which was appointed for its arrival. December 1st was a very cold day, but in a day or two the weather was
suggestive of June, and the school vases are but rarely empty of
roses. Now they are also enlivened by green sprays thickly set with
beautiful scarlet "Christmas berries." My school stove was only set

up yesterday, but I had needed it before.[9] It may sound oddly to you to hear of going out of doors to get warm in December, but it is a common thing here. When the man came to set up the stove, it was in the heart of a "cold snap," and I had succumbed to the cold within, and had adjourned my school to a sunny spot in the yard. There the boys had built a small fire of dry wood and corn husks to heat their feet, and I was hearing their lessons as well as I could for the puffs of smoke which half blinded us at times. But we are all right now. Our stove is up, and last night it did good service in the evening school. I have sixty-two day-scholars now, and twenty-eight at night. My daily average this month is fifty-one and at night about twenty are usually present. A class of seven who began the Alphabet the evening of Nov. 11th, and have only had three lessons a week since, now read well in three lettered words. One day-scholar reads without spelling the words, who began with the Alphabet Nov. 3d. One boy, whose defective eyesight only enables him to see about four inches off, and half a line of his reader at a time, has plodded on to the Third Reader, and now gets both Arithmetic and Geography lessons with the book at the end of his nose, and moved from side to side as he follows the lines. Is not that equal to any white person's application?

But I must now go back to Thanksgiving day. The folks in town sent for me, and I went in just in time to attend the morning service at the colored Congregational church—or rather with the church that worships in Military Hall. The pastor—a Rev. Mr. Jackson from Martha's Vineyard[10]—now a member of Mr. Cardozo's family, preached a most excellent sermon from Isaiah sixty-second, tenth verse. At its close he merely suggested that as a Thanksgiving offering, each should give all that was possible toward raising a fund to buy a lot, and begin a church which they need much. The church has been organized about ten months, and it has now two hundred members. I expected a dragging, tardy, insignificant subscription, but to my surprise the people came forward as fast as three could take their names, and in twenty minutes or less four hundred and twenty dollars was raised. Are these the low people who in freedom were to relapse into barbarism? Things do not look like it here.[11]

Then we hear a great deal of cant about "negro domination" and "negro insolence," but I am bold to say that I am very pleasantly situated on a black man's farm, with no white neighbors, and rarely seeing a white face, and I was never better treated.

I have a nice Sabbath school, although they have neither books nor papers to make it interesting. I do wish that the best library books were issued in a form which would bring them into the places where they are most needed, and I am not the only one who has felt the need of a better provision for poor and mission schools. Just now we would hail with delight a box of Sabbath school books, even if they were old and worn. I think that the donors would feel paid could they see them received, for these excitable, emotional children of nature will turn summersaults out of the school yard, thanking the Lord that they have "got out of a,b,c's," when I promote them to my first primer class, and you can fancy how they would receive a box of books. It is pleasant work to teach them, and I feel repaid day by day. I get but little spare time, for I attend two meetings a week, and expect now to open a third—a scholar's prayer-meeting, and I teach three nights weekly, and my school holds till half past ten each night, yet I feel well, and I look well I am told.

The Gadson family of whom I spoke, now send one more, making eight in all, and the family baby drops in on bright days besides. They yet work for their former owner—Mr. G. being head man on the place, and the father and sons fish, get oysters, and do some planting in odd hours besides their work, yet people tell us that "negroes won't work." However, these Gadson's are black, and I do not find them exceptions to the general rule of conduct, except that they have had and still have a better education than common. But now I will close as it grows dark.

Sarah J. Foster

Letter from the South

Charleston Neck, Jan. 9th, 1868. [Jan. 22]

Dear Advocate:—Although I have not seen your welcome sheet for several weeks, I will not forget to wish you a "Happy New Year." I suppose that you have had a long spell of cold weather ere this, while I yet feel as if winter had not begun. True, we have had some cold days, but a week of June-like weather has made atonement for that, and I cannot realize that it is winter while the roses and japonicas that daily adorn my school vases are so lavishly provided. It is growing cold again now, but yet it is not such cold as you have up there. My school is gaining a little now, and the average attendance is excellent. With a list of sixty-one last month, I had an average attendance of fifty, and they have begun as well this month.

I spent most of the holidays at the Home.[12] Christmas morning I attended the festival at the Wentworth St. colored church. They had some very interesting exercises, which were pleasantly closed by the stripping of a beautifully decorated Christmas tree. I was particularly pleased with the speaking of the children. They spoke loudly and well, and showed that they had had good training. They were drilled by a young Mr. Weston—associate pastor of the church (colored) and would have done credit to any instructor.[13]

The Christmas tree projected by the teachers at Mr. Cardozo's home, for their Sunday school in Military Hall, was delayed on account of the non arrival of some boxes from New York, until it was not even a New Year's tree, but was only dressed for the eve of January second. But I wish that you could have seen it. It was a splendid thing. Besides the gifts and the festooning of parched corn, there were colored glass balls on many of the limbs that caught and threw off the rays of light from the wax that lighted it wherever it was safe to attach them to the boughs. It was a very pleasant evening to me. Fancy hearing over two hundred children in the heart of Charleston, S.C., singing with a will,

"The Union forever, hurrah, boys, hurrah,
Down with the traitor, and up with the stars,
While we rally round the flag, boys,
Rally once again,
Shouting the battle cry of Freedom."

Truly we are living in a strange historic period.

I have made thus far about fourteen calls since the holidays. The people are the farm hands mostly, and they are feeling the pressure of hard times now, and many of them cannot get the pay for their year's work, while I fear that when they have been paid the system of stores on the large places has been made to defraud them.[14] But they are cheerful and hopeful. Said one woman to me last week: "We lost a heap o' money when de Union come in. I done had a hunder dollars of de Confederate money, an' 'twas all no 'count; I jess gi'um away, but I say lef um go, and I tank God I'se free." And that is the way they all feel.

Last Saturday I spent at the place of a Dr. Horlbeek, a mile or so above here where my favorite pupils—the Gadson's live.[15] I saw that day some of the grandest live oaks imaginable, and was charmed with the sequestered loveliness of the place, which is approached by a long winding avenue, closely shaded by mossy trees, and with any

quantity of Christmas berries, displaying their gemlike beauties by
the wayside, together with wild roses, now in bloom, and jasmine
not blossomed yet. There is no white person living on the place,
which is in charge of Mr. Cadson, as it has been for twenty-eight
years, all but one of his nine children having been born there. He
says that he wants now to buy or hire a small place that he can work
with his own family for hands, but can find none. The South Carolin-
ians do not want the negroes to get a hold on the land, but we all
hope and pray that the pressure may drive them to sell or rent soon.
You ought to hear old Father Haynes talk. He does not want confiscation, but thinks that soon, if things are left to work out natural
results, the largest land-owners will have to sell small farms to get
money, for, as he wittily says, "They can't eat dirt or fence rails." [16]
Oh, why don't people see that if monied help is to be given, it
should be given to the colored soldiers and their families, and not to
their oppressors? The Charleston *Daily News* says that Gen. Howard
thinks of aiding planters with surplus funds in the Bureau. Can that
be? God forbid! It should all go to build school-houses. I have day
scholars who come three miles, and those above who can't come
have no school to feed their hungry minds.

In conclusion, does anybody want to send me a box of children's
clothing, shoes and stockings, etc., and papers and books for my
Sunday school? If so, send it to 53 John St., New York City, to be
forwarded to me in care of Rev. F. L. Cardozo, Charleston, S.C. [17]
Next time I'll describe our meetings more particularly that I have
and give specimens of their "Spirituals." Now I will close. I am well,
but a very busy, hard-worked individual, as I teach nearly six hours
daily, and till half past ten three nights a week, besides extra lessons
to Father Haynes twice a day. But then I enjoy it all, and I don't see
a white face more than once a week either.

Yours,
Sarah J. Foster

A Charleston Letter

Undated [Feb. 12]

Dear Advocate:—A note, just at hand from S. H. Record, Sunday
school missionary of Rhode Island, in which he offers my school
here one hundred and forty Sunday school books, because he had

read my letter of Jan. 1st to your columns, gives me both encouragement and incentive to try again. I will therefore improve the leisure
of a very rainy morning to send you a short sketchy letter. Shall I
have a school? Yes. I shall have by-and-by nine or ten of the nearest
or the most adventurous of my pupils, and some five or six of the
night scholars, whose work is stopped by the rain, will come also,
and I shall, of course, give them extra attention, and the day, so
dreary at home, will pass here like a dream. All the farmers are
plowing and hauling manure, and they would, if the weather would
dry up once more, at once put in their Irish potatoes and such crops.
Getting two and three crops a year from the soil, of course it must
be heavily dressed, and for weeks now the farm wagons about here
have been bringing from town two and three loads a day of manure.
This and plowing, etc., has fatigued them all so that my night school
has fallen off in numbers, and those who do come cannot get here till
past eight. I see so much that I want to do for those who do come
that my tasks are no lighter for the decrease. In the day school there
has been some change. Some families have moved away to form new
contracts for this year, and others have come in.[18] Thus I have lost
some scholars, and have thus far had about an equal number of
new ones.

    I have started a Bible class in connection with my Sunday night
prayer-meeting, and it has made a favorable beginning. We use the
Union Questions on the Gospel of St. Luke. As yet they are rather
diffident about expressing their thoughts, but I see gleams of originality that encourage me, and in Father Haynes we have a vigorous
thinker to help us. We have our little prayer-meeting first, and the
young men and women freely join in prayer, and then we take the
Bible lesson. I like the meetings here much. The people gather as
early as they can, and while waiting for the full number so as to open
the meeting, they sing their simple and beautiful "Spirituals." At
about eight the meetings open. A hymn is lined off and sung, and
then they kneel in prayer. The confusion of kneeling is usually covered by a refrain of the last two lines, which are concluded on their
knees. They usually remain kneeling while three prayers are offered.
Each man or woman who wishes to pray sings a verse of a hymn in
which all join still kneeling. At the close of the third prayer they rise.
Father Haynes or the assisting leader may address them, and a hymn
is then lined off, when they again kneel for three prayers more; or
perhaps I read a chapter, which Father Haynes takes as the topic of a

most excellent discourse. Class nights they have a few prayers, and
then Father Haynes talks to them. Next the class is personally examined. This is usually done by Father Haynes and three or four assistants all at once, the confusion covered by a full tide of melody, as
all sing who are not talking, and the musical tide, now rising now
falling, and anon broken a little by some loud voice ever reminds
me of a powerful torrent pouring over a rocky bed. Some of these
"Spirituals" are too good to be lost. I mean to collect a few to save,
and will here give some samples:

> "I want to climb up Jacob's ladder,
> Jacob's ladder, Oh Jacob's ladder;
> But I cannot until I make my peace with the Lord,
>   Then, O, praise ye the Lord,
> Yes, I'll praise him till I die, yes, I'll praise him till I die,
>   To sing Jerusalem."

> "I want to walk and talk with Jesus," &c.
> "I want to see my mother Mary," &c.
> "I want to see my General Jesus," &c.
> "I want to dwell with God the Father," &c.

Another is this:

> "Oh you high head member, you can't get along,
>   Roll, Jordan, roll,
> *I want to know:* How long will you hold on?
> *I want to know:* How long will you hold on?
>   Roll, Jordan, roll,
> *I ask the Lord:* How long will you hold on?
> *I ask the Lord:* How long will you hold on?
>   Roll, Jordan, roll."

The italicised words are put in by a few leading voices, and the rest
respond. The effect is beautiful. Other verses follow such as:

> "If you turn back, seeker, you can't get along,"

or

> "Oh, you nine months' seeker, you can't get along."

and it is susceptible of indefinite extension.
   A few Sabbaths ago I witnessed a "shout" to the above and similar
melodies—for instance:

> "If Satan takes my bloody flag, —
> Jerusalem in the morning, —
> I'll follow with the naked staff, —
> Jerusalem in the morning."

They formed in circles around a sort of pivot of one or two in the center of the floor, standing close till the outer circle was as large as the floor would allow, and then the living mass began to sing and revolve, going around with various rhythmic twistings and shufflings in time to the melodies that were sung. At the close of the meeting there is a sort of musical hand shaking gone through with, that is very beautiful. They join hands and beat time in unison to a strain of a "Spiritual," and then courtesy and separate to join with others until they have thus noticed all. I am not slighted, and, hoping that my hand is more susceptible than my ear, I trust I shall get the tune and measure of a few of these original melodies. One embalms their idea and method of seeking the Savior. It is this:

> "If you want to save your soul,
> Go in the wilderness, Go in the wilderness,
> And wait upon the Lord,
> And wait upon the Lord my God,
> Who taketh away the sin of the world."

They used to believe that a seeker should never go to bed till he finds peace. He must watch by the fire, and go out to pray whenever he hears the cock crow. They wandered off in the wilderness under religious excitement, and most of them met with strange mental experiences there. At a recent night meeting or "sitting up," I heard a man say that in the wilderness the devil met him wrapped in moss, and another said that he had to go down to the lowest pit of hell to find his own lost soul, and both were in earnest. These night meetings are relics of the old slave days, when they could only worship unmolested at night. The meeting really opens at twelve, when after refreshments a short sermon is preached, and then after remarks by leading brethren, the people take the meeting till daylight. I was at one a while since, and it was a delightful season to me. It was an experience meeting that was unflagging in its interest, and marked by strong individuality. At the close those who desired prayers were called forward, and several souls found peace then and there.

A yellow man named Everett administers sacrament here monthly, and for the rest two white gentlemen from town named

Miller [19] and Myers supply the desk most of the time. Both are deep thinkers, and of that educated middle class of Charlestonians who best accept the present. Of the Convention [20] I cannot now speak, but, as Mr. Cardozo is a delegate, will tell you something by-and-by.

Yours,

S. J. Foster.

Letter from the South

Charleston, April 8th, 1868 [April 22]

Dear Advocate:—If I could only send you a bit of the forest and wayside beauty that I have been seeing of late it would seem worth while to write. If the moss was beautiful when it only draped the otherwise bare boughs of the trees, it seems more so now in contrast with the tender green of the new foliage. They tell me that this atmospheric moss marks malarial districts, but, determined to defend what I so much admire, I always suggest at the close of such information, that if it feeds and grows on miasma it must be a benefit to the atmosphere after all by thus acting as an absorbent of malarial influences. But the moss is not now the chief beauty. The yellow jasmine swings its golden censers laden with fragrance in every place where it has not been rifled by the bouquet hunters, who now come out from the town in crowds to enjoy the forests; and the Cherokee roses now too in their glory adorn the fences, and even the tall trees are often festooned with them as thickly as if it had been raining stars. Then there are the dogwoods and the sassafrass, not to mention the violets and some other blossoms. Three weeks ago I was coming into town (I am in town now spending vacation) and a very pretty little brown girl looked very longingly at my immense bouquet of jasmine. I divided with her, though only her eyes asked me. Last week I met her again, and she told me with a bright smile that she "had got the flowers yet." I was deeply touched. Will the child always keep the dried blossoms because they came with a few kind words from a stranger? Since then I gave away to four little girls a bouquet of honeysuckle and rosebuds. I wonder if they will be thus precious to either of the recipients. I only know that I never saw more sensitive children, and the longer I know them the more my soul revolts at the tyranny which would fain deny them the right to all human feelings and passions.

Last Saturday night I was at another night meeting. It was nearly or quite as interesting as the other, and I heard even a greater number and variety of "Spirituals." I do not now think these meetings beneficial, as they exhaust people before the Sabbath, and many sleep on the Lord's day because they have been out. But I kept up, and I feel no ill effects of my vigil. I merely went out of curiosity, as I wanted to study the people in their own peculiar assemblies, and I set them the good example of neglecting no duty the next day.

Last month my school numbered fifty-two and the average attendance was forty-one. They progress finely. I wish somebody wanted to give a home to an orphan boy, about twelve years of age. I have one Stephen Lesesne, who learned his letters of me, and has finished the Primer, and is halfway through the National First Reader. Doesn't somebody want to give a home to such a boy as that? He has only a brother to care for him, and of late has had to work a great deal. He is very handy in waiting upon folks about house. He is very tender in his feelings, and I think quite a good boy, and his mother was an excellent Christian.

A box of Sabbath school books from S. H. Record of Rhode Island, have come to hand, and were gladly received by our Sabbath school. Now I want to get up a picnic for the last part of May, and wish that those who will help me do it by contributions, will communicate with me at Box 175, Charleston, S.C. May be some Sabbath school could get us up a box of cakes and such things. Do not say that these things are unimportant. Oh you cannot measure the value of *little* gleams of sunlight to those who live in gloom. The planters combine to keep down the farm hands, and the people in the country are very poor. How can it be otherwise when women have to work with heavy Southern hoes all day for the paltry pittance of thirty cents? which is the usual rate of pay now.

It is hoped, I believe, that the Constitution will be accepted by the people. Mr. Cardozo is candidate for Secretary of State. I think that he would well fill the office, and we all hope that he may get it.

The rest are to take another week of rest, but I shall resume on Monday next, thus taking one week in place of two, since I will have to run from the anticipation of country fever at the close of May, while the others are to be here a month longer at least. I am as yet very well indeed. I have not been indisposed in the least since my arrival and I am not at all fatigued either. My night class has gone down to six or seven, and one at least of that number is to leave.

I hope to retain a few, however, while I stay, as it well supplies the place of the society which I lack for the three nights weekly which it occupies. With that, Father Haynes' lessons, two meetings a week, and coming here on Saturdays, I make out nicely, and don't get either homesick or lonesome. Father Haynes has begun to read in the Testament, and he can hardly find time enough for the pleasant task of learning. It is a real joy to teach the good old man. But I will not overtax your patience. Pray for my work.

                                                                Sarah J. Foster

Letter from the South

Charleston, May 8th, 1868. [May 20]

Dear Advocate:—Since I last wrote to you, at least three pleasant things have happened. First, after two unsuccessful attempts, we all went to Fort Sumter and Morris Island[21] on Saturday, May 2d. Second, I received that day a letter from an *Advocate* reader, containing the first (I hope not the last) donation for our desired picnic; and last, but by no means least, yesterday we had the dedicatory services at a new school building, on Bull St., in Charleston, to be occupied by the American Missionary Association teachers there, and called Avery Institute.[22] As every scribbler gives a batch of reflections on visiting such historic places as Morris Island and Fort Sumter, I will spare you the infliction of mine, which were of the usual sort I presume, (mostly referring to the important question what to take as relics) and pass on to describe the dedication. That it was a period of thankfulness you will not doubt when I say that the building should have been done February 1st, but has been ever since in getting done. The noisy, inconvenient building which they occupied meanwhile had nearly worn them out, and they gave up Military Hall April 3d, and a portion of the rooms were at once taken by the school of the National Freedmen's Association. They then expected to have their new school in two weeks, but have only occupied the classrooms one week now, while the chapel is but just completed. The building has eight school rooms which will seat from sixty to eighty pupils each. The chapel which is in the second story will seat about six hundred persons I think, and will be used at present by the Plymouth (colored) Church as a house of worship. All the stair cases are outside in order that passing in and out may not disturb those classes that may be in session.

On this occasion the large and pleasant chapel was appropriately and tastefully decorated with evergreen and flowers, the girls and even the boys showing marvelous taste in the arrangement of wreaths and bouquets, and hardly needing a suggestion from us as to what was appropriate.

Rev. Mr. Adams (colored)[a] opened the services by reading a part of the eleventh chapter of Isaiah, and also a portion of the eighth of Proverbs, both very suitable I thought. Rev. Mr. Pease,[24] who has now taken charge of the Plymouth church, followed with a short and feeling prayer, then a select choir of the scholars sang a hymn called "The Latter Day." Well might they sing:

> "We are living; we are dwelling
> In a grand and awful time."

The address was then delivered by Rev. Dr. Hicks of Brooklyn, N.Y. As far as his address referred to education it was excellent, but some allusions to the workings of the Freedmen's Bureau were perhaps a little ill-timed, since they could not possibly refer to such men as General Scott, who was present, nor in fact anyone here I fancy. General Scott, who had been very influential in securing the erection of the building, was offended, as were several other gentlemen, while it appeared that the representatives of the Charleston press who were there were quite well pleased. But the address was good, let who would like or dislike it, only that a small portion of it might have done more good and no hurt if delivered elsewhere.[25] The children at the close of the address sang:

> "Sound the loud timbrel o'er Egypt's dark sea,
> Jehovah has triumphed; his people are free."

Mr. Cardozo, who had presided over the services, then made a few brief remarks. One of the girls of the school presented a beautiful basket of moss and flowers to Dr. Hicks, and another to Mr. Cardozo. The choir sang "America," and the occasion closed quite happily, Dr. Hicks taking an immediate opportunity to disclaim any idea of personality in his remarks so that I think no permanent offense was taken.

Blackberries are now quite abundant, and green peas an old story altogether. Roses are—well—nearly as thick as the sand flies, and Irish potatoes already in the market. It seems to be fully summer now. My school yet goes happily on, and I almost dread to leave. As

yet I do not suffer from the heat, and though my pupils have had
fever spells, I have not had any, nor have I had any illness at all.
I will send specimens of atmospheric moss to such people as desire it, and will send me with their addresses, donations for my picnic. Even the smallest bits of change are welcome. Some Northern
ladies who had a Sabbath school here last season, gave a picnic, and
I cannot help it if I would, without a sorer disappointment than I
care to inflict. It will occur on June 1st. The Sunday preceding I design to bid the people good bye, with a few words based on Paul's
words, 2 Cor. xii : 11. I am now working at the theme in my leisure.

Very hastily yours,
Sarah J. Foster

Notes

1. Francis L. Cardozo (1837–1903) was born in Charleston, the son of a
white businessman father and a free black mother. He left school at age
twelve to become an apprentice carpenter. Nine years later he saved
enough money to enable him to continue his studies in Scotland and England where he trained for the ministry. In 1865 he was appointed director
of the AMA school in Charleston. It was widely acclaimed as the outstand-
ing school for black youth in South Carolina and one of the best schools in
the South. After touring schools throughout the South in 1867–68, one ob-
server awarded Cardozo "the preeminence as principal." His administration
was characterized by "promptness, order and system." In 1868 while SJF
was teaching at her plantation school, Cardozo left his post after being elected South Carolina's secretary of state (Wilhelmena S. Robinson, *Historical
Afro-American Biographies*, International Library of Afro-American Life
and History [Cornwells Heights, Pa., 1979], 60; Joe M. Richardson,
"Francis L. Cardozo: Black Educator during Reconstruction," *Journal of
Negro Education* 48 [Winter 1979]: 73–83).

2. Cardozo's school was called the Saxton School until it was renamed
the Avery Institute when a new building was dedicated in May 1868 on Bull
Street. Military Hall, designed to look like a medieval fortress and used for
military meetings and drill when it was built in 1847, was on Wentworth
Street (Richardson, "Cardozo," 75; SJF, "Letter from the South," May 8,
1868, ZA, May 20, 1868; Kenneth Severens, *Charleston: Antebellum Architecture and Civic Destiny* (Knoxville, Tenn., 1988), 131–32.

3. "Father Haynes" was Wally or Warley Hayne, an elderly, illiterate
black man whom SJF taught to read the Bible. Wally Hayne and Monday
Green leased a farm known as Livingston Farm on the Ashley River "about

Four Miles from the City" for three years beginning on Nov. 1, 1868, from William D. Livingston and Thomas M. Hazelhurst, trustees for John Ashley Livingston and Emma Livingston. Hayne signed his name with an X. John Livingston of Charleston Neck Parish was listed as the owner of fourteen slaves in the U.S. Census of 1860. Two were sixty-year-old males. Warley Hayne, a farmer and "a person of color," died at Charleston on Oct. 28, 1869. His widow, Lamar Hayne, administered the estate. Property located at Gibb's Farm and credited against the estate's debts included two wagons, three carts, farming utensils, two horses, and a mule. One of those posting bond with Lamar was Rev. Richard H. Cain. An African Methodist Episcopal minister, Cain organized churches in the Charleston area after the war. In a newspaper column in 1867, he listed "Haynes Chapel" as one of three AME churches in Charleston. That is presumably the same chapel where SJF taught and preached. Cain entered politics, and in 1868 he was elected to the state senate to represent Charleston. In 1872 he was elected to the U.S. Congress (SJF to American Missionary Association, teacher report, January 1868; SJF to Rev. E. P. Smith, May 9, 1868, AMAA; Maurine Christopher, *America's Black Congressmen* [New York, 1971], 87–89; Register of Mesne and Conveyance Office, Charleston; National Archives, *Population Schedules of the Eighth Census of the United States, 1860,* South Carolina [slave schedules], vol. 2, Charleston District; Charleston County Probate Court Records, microfilm reel 191-6/194-4, PR-EF-024; "Charleston Correspondence," *Christian Recorder,* June 29, 1867, 1).

4. Cardozo married Catherine Rowena Howell of New Haven in 1864. They had four sons and two daughters, one of whom died in infancy (*Dictionary of American Negro Biography,* s.v. "Cardozo, Francis L[ouis]").

5. SJF helped Cardozo during the end of October, and on the afternoon of Nov. 4 she went with him to organize her school, where she moved Nov. 7. "I think she will be able to do a great deal of good out there," Cardozo wrote to an AMA official. By Dec. 7 Cardozo announced that she had a day school of fifty pupils and a night school of about thirty. Each week Cardozo hired a carriage to transport SJF the three miles from her school to spend the weekend with the other teachers (F. L. Cardozo to Rev. E. P. Smith, Oct. 22, Nov. 4, Dec. 7, 1867; Cardozo to Wm. E. Whiting Esq., Dec. 28, 1867, AMAA).

6. Charleston Neck was the name used to refer loosely to areas of the city north of Calhoun Street, once the boundary of the city (Professor Edmund L. Drago, personal communication; see also Anne W. Chapman, "Inadequacies of the 1848 Charleston Census," *South Carolina Historical Magazine* 81 [Jan. 1980]: 24, 29; J. L. Dawson, M.D., and H. W. DeSaussure, M.D., *Census of the City of Charleston, South Carolina, for the Year 1848* [Charleston, 1849], iv–vi).

7. Before SJF arrived, the school had been attempted several times by "some person who wanted to line her purse with tax money. A short experiment usually sufficed, and when I began, some were slow to send, but the month was long enough it appears to show them that the school had fallen into a Yankees hands and was bound to hold on."

SJF taught and preached in the chapel on the farm. There were no desks and no books or papers for Sunday school. The visits to black homes that she felt pressured to limit in West Virginia were limited here only by her workload and the distance away some pupils lived. She made thirteen or fourteen visits in November and December.

Her school reports for January, February, and April, the only ones extant, indicate her progress. She reported that attendance at her day school averaged forty-two pupils. The number of pupils in her night school averaged fourteen in January and then dropped to six when planting commenced in February. Average Sunday school attendance was thirty-five. In the day school only three of her students were over age sixteen. The majority were in primary studies, although an average of thirteen were classified as intermediate students. The number of students learning to write doubled from eight to sixteen between January and February, four in books and twelve on slates. By April she reported that she had taught thirty-one students to read beginning with the alphabet.

Punctuality and perfect attendance were rare. For example, in February, she reported that only four students were always in attendance and always punctual. She said very few, perhaps only one, of her students were free before the war. In January and February very few paid their tuition promptly, but by April all but four had paid in part.

On each report teachers were asked to respond to the question, "How can we add to your comfort and the success of your work." In January she responded: "I have no special request to make. I find pleasure in my work. I would not change now for a school in town." In February she wrote, "I need maps for my school now, for I have now some fine little boys in Geography." In April the space was left blank (SJF to Rev. E. P. Smith, Jan. 3, 1868; SJF, school reports, January, February, April 1868, AMAA).

8. She wrote in a letter to Rev. E. P. Smith, "I think that I have the blackest school in this section and I can also proudly say that I have not a dull or stupid child in it." The relative intelligence of students of different colors was an issue of the times. The AMA asked on early school reports whether mulattoes performed better than blacker children. The fact that most of SJF's students on Charleston Neck were black, and not "yellow," was of more than passing interest in Charleston as well. The Avery Institute received high praise, but some observers noted that its student body was elitist based on color. "About three-fourths of the scholars are Freedmen, the remaining fourth (comprising the more advanced classes) being com-

posed mostly of those who were born free, and who now constitute an aristocracy of color. . . . It is the design to make this a Normal School for the education of teachers, and the best material only has therefore been retained. . . . Although the greatest number of scholars in the most advanced classes are very fair, all hues are represented from the pale-faced Caucasian to the shining ebony of the native of Dahomey," one analyst observed in 1866. SJF was only one of many teachers who observed that the blackest students were as capable at learning as the whitest (SJF to Rev. E. P. Smith, Jan. 3, 1868, ibid.; Richardson, *Christian Reconstruction*, 52; Litwack, 496–97).

9. Her students brought the wood for the stove in bundles on their heads (SJF to Rev. E. P. Smith, Jan. 3, 1868, AMAA).

10. Rev. B. F. Jackson of Edgarton, Mass. (*American Missionary*, April 1868, 74).

11. The Plymouth Congregational Church was formed in 1865 at Military Hall from a congregation that had met in several places in Charleston since its former meetinghouse, the old Circular Church, had burned on Dec. 11, 1861. A cornerstone for a church building was laid in 1872 at the corner of Pitt and Bull streets (American Missionary Association, *Twenty-Fifth Annual Report* [New York, 1872], 30–31).

12. "Cardozo not only taught several classes and supervised Saxton School, he was also responsible for watching over the 'mission home,'—buying food for the 'family' and giving religious direction to students. The AMA provided special living facilities for the Saxton faculty since Charleston whites tended to oppose Black education and northern teachers were occasionally ostracized and occasionally threatened. During Cardozo's tenure as principal there was remarkable harmony in the 'family'" (Richardson, "Cardozo," 76).

13. The Wentworth Street colored church was the Centenary Methodist Church located at 60 Wentworth Street across from Military Hall. It was acquired from white Baptists in 1866 by the AME church. Rev. William O. Weston also taught at the Avery Institute (Samuel Gaillard Stoney, *This Is Charleston: An Architectural Survey of a Unique American City* [Charleston, 1987], 110; William O. Weston to Thomas Cardozo, June 24, 1865, AMAA; W. H. Lawrence, *The Centenary Souvenir, Containing a History of the Centenary Church, Charleston, and an Account of the Life and Labors of Reverend R. V. Lawrence, Father of the Pastor of Centenary Church* [Philadelphia, 1885], xv–xvi).

14. The years 1865–68 were bad years for farmers in South Carolina, and the Freedmen's Bureau found it necessary to mount an enormous relief effort for both whites and blacks. In some cases workers actually found

themselves in debt after a year's sharecropping. One Freedmen's Bureau agent told of twenty-four workers whose proceeds for the cotton crop came to $543.43. After deductions for the supplies advanced during the year by the planter, seven were entitled to shares ranging from $4.51 to $8.15 for the year's work. The other seventeen owed from $1.71 to $73.62 (Abbott, 41–42).

15. There were five Horlbecks in the *Charleston City Directory for 1867–68* who were either physicians or else had the title Dr. before their names. Only one of them, Dr. H. B. Horlbeck of 10 Coming Street, was identified also as a planter.

16. The subject of confiscation and distribution of white farmlands to the freedmen was debated intensely during this period. At the end of the war the Freedmen's Bureau owned 300,000 acres of land in South Carolina. Some bureau officials were determined to provide freedmen with 40-acre homesteads for sale or rent. President Andrew Johnson, however, determined to restore the lands in full, and his will prevailed. As late as the beginning of 1868, however, thousands of freedmen still believed they would get free farms in a general land distribution (Abbott, chap. 4).

17. 53 John Street, New York City, was the address of the American Missionary Association.

18. The Freedmen's Bureau promoted a system of contract labor designed to get the landless freedmen a fair return for their work to help them rise above subsistence and acquire land of their own. A model contract drawn up by the bureau spelled out that the worker would be entitled to a place to live, food, medical care, fuel, and a share of the crops, preferably one-half. The reality, however, did not always meet such an ideal, and sometimes the farmhand had little or nothing to show for his work (Abbott, chap. 5).

19. SJF described Miller as "a white Methodist Exhorter from town. . . . He is a carpenter by trade, and, although a South Carolinian is a great worker for the real good of the colored race. He has often dined here with me when colored clergymen and Father Haynes were at the board and with no offensive air of condescension" (SJF to Rev. E. P. Smith, Jan. 3, 1868, AMAA).

20. Cardozo's election as a delegate to the South Carolina Constitutional Convention marked the beginning of his political career (Edward F. Sweat, "Francis L. Cardozo: Profile of Integrity in Reconstruction Politics," *Journal of Negro History* 46 [Oct. 1961]: 219).

21. Morris Island was a fortified island near Fort Sumter at the mouth of Charleston Harbor (Arthur M. Wilcox and Warren Ripley, *The Civil War at Charleston* [Charleston: Evening Post Publishing Company, 1986], 14).

22. The Avery Normal Institute, the successor to the Saxton School, was operated by the AMA until 1947 when it became a public school. It was closed in 1954 (Edmund L. Drago and Eugene C. Hunt, "A History of Avery Normal Institute from 1865 to 1954," paper sponsored by the Avery Institute of Afro-American History and Culture and the College of Charleston, n.d.).

23. Rev. E. J. Adams assisted Cardozo in organizing the Plymouth Congregational Church (American Missionary Association, *Nineteenth Annual Report* [New York, 1865], 23–24).

24. Rev. Giles Pease (*American Missionary*, July 1868, 148).

25. Rev. W. W. Hicks's comments were summarized May 8 in both the *Charleston Daily Courier* and the *Charleston Mercury*. It is unclear from the papers' accounts exactly what angered Maj. Gen. Robert K. Scott, who was assistant commissioner for the Freedmen's Bureau in South Carolina until he was elected governor in 1868. But F. L. Cardozo wrote to the AMA that he regretted having invited Hicks to deliver the speech. "His reference to the Freedmen's Bureau and Politicians (which are somewhat smoothed over in the copy as fully printed) are so sweeping and unqualified that Gen. Scott and other good friends took offence.

"Mr. H. is a Southerner, and as soon as he got here began to be acquainted with Southerners. He heard all their views and complaints, and is now an ardent champion of their side, and is certainly a bitter partisan of theirs.

"I liked Mr. H. at first very much, but his supercilious and disdainful manner of discussion, which indeed characterise most Southerners, soon made him very offensive to me" (Abbott, 18; F. L. Cardozo to Rev. E. P. Smith, May 12, 1868, AMAA).

MAINE, 1868

Our Charleston Letter

Gray, Me., June 19th, 1868. [June 24]

Dear Advocate:—You will see by date that I am at home. I arrived here last week and have got nicely rested.

I was not able to have a picnic as I only received four dollars. This amount I spent for prizes, giving them to those who were best in deportment, Arithmetic and Geography, with a few ribbon badges for minor merits, and a part of these I had to furnish myself. But the day went off well. The Sabbath preceding my departure I addressed the people from the words: "Finally brethren farewell; be perfect; be of good comfort, be of one mind, live in peace, and the God of love and peace shall go with you." Two white men were in the audience—our favorite Mr. Myers, and a Mr. Bunch. Mr. Bunch followed me with excellent remarks and Mr. Myers closed with a prayer. In the afternoon a colored man from a remote district preached. His doctrine was excellent, but right in the midst of it he turned abruptly to me and said with deep feeling:—"'Taint likely that we'll ever meet again in this world but I'll pray for you ma'am, I'll pray for you, and God haint never refused me anything that I've asked in faith for these thirty-six years." I was deeply touched, for it was done in a natural unaffected manner.

I had been requested to take charge of several colored children going on to New York from the Shaw Orphan House.[1] Last week we found them located at the old Slave Mart,[2] but the orphans now occupy the old Elliot Mansion. It is a fine old stone dwelling house and has a nice shaded yard and a large garden adjoining, which the children work for sport, and which has a border of fig trees from which they hope to get about a hundred bushels of figs. There is there an organ left by somebody of old and a marble topped table once used by Lafayette. The walls of some rooms have very ancient paper hangings which represent hunting scenes and personages of ancient mythology.

There is a spiral staircase of stone, eighty feet in height, which is the basis of a ghost story. It is said that a colored woman was once dragged down those steps, which caused her death, and that she

haunts the halls and passages, and indeed a guilty conscience might
well render ghostly the strange echoes awakened in those high and
wide passages. Among other relics, Mr. Wolhurpter, the superintendent, has found an authentic love letter connected with an old
romantic affair of the founder of the home, and which he pronounces
wonderfully sensible, indeed, "having no nonsense about it." There
are one hundred and thirty-five children there now, and the old
punch bowl—very large, of carved marble, is now degraded into
their *kneading trough.*

A week or two before I came home I visited the place of a colored
man named Blake about four miles further up on the Ashley river.[3]
He lives in a grand, live oak grove, where of late he has induced
Mr. Miller to hold services out of doors in fine weather. I accompanied Mr. Miller over, and enjoyed it so well that I made another
visit before leaving. They want a school, and Mr. Blake will give
more than the board to secure one.

June 6th, I sailed in the Steamer Charleston, Capt. Berry. The
steamship regulations only allow deck or steerage passage to colored
people, but the captain kindly exerted himself to find sheltered
places in which to locate my three charges—nice little girls of about
twelve. I got to New York June 9th, in the morning, and by hasten-
ing on in spite of bad weather that day, I got home the next night,
and my head ached too much to allow me to walk out while awaiting
the stage, and I reached home very tired and with a severe cold. I
am getting finely rested, and my cold is wearing off.[4]

Does any one ask if I liked? Yes, very much, and I now plan to go
again, and perhaps to the same place. The Charleston teachers leave
the last of June. Mr. Cardozo has been already some weeks in Columbia, his connection with the school at Charleston having closed
at the dedication. His place is now filled by Miss Ellen M. Pierce, of
Salem, Mass., who also, with the help of another teacher, superin-
tends the housekeeping.

My number the last month dwindled to thirty-six, but they were
good, and, as I knew that poverty drove the rest to work, I could not
blame them. I miss them now, and would like to have them again in
charge.

> Yours as ever,
> S. J. Foster.

Notes

1. The Shaw Orphan Asylum was located on the south side of Queen Street between East Bay and Church streets. The superintendent was G. Pillsbury (*Charleston City Directory for 1867–68*).

2. The old Slave Mart was a slave auction house located at 6 Chalmers Street. It became a museum in 1938. It was recently closed and sold to the city of Charleston (Edmund Drago and Ralph Melnick, "The Old Slave Mart Museum, Charleston, South Carolina: Rediscovering the Past," *Civil War History* 27, no. 2 [1981]: 138).

3. The Ashley River bounds Charleston peninsula on the southwest.

4. SJF apparently wished to see her old friends in West Virginia on her way north. In a letter to the AMA in early May written under the pretext that she lacked an official blank with which to file her monthly school report, she asked "if it will be possible for my transportation to be made out in such a way that I can stop at Baltimore, as I desire to make a short trip westward" (SJF to Rev. E. P. Smith, May 9, 1868, AMAA).

SARAH JANE FOSTER, 1839-1868

Miss Sarah Jane Foster

It becomes our painful duty to announce the sudden death of this estimable young lady. For several years she has been a regular contributor to the columns of the *Advocate*, and thousands have read her articles with admiration. For a few years past she has devoted herself to instructing the freedmen. For some months she was in the vicinity of Martinsburg, and Harper's Ferry, West Virginia. While there she was a regular correspondent of the *Advocate*, and her letters abounded with interesting information, respecting the condition and needs of that section of our country. Early last autumn she went under appointment to South Carolina, and with great success conducted a school for the colored children near Charleston. Her letters from that place we have published and our readers know how interesting they have been. A few days ago she returned to this State, to spend the summer and recruit her energies for the work she loved so well. In our last paper was a letter from her, written in her easy, graceful style. She was with her friends in Gray, and passed from the scenes of earth, on the evening of June 25th. She not only possessed unusual talents as a writer, but was a most earnest and devout Christian. Her religious character was well established and uniform, and her efforts for the spiritual welfare of her pupils and others were constant and unwearied; and though death came at an unexpected hour, it found her with her work well done, and prepared for the joy of her Lord. We feel that we have lost a valued personal friend, and sympathize with her relatives in their heavy bereavement.

Zion's Advocate, July 1, 1868

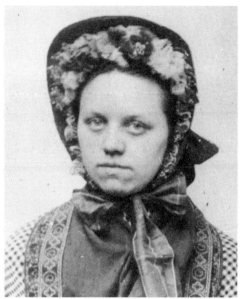

Sarah Jane Foster. (Courtesy of Carolyn Reilly)

Pages from Sarah Jane Foster's diary

N. C. Brackett. (Courtesy of
the American Baptist Archives
Center, Valley Forge, Pa.)

Anne S. Dudley. (Courtesy of the George
and Helen Ladd Library, Bates College,
Lewiston, Maine)

The Lockwood House, Harpers Ferry, Sketch by J. E. Taylor in Frank Leslie's
Illustrated Newspaper, Sept. 3, 1864. (Courtesy of Harpers Ferry National
Historical Park)

Distant view of Harpers Ferry, sometime between 1870 and 1883. (Courtesy of Harpers Ferry National Historical Park)

View from Jefferson Rock at Harpers Ferry. Woodprint from William Cullen Bryant, Picturesque America, or The Land We Live In, *1872. (Courtesy of Harpers Ferry National Historical Park)*

Francis L. Cardozo. (Courtesy of Moorland-Spingarn Research Center, Howard University, Washington, D.C.)

Avery Institute. (From the American Missionary, *May 1870)*

APPENDIX:
Poetry and Stories

SELECTED BIBLIOGRAPHY

INDEX

APPENDIX: POETRY AND STORIES

OH, WEAVE ME A STORY.
By Sarah J. Foster.

Oh, weave me a story, warp and woof,
While the snow's white feet are on the roof,
While its robes are floating on the breeze,
And the wild winds harp among the trees.
My faith is weak, and my courage low,
When I think of graves, where winter snow
Hides all of beauty that love could bring,
To wait for the warming breath of spring.
Tell me a tale of the olden time, —
A tale that with wind and storm will chime;
Of truths that battled with giant wrong;
Of victories crowning the contests long;
Of hearts which were noble, brave, and true,
And the matchless deeds they dared to do;
For all of life is a drama grand,
And time's a scroll where a mighty hand
Hath written lessons I cannot see,
For the great hot tears are blinding me.
Help me to see that Now is small,
And God's eternal scale weighs all;
That lives can never be sublime
Which look not past the present time.
Teach me that living is not life,
If lived apart from noble strife,
That I may feel how grand the hour,
Which awes me with its awful power.
Yes, weave me a story, warp and woof,
While the ghostlike snow treads on the roof;
While requiems lade the evening breeze,
And sob and sigh 'mong the leafless trees.
Oh, teach me that life is to do and dare;

That the glory of life is not to spare
A boon that Now to the Future can lend,
Not even a soul, which, the right to defend,
Must venture to fathom the awful gloom,
Which lieth beyond the gate of the tomb.
Then shall I reckon that nothing is lost,
If freedom be gained, though blood is the cost.
Then, then shall my spirit be brave again,
O'erliving and crushing its dreadful pain.
As the white snow buries the frost-browned earth,
Or filmy ashes the desolate hearth,
So my heart shall its buried pleasure dress
As calmly as though it had none the less.
But help me to see that a ladder is thrown,
From the distant skies to my pillow of stone.
Awaken my faith, for my eyes cannot see
How good in a thing that is evil can be,
How the rough and the bitter, the wild and the strange,
To the pure, the sweet, and the truthful can change.

Home Monthly,
January–July 1865

MY DISAPPOINTMENT
By Sarah J. Foster

"The girls are going to have a picnic in Beech Grove this afternoon, and—"

"And what?"

For more than a week I had been trying to announce the coming picnic to my task-mistress, Mrs. Armitage, and now, before I could frame a request, it was frozen on my lips by her hard, metallic question, "And what?"

"Why don't you speak? What are you waiting for?" and the cold stare of her steel-blue eyes gave a fitting point to her words. Confusedly I tried to respond, and only succeeded in stammering out,—

"I wanted—I thought—maybe—I'd like to go."

"You don't seem to know your own mind very well. You had better stay at home; I have work for you to do."

"Well, what, ma'am?"

I had not expected any such relaxation. So very submissively I took up again my burden of care. Mrs. Armitage never scolded. It was not necessary. She was one of those moral icebergs who can petrify all who come near them into serviceable automatons. If any one awoke to natural desires, it was easy for her to administer such a mental shower-bath as she had given me.

Seeing that it had taken effect, she went on with perfect composure to say,—

"We move next week, you know, and I want you to sort over the rags and waste papers in the woodshed chamber."

"Now?"

"No, after dinner."

The little friction was over. The wheels of life resumed their monotonous hum, and dinner was prepared, eaten, and cleared away in the usual manner, only my thoughts were a little busier than common.

Six years before I had become an inmate of the family, and mem-

ory now ran back to that time,—yes, and farther back. I recalled my
East Indian home. I lived again the agonizing moments when Death
was achieving his dread conquest over my dear parents. Then I
recalled my voyage back to the fatherland, which was not home,
because my aged grandfather had long been severed and totally
estranged from the land of his birth. But when the newer joys faded
and left his heart aching and desolate, he went back and I with him
to renew the old associations. Time had wrought sad changes, however. Nothing remained to link past and present. There was nothing for the heart tendrils to cling to, and very soon we took our
lonely way to the New World.

The old and careworn may love the young and thoughtless; but
their relations are never confidential. Thus I had known nothing of
my grandfather's relations to the world. I had not known want, and
had a vague idea that a certain little black trunk must contain fabu-
lous sums of money. I had heard my grandfather speak of a brother
in the new land of our destination. But years agone there had been
some disagreement, and his name had never been a household
word. I had heard him called "Jack," but knew that was not his
name. I had either never heard, or else had quite forgotten, his
name and place of residence.

Landed in the strange, unhomelike land, we set out for the West.
But here came a fearful pause in my life history. Somebody on the
great railroad was careless,—who was not decided. There was a
collision, a crash. An hour afterward I was drawn forth from the
ruins, stunned and helpless, to find myself alone among strangers.
Only ten years old, I was passive in the hands of others. Mrs.
Armitage was in the train, and she it was who first broke to me the
news of my utter desolation, while her hand slowly stroked my
hair and forehead with a touch too cold to be caressing. Still numb
and unresisting I went with her to her country home, because she
carried for interment the mortal remains of my last and best friend.

Weeks passed before I recovered from the shock sufficiently to
care aught for my worldly estate. When I did awaken to my situation, I found that I was dependent. The black trunk which held my
earthly all was gone. The awakening was six years agone; but what
a weary time it was since then!

The family contained only Mrs. Armitage and her son Stephen, who entered college in my thirteenth year, and of whom I saw little at any time.

Memories of all this, and thought born of those memories, were singing to and fro in my mind through the busy while that I was preparing to go up to my unwelcome task. Denied all outward expression, my hot passions were consuming my very heart. My icy reserve was but a surface crust. Beneath was a boiling crater into whose angry depths I dared not look, while sometimes conscience shrank back aghast at wild wishes that cared not shape themselves into deeds.

At last I went up into the hot, low-roofed chamber. Dusty, festooned with cobwebs and lumbered with all sorts of accumulated rubbish, it was always an uninviting place. Now it was intolerable; I did not mean to contrast it with Beech Grove; but I could not help it. The farther window commanded a good view of the fine wooded hill thus named, and thither some obstinate impulse drew me to feed the gnawing discontent that already maddened nerves and brain. Up over the slowly rising ascent of the field before me groups of merry children were trooping, bound for the grove which was already astir with zealous preparation. How bitterly I thought of their lots in life as compared with mine! I did not consider how often I had been angered at real or fancied slights from the youths and children of the village. I only mourned a lost prospect of pleasure. It was unusual for me to be invited to a merry-making. Such an invitation I had now received, and a refusal of my stammering request was a shaft to rankle sorely in my wounded breast.

How long I might have dallied by the window I know not; but I very soon heard a frank, boyish voice ask, —

"Cannot Mallie come to the picnic?"

I bent eagerly to listen. Ainslie Carruth was the only son of our new clergyman, and I wondered if Mrs. Armitage could chill his mirthful temperament as she did mine. I was not left long in doubt. She did not try. It appeared that she was dressed or dressing to go out; for she said, —

"Strange that she should have cared so little about it. She hardly said a word. I was going away, and she had considerable to do.

Well, then, if I had imagined—I'm terrible sorry that she hadn't
ha' known that you was coming after her. Now she really can't go."

Meanwhile she had got out on the door rock, I heard the key
click in the lock.

"I always lock up this front-door when I go out," she explained.
"Mallie's away up in the woodshed chamber, and mightn't hear
anybody that come here."

As "this door" was the front porch–door,—the front-door for excellence never being used at all,—I was a veritable prisoner. I felt
it bitterly. Of course, Ainslie would go up to the grove and have a
merry time, while I was locked in to my tiresome task. Then I
carried the vexatious contrast still farther out on life's journey. We
were of an age; but he was the petted child of influential parents.
He would be well educated. He would be able to move in the best
society. Appreciation, approbation, success, awaited him everywhere. With *me* how different was life! Tied down to an irksome
drudgery, kept back from all improvement, growing worse day by
day,—whither was I tending?

Throwing down the rags which I had begun to separate into
heaps of white and colored, useful and useless, as I had been directed, I arose and paced the floor, like a caged tigress growling in
a defiant undertone the rage that had never before found expression. I noticed nothing, thought of nothing, save my own grievances, until my passion had spent its fury and at last quenched
itself in a torrent of tears. Then, dropping on the floor, I pillowed
my head on the heterogeneous mass, and sobbed violently.

"Come Mallie, dry your tears," said a pleasant voice at my side.
"As picnics are nothing new to me, I have decided to pick rags for
this afternoon's amusement. Won't you help me?"

"How did you get up here?" I asked in wonder, glad that Ainslie
had invaded my solitude, but at a loss to tell how he had entered.

"Easily enough," he replied. "There are several loose boards
over the woodpile there, and, when I came in, you were in such a
tragic state of mind that an earthquake wouldn't have disturbed
you. How you did run on though! I'm glad you can rave. It shows
that you are not frozen completely."

"Are you really going to stay here?" I asked, not much abashed
at the fact that he had witnessed my passionate outbreak. Long-
forced repression had given me an idea that unrestrained passion
was heroic.

"Stay? Yes, and we'll have a real good time."

I did not believe him; but somehow his good-humor was con-
tagious, and ere long our echoing laughter was startling the spiders
from their dusty lairs. We were actually merry. And the work went
on bravely too. Now and then we appropriated an article to our
own use, until our goods presented a melange curious to behold of
articles ancient and modern, grotesque and ludicrous. But yet we
were not idle, and long ere Mrs. Armitage returned the whole
dreaded labor was done.

Once I had seen Ainslie thrust something into his breast pocket;
but when asked what it was, he merely laughed and said that it
was a relic of our good time that he was going to keep, and he at
once offered me a comical-looking wide-ruffled night-cap for the
same purpose. Thus it passed off, and I soon forgot the little
incident.

"There she comes! Now I'll leave. Good-bye, Mallie," and
Ainslie unceremoniously tumbled down through an opening over
the woodpile as Mrs. Armitage unlocked the outer door. When she
came up, I was demurely sweeping up the "scatterings."

"So you've got through; have you? Why didn't you tell me that
that Carruth boy was coming after you? Strange that you were so
indifferent about it," said she with a hypocritical air, which would
have irritated me beyond endurance, only that sudden contact
with her had frozen over all rebellious feelings. It was impossible
to tell that tall, stony woman aught that would contradict the studied complacency with which her merciless face was masked. So I
swept on rapidly, and attempted no reply. Evidently none was expected; for she at once descended to that kitchen, whither I was
soon summoned to set the supper-table.

Weeks passed on, and the afternoon in the shed-chamber had
proved itself one of those times that make sadness the sadder by
their unfrequent contrast.

We had removed to another town some fifteen miles distant, and
I never expected to see Ainslie Carruth again. I had not even been
able to achieve a stolen good by.

But one day when I had been left alone, while Mrs. Armitage
was gone to a meeting held at a neighbor's, regarding a levee that
was soon to come off, I was startled by a loud rap at the door. Opening it, I almost fell to the floor at sight of a face and figure that
nearly made me believe my dear grandfather had returned to life.

"Don't be frightened my child," said the kind-visaged old man.
"What is your name?"

"Mallville Marret," I found voice to reply, after several efforts.

A half dozen questions drew forth the simple story of my life;
but what could the man mean?

I was not long left in doubt.

"Can't you guess who I am?" asked the stranger, pausing, after
he had exhausted my knowledge of myself. And, looking in his
face, it suddenly came to me who he must be. I replied,—

"You are—you must be my Uncle Jack!" meaning my grandfather's brother Gowan.

"Yes," he replied, "I am your Uncle Jack."

"How did you find out where I am?" I asked in amazement.

"No matter how. I have heard all about your trials, and more
than you know. So I have come to take you home with me. Will
you go?"

"Oh, wont I?"

"Then get your things right off."

"But—" and I hesitated.

"No buts about it. Come with me as soon as you can pick up."

Without any more delay, I obeyed, and in less than an hour we
were on the way to what was henceforth to be my home. As we
passed the house where my task-mistress was holding forth on her
favorite topic of benevolence, Uncle Jack sent in the key of her
house by a passing urchin, and we drove rapidly on. I could not
help peering back and was rewarded by seeing her hasten to the
door and look after us in awe-struck amazement. I laughed at the
sight long and loudly; for, once clear of my task-mistress my spirits
rose suddenly to a strange pitch of excitement.

On arriving at my new home, I found that it was only about ten miles from where I had passed six unhappy, toiling years, and wonder of wonders, the first to welcome me there was Ainslie Carruth! Nor was there any less of wonder in my mind when, three days afterward, my great uncle exhumed the black trunk, and told me that henceforth I was an heiress compared with the farmers' daughters around. Then I eagerly demanded an explanation, and it was cheerfully given.

Some scraps of old papers, found in the rag-bags in the garret on that eventful afternoon by Ainslie Carruth, formed fragmentary but good evidence that Mrs. Armitage had, concealed in her possession, the old black trunk. They were half-burned scraps of letters from Stephen. Doubtless Mrs. Armitage had torn them up and thrown them in the fire; and I remember that once her mother, who was then with her, had caught such remnants from the flame, and, very likely she had put them in the rag-bag. There was also an allusion to the danger of my discovering a relative not far off. Ainslie, chancing to partly know my great-uncle had traced out the matter silently; and, after I was well established in my new abode he confronted Mrs. Armitage with an accusation which her fears magnified to a certainty, and thus rendered effectual. So my trials were all over, and I was free to culture my mental powers to mate with Ainslie Carruth as an equal; and the first gleam of light dated from that gloomy beginning afternoon when I was banished to the woodshed chamber to toil away the picnic hours. Ever since I have looked for brightness in every cloud, and often have I seen light and hope spring forth from things as inscrutable as my disappointment.

Home Monthly,
July–December 1865

SILKEN FETTERS
By Sarah J. Foster

"I wish I could be a missionary," sighed Nellie Stanwood, closing as she spoke "Sears' Illustrated History of India and China."

"Perhaps you can," said her mother softly.

"Me! how can I?" and the young girl looked sadly out of the window.

"A home missionary I meant," explained the mother. Remember, my dear, what you were reading to me last week:—

"No man is born into the world, whose work is not born with him; there is always work, and tools to work withal for those who will."

"But how, mother, can I work—for the reform of the world, I mean?"

"For the reform of your little world, when it needs reform, I think you may find something! Recollect that,—'He who waits to have his task marked out may die and leave his errand unfulfilled.' You will need to seek opportunities, and they are never wanting. Think of Lawrence. Can you do nothing for him?"

With this the mother went out, leaving Nellie still thoughtfully gazing out of doors.

In the yard, within view, stood the only son of her step-father. Her mother had been married three months, but it was only two weeks since she had come to her new home, from the abode of her grandmother which had been her shelter since death removed her father. She was still a stranger.

Lawrence Dana was not old enough when his mother died, to realize his loss. Nor did he mourn for the infant sister, who shared her grave. But he suffered a great loss nevertheless. His father, absorbed in business and unsympathizing, left his little son to the entire control of an elderly female relative with a mania for housekeeping, which failed to recognize the rights of a child. Accustomed to fault-finding, and repulsed from his father's confidence, the poor boy reached the most critical period of youth ere Mrs. Stanwood came to fill his mother's place. That lady soon saw with pain that she could do little for him. Lawrence avoided home,—it had so long been distasteful, and when there, kept himself out of the way as much as possible. Already were the seeds of vice sown in his heart, by the influence of wicked companionship, into which he had fallen; but still the stepmother's unskilled hand felt blindly for the clew which might lead him back to innocence and peace.

At length, Nellie, her only child, came to her new home. Mrs. Dana noted the interest with which her stepson watched every movement of her daughter. Perhaps, thought she, he may be re-claimed, if he and Nellie can be brought to regard each other as brother and sister. But for this, she could only wait and pray. It would not do to dictate to a boy of sixteen, who knew restraint only as a tyrannical, irksome, thing. Nor did she dare to speak to his father of the growing viciousness which she could not fail to perceive, lest she should alienate the heart that she hoped to win, and rouse the father to greater harshness. In this frame of mind she had heard and answered Nellie's query, "How can I work?" and then left the room to pray that God would grant wisdom to the child, and bless her efforts.

Nellie Stanwood was a cripple. Three years before, a sudden cold had aggravated a scrofulous affliction of the right knee, and now the contracted cords would not permit a step. But her trials had been blessed, and though only twelve, she was a sincere fol-lower of the "meek and lowly Jesus."

As Nellie looked out of the window, Lawrence began to labor at the repairing of a large sled, for it was early winter, and snow had already fallen. For some time the girl watched his movements, wishing, yet not daring, to address him. She would not have hesiti-ated so long, had she known that she was uppermost in his thoughts. Yet so it was. Her helplessness had touched his pity; and just then he was wondering how she could bear the close confine-ment of the coming season, and if, through it all, she would keep the same pleasant voice and smile. Still if he desired a closer ac-quaintance, he knew not how to make a beginning. And she, while admiring his manly figure and activity, was striving to think of

some plea for addressing him, for hitherto a formal "good-morn-
ing" had been the only words exchanged between them, with the
exception of now and then a "good-night" when he had chanced to
be at home so early as her hour of retiring.

Thus a half-hour passed. The sled was nearly completed, and
still Nellie had not spoken,—knew not what to say; but nervously
toying with one of her crutches, she felt that the arm piece was
getting loose. She would request Lawrence to fix it for her, then
she could thank him, and ask what she might do in return,—it
would compel some conversation at least, and, without that what
could she hope to do for his benefit? So falteringly, and with a
voice almost below her breath, she called,—

"Lawrence!"

The boy gave a conscious start; but charging the half heard voice
to his imagination, he went on to sharpen with the hatchet the last
stake for his sled. Nellie wanted courage to speak again. "Perhaps,"
thought she, "Lawrence heard, and does not mean to answer." But
just as she came to this conclusion, the hatchet glanced, and a
quick exclamation, together with the blood which flowed from his
left hand, attested the effect of the misdirected blow. With a
child's horror of blood, Nellie hid her face crying out,—

"Oh, mother, come quick, Lawrence has cut his hand!"

"It isn't cut much; don't be scared," interposed Lawrence, for
the comfort of the bowed figure in the window. It aroused a native
manly instinct in his breast, to hear that timid voice raised on his
behalf.

"Call him in," said Mrs. Dana, "I will get a bandage for the
wound."

"Mother says come in. She is getting a bandage for you," Lawrence heard in the sweetest of tones, as he was trying to stanch the
blood with snow.

"I don't need it," he looked up to say, like any boy-man; but
Mrs. Dana came to the door, and seating herself upon the thresh-
old with her bandage in her hand, said,—

"You may take cold, and the trouble of having it dressed now
will be far less than that of a lame hand."

It needed little persuasion, for the contact of the cold snow with the raw flesh had thrilled every nerve with pain; and the fresh roll of linen in his step-mother's hand looked inviting. So he came and knelt upon the lower step, and Nellie with one crutch hobbled across the floor to bring water, as the cut was found to require cleansing.

"Now a little brown sugar, dear," said Mrs. Dana to Nellie, adding to Lawrence while she was gone, —

"That will stay the blood. I see that you have severed quite a large vein, and you ought to be very careful not to handle anything cold for some days."

Convinced that care was necessary, Lawrence said no more until the soft bandage was neatly secured. Unused to kind attentions, he did not naturally thank Mrs. Dana for her care; but he felt sorry that Nellie had been compelled to wait upon him, and this he tried to express.

"I'm sorry; it's too bad that you should have to get things for me."

"Never mind that," laughed she; "you can pay me some time; there will be chance enough."

Upon this, he asked as he put away the washbasin, which he had been using, "Did you speak to me just before I cut my hand?"

"Yes; but no matter now."

"Yes, it is matter," he urged. "I thought I heard you, and then I did not know. What were you going to say?"

Nellie told him of the loose arm-piece to her crutch.

"I'm glad you told me," Lawrence exclaimed with eagerness. "You need a new pair. These are not long enough for you now. I can make you some as well as not; but I'll fix this one so that it will do while I'm at work on them."

In vain Nellie protested that he ought not to work then. Lawrence playfully took away her crutches, and carried her into the sitting-room, where he placed her in a chair, from which she could not escape until he returned with the crutch neatly repaired, but with a large blood-stain upon his clean bandage, telling that it had cost him some discomfort.

Nellie saw it and said,

"I don't know whether to scold or thank you."

"I shall be satisfied if you do either," was his half-gloomy response.

"Why, what do you mean?"

"I mean," said he, "that I want you to act as if you were my sister. I would rather you would scold than not talk at all."

"You never gave me a chance," apologized Nellie.

"I didn't know that you wanted one," returned Lawrence.

And so the ice was broken. Lawrence insisted upon the speedy manufacture of the crutches, and of a sled with seat and cushions for Nellie; and in spite of her fears for his wounded hand, she grew interested in his work. Her interest in turn stimulated his, and thus the lacerated flesh had not time to heal, and the cut grew worse, rather than better.

"What's the matter now?" reprovingly asked his father one night, as Lawrence stole down-stairs at midnight.

"My hand pains me so that I cannot sleep!"

"You should have been more careful," was the paternal response, and Mr. Dana again fell asleep. Not so with the wife. Listening, she heard a suppressed groan, and quietly robing herself, went into the other room; he was painfully trying to build a fire.

"How long has your hand been so sore" she inquired pityingly.

"It has been growing worse for a week," replied Lawrence.

"And you have worked every day for Nellie! It is too bad. I blame myself that I did not inquire daily," and the kind step-mother arranged the fire and prepared a warm poultice as rapidly as possible. The noise disturbed Mr. Dana, and he appeared, just as his wife, after nearly an hour of constant ministration, was wheeling out the sofa for Lawrence to lie down.

"How are you now?" was his first inquiry, which he evidently meant should deserve the credit of being fatherly. But, on receiving a satisfactory answer, he added, "I thought there was nothing serious to pay. Aint you ashamed to be disturbing the house in this manner; and all about a little scratch, caused by your own carelessness?" He then began to question him as to how the week had been passed, Lawrence well knew that he had been imprudent, but the reproof was ill-timed, and the tone and manner such as a high-spirited boy could ill brook. "You are a thoughtless, bad boy, and if you had met with a severe accident, it's no more than you should expect. Providence is dealing with you for your sins; and your mother here is too sympathizing; better let you suffer a little, perhaps it will make a better boy of you. For my part, if I knew you was really suffering, and thought it would do you good, I'd let you suffer." With flashing eyes the son had risen to his feet during the delivery of this ill-natured speech, and was about to reply, when with ready tact, Mrs. Dana prevented him by gently saying to her husband, —

"Permit me to excuse Lawrence in part. He has at least been usefully employed, and from the purest motives. He is suffering. Therefore please to postpone your censure until he can bear it."

"Well, well, I don't care; only I don't want you to stay up with him; it will only encourage him in his evil ways. I do not think it is necessary."

"When I find it no longer necessary, I will retire," was the mild but decided reply of Mrs. Dana; and Mr. Dana went back to his slumbers.

"Thank you—mother,—I shall not need anything else," said Lawrence as at length he felt himself sinking away to sleep,—the effect of the sudden subsidence of pain under the influence of the warm soothing application to his hand and the more soothing words of his step-mother.

It was the first time the step-son had given her that title, and with overflowing eyes she kissed his forehead, and bidding him to call her if he should need anything, she hastily left the room, — perhaps to return thanks that love had at last unsealed the heart of the youth for whom she had prayed so often.

Meanwhile, Lawrence fell asleep with that grateful kiss warming his inmost soul, and filling his dreams with joy born of its pure baptism. And there, on the sofa, Nellie found him when in the morning she entered the sitting-room. His brow was corrugated with pain; but around his whitened lips yet wandered a pleasant smile. At her entrance he started and awoke.

"Oh, Lawrence, what is the matter? Are you sick?" Nellie asked anxiously.

Before he could reply, Mrs. Dana came, and bending over the back of the sofa, replied for him.—

"He has taken cold in his hand by working so much in the wood-shed of late; and I fear that he will have an ague sore."

"Oh." cried Nellie, the quick tears starting, "He must see the doctor. I shall never get over it, if he loses his fingers Uncle James did,—just by working for me."

"Will you speak to Dr. Osgood as you go to the store?" asked Mrs. Dana, of her husband, who had just entered. He bent over his son and carefully examined the inflamed and swollen wound.

"Why, why," said the softened father, clumsily readjusting the bandages, "I had no idea that this was so bad. I am glad that you attended to it last night, Ellen; it needed attention before."

"Please let mother do it up," pleaded Lawrence, "She didn't know that it was so bad. I never let her see it, or said anything about it, because I wanted to finish Nellie's crutches and sled. And now she can't use her sled till my hand gets well."

"Will that do?" asked Mrs. Dana, securing the outer bandage.

"Yes—thank you;" and Lawrence aroused himself and started for the breakfast-table. But Nellie pressed up close to his side to whisper,—

"Never mind about the sled. Now, I can partly pay for it, before I use it at all."

"How?" asked Lawrence.

"Sit down and I'll show you." Nellie returned, and she briskly hopped away on one crutch, and in a moment came back, bringing, Lawrence could hardly understand how, a basin of warm water and a fresh, white towel.

"You ought not to do this for me," exclaimed Lawrence, to which Nellie laughingly responded,—

"It is my turn now. I am not going to allow you the privilege of doing wrong alone all the time, Brother Lawrence."

"Sister Nellie must allow me to have my own way half of the time;" and, with this, Lawrence returned the basin and towel to their places. But Nellie would comb his soft dark hair, insisting that he "must have slept in his wig."

That was to Lawrence a happy morning, though pain would nei-

ther allow him to eat or drink. He had never had a sister since his
remembrance, and Nellie had never had a brother. So the "Brother
Lawrence" and "Sister Nellie" of that morning was to each the
opening of a new relation, and a relation that was doubly pleasant
to Lawrence, because he had just awakened to its need. Nellie was
not thus surprised: she was only gratified at the success of her
labors.

"You must not venture out in the cold," was the doctors's final
charge, after he had told Lawrence that he could only hasten the
development of the sore, which it was now impossible to avoid.
"You must not expose your hand to the air now, and it should be
kept well poulticed."

Lawrence promised caution, and Dr. Osgood left. But the promise seemed hard to keep. He had not been accustomed to indoor
amusements, and Nellie had gone out somewhere. What should he
do? He got a checker-board and played one or two games with an
imaginary partner. Then he wearied of that, and tried dominoes
with a like result. Still Nellie did not come. He went up-stairs to
get a puzzle-board which he had made long ago; for all his games
were of his own manufacture. When he returned, by the chair he
had occupied, a pair of embroidered slippers, with a little note
attached, caught his eye. Taking up the note, he read,—

"Will my Brother Lawrence accept these slippers from his
Sister Nellie, as a partial return for the crutches and sled?
"Nellie Stanwood."

"Come here, and let me question you," cried Lawrence as he caught
sight of his step-sister hidden in the bay-window. She came timidly to his side, and he drew her upon his knee, asking,—

"Where did they come from?"

"I made them myself," whispered Nellie.

"When?"

"Last week, mostly. I hid in mother's room and finished them
this morning, because she thought you would need them now."

"You are very kind;" and Lawrence's voice was deep with feeling.
"You must thank mother, and not me."

"Why?" asked Lawrence; "didn't you want to do it?"

"Yes," was the childlike reply; "but I did not think of it till mother,"—and here she paused.

"What did 'mother' do?" Lawrence inquired.

"She made me think of them;" but Nellie was evidently keeping back something that had been said, which roused the curiosity of Lawrence, and he continued requesting to know what it was, until Nellie timidly repeated the substance of the conversation, which was this: after breadfast, Nellie, who was an adept in a thousand little arts of knitting and needlework, was about to begin to crochet a new and very beautiful pattern, when her mother said,—

"You can find better work than that for to-day, perhaps for all this week, or longer."

"What do you mean?" Nellie had asked.

"In the first place, you can finish those slippers for Lawrence."

"Yes, but I can do that in half an hour, or hour at the farthest, and you said that I could find better work for all this week, and perhaps longer. I don't understand."

"Do you remember," asked Mrs. Dana, "our conversation the morning before Lawrence cut his hand?"

"Yes'm," returned the little girl, thoroughly interested.

"Well," continued the mother, "your mission work can begin at once. Lawrence must stay indoors now, and you will never have a finer time to awaken his love of home."

"But how shall I do it?" queried this would-be missionary, and her mother had made answer,—

"Try and think of some way while completing the slippers."

"So your mother thinks that I am a heathen; does she?" remarked Lawrence as the blushing child hid her face on his shoulder at the close of her recital.

"Oh, no," was her prompt reply; "but she thinks that John Sherman, Warren Marks, and Leigh Symonds, are very poor companions for you, and"—

"And what?"

"You wont be angry?"

"Not with you!"

"Nor with mother?"

A thought of the loving care of the previous night crossed his mind, and Lawrence replied,—

"No, I will not."

"Then," said Nellie, "she thinks you had better go to work with father, in the store, when your hand is well"

A cloud darkened the boy's face at that, but, with quiet tact, Nellie changed the subject. All through that long day and evening she played checkers, puzzles, and dominoes with Lawrence, laughing at her own ignorance of the games, and hiding her want of interest as skilfully as she concealed her wish for her favorite employments.

That night Lawrence was to sleep on the sofa, if pain would allow him a moment of slumber.

"How have you enjoyed the day, my dear?" he heard Mrs. Dana ask, as Nellie was being helped up-stairs.

He was no eaves-dropper, but he could not avoid holding his breath to catch the reply,—

"Very well indeed, mother; for I think that I have made Lawrence happy."

"Strange," thought he, "very strange that my step-mother should think it Nellie's duty to amuse me. Well, I am glad that she does;" and in a happy frame of mind he tried to compose himself to sleep after the poultices had been renewed upon his hand. But he could not sleep until quite worn out; and he was not sorry to have his step-mother come out to inquire how he was, and stop to loosen, or rearrange the bandages for him, as she did five or six times during the night. She had quite won his heart.

Time wore slowly on, and the blustering March had come before Lawrence could work again, and even then, his hand was partly disabled. All that while had Nellie patiently ministered to his wants, soothing his restlessness, and whiling away the wearisome hours by conversation, reading, or singing as suited him best; and he was not ungrateful. In those long days of forced quiet, he came to realize the baneful influence which his old associates had exerted upon his mind; and gradually, by an acquaintance with purer pleasures, he lost all relish for such vicious society.

"Father," asked Lawrence one evening after tea, "am I not able to go into your store now?"

Mr Dana looked up in surprise, and helped himself absently to butter, forgetting that he had done eating.

"Lawrence wished to know if he could enter your store, John," remarked Mrs. Dana.

"Yes, yes! I heard him," said Mr. Dana. "I was astonished at his wanting to work,—that is all. He may come in to-morrow, if he likes."

So the next day Lawrence began his working life. Nor did he repent his choice. As constant as his father during the day at the store, his evenings were spent with Nellie in useful reading, or in singing, in which both excelled.

"How did you make out to tie Lawrence up to work and study?" asked a neighbor, who hoped to gather an idea that Mrs. Dana had been tyrannical, or had encouraged her husband to be so.

"Nellie and I have bound him with silken fetters," was the smiling reply, which was no answer at all to Mrs. Jones, who could not comprehend how affection can bind the rude and reckless more thoroughly than authority possibly can.

Nellie is yet a cripple, and her dream of becoming a missionary is unfulfilled; but by her influence, Lawrence has become a Christian man. In his stirring business life he interprets the visions which Nellie had of extended usefulness, so that the world has reason to rejoice that Nellie Stanwood has lived, even though she is, and ever must be, largely dependent upon others.

One evening not long since, when Lawrence came in from the store, Nellie was singing,—

> "God moves in a mysterious way
> His wonders to perform."

He stood until she had closed singing this stanza:—

> "Judge not the Lord by feeble sense,
> But trust him for his grace;
> Behind a frowning Providence
> He hides a smiling face."

"I was thinking of much the same thing, dear Nellie," he said, coming forward and taking a seat by her side. "My lame hand, and the kindness that I then so unexpectedly met, have proved my salvation."

"And I was singing that hymn," Nellie returned, "because I thought it appropriate to that part of our history. I felt so sad to think that your first kindness should have caused you so much pain; but, since then, I have fully realized that your confinement was God's way of reclaiming you from vice."

"Yes," said Lawrence, with feeling, "I should have been ruined, as my three old friends were, had my father, with his notions of authority, been left to manage me. But, after my forced confinement was over, I never had a moment's desire to escape from the 'silken fetters' in which mother bound me, or to disappoint her hopes and yours."

"Now let us sing, 'Full and harmonious.'"

And so they sung and chatted away the evening. Leaving them thus, we only pause to ask if none of you, dear readers, have friends whom you can bind with "silken fetters"? Think for youth flies fast.

Home Monthly, January–July 1865

APPRECIATION.
By S. J. F.

"I don't expect that you'll ever make much out of Johnnie."

Miss Winship looked up when Mrs. Preston made the above remark, to see if it might not be one of those assertions so commonly thrown out to catch a polite denial. But the mother's face forbade that idea. Her countenance was sad and hopeless as she again bent over the task of patching a jacket for the said Johnnie. The young teacher hardly knew what to reply; for she had not opened her school. During the two days since she had been left at Mr. Preston's door by a friend who was travelling past, she had heard much condemnation of Johnnie, and more praise of Thomas, Mary, and Susan. But the subject was not yet exhausted.

"Now Thomas," continued the mother, "could read right off without spellin', when he was four years'n'a half old; and he studied 'rithmetic too. Why, Johnnie is ten and he aint much further along now. Sometimes I'm 'most discouraged. The other three all kep' school before they was sixteen, and here he is ten and don't like anything but to whittle and make things."

What more the discouraged mother might have said is not known; for just here Miss Winship, looking, saw Johnnie standing in the porch. He was looking in with a downcast air. In his hand he held a skillfully made toy-bedstead, nicely painted and finished. He had evidently been arrested by his mother's last words while on his way in to display his work for approval. So she replied to Mrs. Preston, "It is not every one who can make things as well as he does. The world needs mechanical as well as professional genius. Who knows but he may become a great machinist, perhaps an inventor of something useful to the whole country?"

The mother looked a little relieved; but hardly convinced, while the boy's face underwent a strange transformation,—a change from an expression of sullen indifference to one of grateful, intelligent interest. Miss Winship had found the key to his heart. She stepped out into the porch, and taking the toy from his hand, said,—

"This is very prettily done. Did you do it all yourself?"

"Yes, every bit," was the pleased reply.

"Whom is it for?" pursued the teacher.

"For brother Thomas's little girl. It is just big enough for her doll."

"Where does your brother live?"

"In Wilton. He is clerk in the counting-room of a large machine-shop. I wish I could go there to learn a trade. I don't love to go to school!"

Miss Winship smiled, and Johnnie grew a little confused, but soon rallied under her kindly manner, and went on,—

"I guess I shall like to go to your school pretty well; but then I can't learn fast. Is it wicked not to like to study?"

Miss Winship saw that she should not have a better time to awaken the boy's ambition to acquire knowledge. So, drawing a chair for him, she seated herself by his side.

"Now," said she, "I am not going to answer your question at once. Perhaps I shall ask you a number of questions first. To begin with: Would you be willing to grow up to manhood without knowing more than you do at present"

"Why—no, I suppose not."

"You do not think that you are old enough to go and learn a machinist's trade now?"

"Oh, no; but then I want to go when I am sixteen."

"And after you go, you do not expect to have much time for study?"

"Why, no; I guess I should have to work fourteen hours a day."

"Very likely you would; and after that, you would often be too tired to read even, and yet evening reading would be all the education, outside of your business, that you could get."

"But, if I could learn such a trade, what would I need so much education for?"

"Of course, Johnnie, you are not going to be satisfied always to work in making machines, which other people have invented. You will make some discoveries yourself, and then you will need to be educated in order to be able to introduce them to the notice of

cultivated and intelligent men. You would not like to have them
admire your work, but ridicule your ignorance all the time; would
you?"

"Oh, no, I never thought of that. I shall want to study; but can I
learn enough in six years? I never did learn fast, and I want to go
to my trade as soon as I'm sixteen; but then, I don't believe that I
can go at all."

"Oh, yes, Johnnie, I guess you can go by that time, and I think,
now that you see the importance of education, you can learn as fast
as any one."

Here the conversation met with a twofold interruption. Mrs.
Preston had completed Johnnie's jacket, and called him to put it
on, while, at the same moment, Miss Winship caught sight of a
little girl passing with whom she wished to speak. She had met the
child twice and saw that her future health and happiness were
being endangered by too close aplication to books. So, going out
into the yard, and calling the child up under the shade of the fragrant and dewy evergreens which bordered the ample enclosure,
she tried to recall her mind from its painfully old thoughts and
occupations, and to give her an interest in present child-life. And,
in part at least, the teacher succeeded; for she went, by sympathetic inquiries, down into the child's hidden fancies and aspirations. Then she told her that, if ever she would awaken the masses
with her pen, she must have known, from childhood to womanhood, those active, kindred associations which make void all differences of power and station. It was a new idea to Susie Marsh, that
play was necessary to a sound education, and Miss Winship was
pleased to note her kindling eye and animated voice as the conversation, by degrees, changed to the forming of plans for the summer's amusement.

Three days later, the school opened. It is not our purpose to
follow closely its progress. We only deal with results. Susie Marsh,
from a thin, querulous child-woman, changed to a rounded, sym-
metrical, and playful little girl. Nor was the change less marked in
Johnnie Preston. He made astonishing progress in all his studies;
but did not give over his devotion to mechanical employments.
For this faculty the kind teacher found abundant occupation. He

was commissioned to arrange a ventilator for the schoolroom, and
to prepare the windows to let down at the top, beside conducting
the water of a mountain brook to a shaded reservoir near the school-
room. All of the children were met upon their own ground, and
felt sure of sympathy and encouragement. Each day made them
love their kind teacher more and more. But were the parents satisfied? Hardly. Mr. and Mrs. Marsh were unwilling that Susie
should be interested in such games as "I spy," and "Hide and go
seek," and would not see their darling had been saved from
insanity, or a too early grave, by the recreation which they condemned. Mrs. Preston, forced to acknowledge that Johnnie
learned wonderfully well, yet put in her mite of condemnation, by
saying, that Miss Winship had "set him out to whittle and tinker
worse than ever."

Hilton school had a male teacher in the winter, and Mr. Marsh
getting the agency, Miss Winship did not secure it again; yet her
work did not die. For evidence, we will look over her shoulder one
happy evening twelve years later. We thus obtain the privilege of
reading two letters,—the first as follows:—

                    "W——, May 30th, 18—.
"Dear Miss Winship,—I have at last secured my patent, and
now the road to fortune is open. But what can I do to repay
you? for I must acknowledge that I am solely indebted to your
influence for the success which has finally crowned my efforts.
But for your kind appreciation twelve years ago, and your
subsequent encouragement, I might have gone through life as
dissatisfied and unsuccessful as my brother and sisters, only
far more ignorant than either. Please indicate some way in
which I can serve you. Wishing that I could repay your kindness, I remain,
                            "Your grateful Friend,
                            "John Preston."
To Miss Alice Winship.

The other, dating from one of our large cities, was almost
equally welcome to the faithful teacher, who though sometimes
worn and weary, still continued her labors. It was this:—

"———.May, 18—.

"My dear Miss Winship,—I send herewith a copy of my new
book, and some of the book reviews and criticisms thereupon.
You will perceive that they all praise my fidelity to nature,
and to life as its exists. As far as I have merited these en-
comiums, the first credit is due to your influence upon me
years ago, in awakening—what I had nearly lost, even thus
early—an interest in common life and its occupations and surroundings. Nor must I forget to thank you for my present
robust health, which I am sure is owing to the active exercise
which I should never again have taken, had you not led me
out of the unnatural and morbid mental state in which you
found me on opening your school at Hilton.

"Enclosed you will find tickets for all the necessary means
of conveyance between yourself and me. Make use of them, I
beg, and thus receive the personal thanks of

"Susan Marsh."

Was not the good teacher well rewarded? Is it any wonder that a
hymn of thanksgiving welled up from her full heart? Tired and
lonely though she was, all unknown to the public as she must ever
be, was it not a pure joy that two, whom the world delighted to
honor, had humbly laid their laurels at her feet?

May not this encourage the faithful and warn the careless teachers of our land. Our future statesmen, heroes, poets, and sages are
in the humble country schoolhouses by the dusty roadside. But
ere these buds can blossom, they must meet, from some older
friend, from either parent or teacher, the kindly breath of
appreciation.

Home Monthly,
July–December 1864

SELECTED BIBLIOGRAPHY

Manuscripts

American Missionary Association Archives. Amistad Research Center, Tulane University, New Orleans.

Sarah Jane Foster's Diaries, 1864 and 1866. Private collection.

Emma Ann Foster Thompson's Diary, 1864. Private collection.

Collection of Storer College. Harpers Ferry National Historical Park, Harpers Ferry, W.Va.

Government Documents and Annual Reports

American Missionary Association, *Annual Reports*. New York.

Charleston City Directory for 1867–68.

Charleston County Probate Court Records. Charleston, S.C.

Dawson, J. L., M.D., and H. W. DeSaussure, M.D. *Census of the City of Charleston, South Carolina, for the Year 1848.* Charleston: City Council, 1849.

Freewill Baptist Home Mission Society. *Thirty-second Annual Report.* Dover, N.H.: Wm. Burr, Printer, 1866.

Harpers Ferry National Historical Park map, National Park Service, U.S. Department of Interior.

Keesecker, Guy L. *Marriage Records of Berkeley County, Va. and W.Va.* Martinsburg, W.Va., 197–.

Maine State Seminary. Catalogs, 1862, 1866–68. Lewiston: Daily Journal.

National Archives. Population schedules for the eighth and ninth censuses of 1860 and 1870 for selected communities in Maine, West Virginia, and South Carolina.

———. Records of the Veterans Administration, Record Group 15 (pension files).

Register of Mesne and Conveyance. Deeds. Charleston, S.C.

Magazines and Newspapers

American Missionary (New York)

Charleston Daily Courier

Charleston Mercury

Home Monthly (Boston)

Martinsburg News

Morning Star (Dover, N.H.)

New Era (Martinsburg, W.Va.)

Zion's Advocate (Portland, Maine)

Books and Pamphlets

Abbott, Martin. *The Freedmen's Bureau in South Carolina, 1865–1872.* Chapel Hill: University of North Carolina Press, 1967.

Aler, F. Vernon. *Aler's History of Martinsburg and Berkeley County, West Virginia.* Hagerstown, Md.: Mail Publishing Company, 1888.

Anthony, Kate J. *Storer College.* Boston: Morning Star Publishing House, 1891.

Auburn Centennial History Committee. *Auburn, 1869–1969: 100 Years a City.* Lewiston, Maine: Twin City Printery, 1968.

Beasley, Maureen Hoffman. *The First Women Washington Correspondents.* G. W. Washington Studies, no. 4. Washington, D.C.: George Washington University, 1976.

Burgess, Rev. G. A., and Rev. J. T. Ward. *Free Baptist Cyclopaedia.* Chicago: Women's Temperance Publication Association for the Free Baptist Cyclopaedia Co., 1889.

Burrage, Henry S. *History of the Baptists in Maine.* Portland: Marks Printing House, 1904.

Butchart, Ronald E. *Northern Schools, Southern Blacks, and Reconstruction: Freedmen's Education, 1862–1875.* Westport, Conn.: Greenwood Press, 1980.

Christopher, Maurine. *America's Black Congressmen.* New York: Thomas Y. Crowell Company, 1971.

Cogan, Frances B. *All-American Girl: The Ideal of Real Womanhood in Mid-Nineteenth-Century America.* Athens: University of Georgia Press, 1989.

Davidson, James Robert. *A Dictionary of Protestant Church Music.* Metuchen, N.J.: Scarecrow Press, 1975.

Degler, Carl N. *At Odds: Women and the Family in America from the Revolution to the Present.* New York: Oxford University Press, 1980.

Doherty, William Thomas. *Berkeley County, USA: A Bicentennial History of a Virginia and West Virginia County, 1772–1972*. Parsons, W.Va.: McLain Printing Company, 1972.

Drago, Edmund L. *Initiative, Paternalism, and Race Relations: Charleston's Avery Normal Institute*. Athens: University of Georgia Press, 1990.

Evans, Willis F. *History of Berkeley County, West Virginia*. Martinsburg, 1928.

Hamilton, J. G. de Roulhac. *Reconstruction in North Carolina*. Columbia University Studies in History, Economics, and Public Law. 1914; rept. Gloucester, Mass.: Peter Smith, 1964.

Hill, George T. *History, Records, and Recollections of Gray, Maine*. Portland: Tower Publishing Company, 1976.

Holt, Thomas. *Black over White: Negro Political Leadership in South Carolina during Reconstruction*. Urbana: University of Illinois Press, 1977.

Jones, Jacqueline. *Soldiers of Light and Love: Northern Teachers and Georgia Blacks, 1865–1873*. Chapel Hill: University of North Carolina Press, 1980.

Keller, Allan. *Thunder at Harpers Ferry*. Englewood Cliffs, N.J.: Prentice-Hall, 1958.

Kelley, Mary, ed. *Woman's Being, Woman's Place: Female Identity and Vocation in American History*. Boston: G. K. Hall & Co., 1979.

Lawrence, W. H. *The Centenary Souvenir, Containing a History of the Centenary Church, Charleston, and an Account of the Life and Labors of Reverend R. V. Lawrence, Father of the Pastor of Centenary Church*. Philadelphia: Collins Printing House, 1885.

Litwack, Leon F. *Been in the Storm So Long: The Aftermath of Slavery*. New York: Vintage Books, 1980.

Logan, Rayford W., and Michael R. Winston. *Dictionary of American Negro Biography*. New York: W. W. Norton & Company, 1982.

McKitrick, Eric. L. *Andrew Johnson and Reconstruction*. Chicago: University of Chicago Press, 1964.

Morris, Robert C. *Reading, 'Riting, and Reconstruction: The Education of Freedmen in the South, 1861–1870*. Chicago: University of Chicago Press, 1981.

Mott, Frank Luther. *A History of American Magazines*. 5 vols. Cambridge, Mass.: Harvard University Press, 1930–68.

Neidhardt. W. S. *Fenianism in North America*. University Park: Pennsylvania State University Press, 1975.

Pine, Frances Staubly. *History of the First Baptist Church*. [Martinsburg, W.Va., ca. 1958].

Rev. N. C. Brackett. PH D. Undated pamphlet at American Baptist Historical Society, Valley Forge, Pa.

Richardson, Joe M. *Christian Reconstruction: The American Missionary Association and Southern Blacks, 1861–1890*. Athens: University of Georgia Press, 1986.

Robinson, Wilhelmena S. *Historical Afro-American Biographies*. International Library of Afro-American Life and History. Cornwells Heights, Pa.: Publishers Agency, 1979.

Rose, Willie Lee. *Rehearsal for Reconstruction: The Port Royal Experiment*. Indianapolis: Bobbs-Merrill Company, 1964.

Ryan, Mary P. *Womanhood in America, from Colonial Times to the Present*. New York: New Viewpoints, 1975.

Sears, Stephen W. *Landscape Turned Red: The Battle of Antietam*. New Haven: Ticknor and Fields, 1983.

Severens, Kenneth. *Charleston: Antebellum Architecture and Civic Destiny*. Knoxville: University of Tennessee Press, 1988.

Southern, Eileen, ed. *Biographical Dictionary of Afro-American and African Musicians*. Westport, Conn.: Greenwood Press, 1982.

Stoney, Samuel Gaillard. *This is Charleston: An Architectural Survey of a Unique American City*. Charleston: Carolina Art Association, 1987.

Stowe, Harriet Beecher. *Sunny Memories of Foreign Lands*. Boston: Phillips, Sampson, and Company, 1854.

Swint, Henry Lee. *The Northern Teacher in the South, 1862–1870*. New York: Octagon Books, 1967.

Wiley, Rev. Frederick L. *Life and Influence of the Rev. Benjamin Randall, Founder of the Free Baptist Denomination*. Philadelphia: American Baptist Publication Society, 1915.

Williamson, Joel. *After Slavery: The Negro in South Carolina during Reconstruction, 1861–1877*. Chapel Hill: University of North Carolina Press, 1965.

Articles

Chapman, Anne W. "Inadequacies of the 1848 Charleston Census." *South Carolina Historical Magazine* 81 (Jan. 1980): 24–34.

Drago, Edmund, and Ralph Melnick. "The Old Slave Mart Museum, Charleston, South Carolina: Rediscovering the Past." *Civil War History* 27, no. 2 (1981): 138–54.

Du Bois, W. E. Burghardt. "The Freedmen's Bureau." *Atlantic Monthly* 88 (March 1901): 354–65.

Richardson, Joe M. "Francis L. Cardozo: Black Educator during Reconstruction." *Journal of Negro Education* 48 (Winter 1979): 73–83.

Stealey, John E., III. "The Freedmen's Bureau in West Virginia." *West Virginia History* 39 (Jan./April 1978): 99–142.

——. "Reports of Freedmen's Bureau Operations in West Virginia: Agents in the Eastern Panhandle." *West Virginia History* 42 (Fall 1980–Winter 1981): 94–129.

Sweat, Edward F. "Francis L. Cardozo: Profile of Integrity in Reconstruction Politics." *Journal of Negro History* 46 (Oct. 1961): 217–32.

Welter, Barbara. "The Cult of True Womanhood, 1820–1860." *American Quarterly* 18 (Summer 1966): 151–74.

Thesis

McLain, Mary Ellen. "Storer College, Harpers Ferry, West Virginia (1865–1897)." Honors Thesis, Linfield College, 1974.

Index